PELICAN BOOKS

AGAINST ALL REASON

Geoffrey Moorhouse was born in Bolton in 1931 and educated at Bury Grammar School. After service in the Royal Navy he became a journalist, and for thirteen years was on the staff of the *Guardian*, where he was Chief Features Writer until 1970, when he left to concentrate on writing books. His assignments in that time had taken him to twenty-five countries. He climbed the Matterhorn for his paper, reported from Rome during the Vatican Council, from Bethlehem during its first Christmas under a Jewish governor, from Czechoslovakia during eight crucial weeks of 1968, from Moscow on Lenin's centenary. His first book, *The Other England*, sold 25,000 copies before going out of print. *Against All Reason* has been translated into French and German. His latest book, *Calcutta*, appeared in 1971 and he is now working on a history of the missionaries in Africa. When he is not writing he likes to walk in hill country, look at buildings and listen to music.

AGAINST
ALL REASON

GEOFFREY
MOORHOUSE

PENGUIN BOOKS

Penguin Books Ltd, Harmondsworth, Middlesex, England
Penguin Books Australia Ltd, Ringwood, Victoria, Australia

—

First published by Weidenfeld & Nicolson 1969
Published in Penguin Books 1972
Copyright © Geoffrey Moorhouse, 1969

—

Made and printed in Great Britain
by Hazell Watson & Viney Ltd,
Aylesbury, Bucks
Set in Linotype Baskerville

Contents

Acknowledgements
Foreword

PART 1

1 Taizé   3
2 The Tradition   21
3 Towards a New Dissolution   57

PART 2

4 The Structure Today   95
5 Prayer   130
6 Authority and Obedience   163
7 Vocation   202
8 The Turning-point   241
Bibliography   271

Appendix 1   The Religious Population
    among Roman Catholics   275
Appendix 2   Declaration by the General
    Chapter of the Cistercian Monks of the
    Strict Observance (The Trappists) in
    March 1969   278
Appendix 3   The Rule of the Community
    of the Sisters of the Love of God   282
    Sources   296
    Index   304

Acknowledgements

I OWE a very big debt to a great number of people in religion. I do not expect any of them to share all the attitudes I have expressed in the book; I only hope that none of them is too shocked by some of my comments and conclusions. The largest debt of all is to those men and women – about a hundred of them – who answered a questionnaire primarily designed to find out why they became religious; some of them wrote small biographies in reply and some exposed themselves as very few human beings in my experience are prepared to, at some cost and at some risk of being hurt; they moved me more than I can say and Chapter 7 could not have been written without them, or without the permission of several superiors who generously let me circulate my questionnaire round their communities.

Apart from those helpers who must remain anonymous, people who talked to me as well as people who answered questions in writing, there are others I have to thank. More than anyone, perhaps, Dom Cyprian Martin OSB for his tireless and stimulating correspondence (not always answered promptly, I'm afraid) across three years. I'm also grateful to Fr Vincent Strudwick SSM, who allowed me to see the results of his own questionnaire on Anglican religious deployment; to Mother Mary Clare SLG, for more insights into the religious life than I can count, as well as for permission to reprint the Rule of her community as an appendix; to Dom Ambrose Southey OCSO, for much advice and encouragement; to Fr M. Basil Pennington OCSO for supplying me with the Trappist Declaration which appears in Appendix 2; to Fr Peter Ball CGA, for allowing me to reprint an extract from his community's constitutions; and for various help and counsel to Sister Marcia CSC, Fr Arthur Longworth CR, Fr Hugh Bishop CR, Fr

Donald Patey C R, Dom Edward Crouzet O S B, Dom Alberic Stacpoole O S B, Professor David Knowles O S B, Fr Herbert McCabe O P, Fr Peter Hebblethwaite S J, Fr Brocard Sewell O Carm., Brother Thomas of Taizé, Brother Guy Jarrosson of the Petits Frères and Fr Jonathan Young S S J E. I should also like to salute the late Jonathan Graham C R, who didn't believe I ought to attempt this book, but who told me to forget that and go ahead. Lastly my thanks to three people outside the religious life. To Mrs Mary Buck, of the Catholic Central Library in London, and to Mr R. K. Browne, Librarian of the Jesuit Provincial headquarters at Farm Street, London, both of whom helped me to find the right books and papers when I was looking for them. And to Ann Shearer, who in the middle of her own writing made time to translate from the French two books which have not been published in English; the chapter on Taizé is for her.

Foreword

THIS book is not about Christianity in general: it is about 'the religious life' in its technical sense. Much of it is about monks and nuns, but they form only part of the religious world, which is also inhabited by friars, 'sisters', 'brothers' and several other varieties of profession. In crude and worldly terms the book is about those Christian bachelors and spinsters who live together in monasteries, convents or other communities, and who mostly wear medieval clothes. With very few exceptions, which I hope are clear from the context, the word 'religious' in this book applies to them and their life alone; in this technical sense 'a religious' is some-one who is 'in religion' as a result of having taken vows or made promises to live in poverty, obedience and chastity with others of a like mind.

This book isn't about all the Christian religious in the world. Except for passing references it excludes the religious of eastern Christianity, of whom the Greek Orthodox monks living on Mount Athos are the best known. It is an attempt to survey the religious life today of western Christendom, of the world under the influence of Catholic and Protestant Christianity. It is an attempt to examine a way of life and a philosophy, the reasons why individuals have taken up that life and the effect it has on them. It is about one and a quarter million human beings. The book has been written at a dramatic point in the history of the religious life, which is changing quite radically for the first time in perhaps fifteen hundred years – since St Augustine of Hippo constructed the doctrine of perfection on which the religious life has been based. No one can yet be sure which way it is going from now on. But it is going. This book, in part, is therefore a last look at a deeply traditional way of life that may not be with us much longer. It is also, in the last chapter, an attempt to see where the religious life might go.

For this Penguin edition there has been some revision of the appendices which appeared in the original hard-cover edition. The lengthy Trappist Usages, which formed Appendix 2, were abandoned by the Order in its General Chapter almost at the moment of the book's publication. The documents which now appear as Appendix 2 were substituted by the Chapter in place of the Usages. The Dominican Questionnaire, which formed Appendix 4, has been omitted because it was felt that it has now outlived its usefulness. Apart from these alterations, the text of this edition is substantially unchanged.

PART ONE

TAIZÉ

'We must strive for a Christian engagement in the human society around us. We must discover in our own field, in our place of work, the means of radiating – perhaps without a word – the presence of Christ. For you must accept a man where you find him, how you find him, in order to enter into his humanity and understand him from within.' – ROGER SCHUTZ, Prior of Taizé, *Living Today for God*, p. 66*

THIS is one of the most memorable places in Christendom. Seen from the hillside opposite it is just another attractive French village, slipping off the end of a ridge in a scatter of warm brown walls and pink pantiled roofs, with a Romanesque church tower poking higher than anything else. All around is the rich, cultivated and undulating landscape of Burgundy; patched with woods, with vineyards, with cornfields and with pasture. In a meadow below the church cream-coloured cows idle in the grass. Over a wall a peasant plods up and down his allotment, hand-sowing seed upon the crumbled red earth. It is a very peaceful place and the only loud noise it hears is made by the occasional train passing the maire's cottage at the bottom of the hill, on its way from Dijon to Macon. Seen from a distance the village looks as if it might be vegetating as thoughtlessly as the fields and slopes that surround it. But it is the vibrant centre of an influence which for a quarter of a century has been gradually spreading across the world and which is helping to transform one of the most ancient segments of Christian civilization. Peasants in Chile have been touched by its presence and so have petit-bourgeois in Japan. And when, in solemn conclave beneath the dome of St Peter's, old men at the last Vatican Council attempted to shift the Church of

---

* Full details of books referred to are given in the bibliography.

Rome from some of its antique rigidities, they did so at times and in part from an awareness of this place and its significance.

The village's name is Taizé. It is so memorable, so influential and so significant because it contains what the world would call a monastery, but what, by the strictest legalistic canons of Christendom, is more precisely a religious community. It cannot technically be a monastery because to the purists monasteries do not exist outside the Catholic and Orthodox Churches. The Taizé Communauté is Protestant. It is nevertheless the home of about seventy men who have renounced the possibility of marriage, abandoned all private possessions and vowed themselves to be obedient to a rule of conduct for the rest of their lives. They have put themselves almost as far as it is possible to go from the social norms of the mid-twentieth century. To most of the world outside their lives must seem a waste or a farce or a mixture of both. To Axel, Léonard, Rudolphe, André, Clément and the other men of Taizé it is something between a duty and a fulfilment; they call it a vocation to a particular form of Christian life. In its essentials it merely follows a pattern established ages ago by men who decided that poverty, chastity and obedience provided a framework within which they would worship their God. Taizé is memorable because of its interpretation of this life, because it is Protestant, because it is dedicated to the destruction of all Christian sects and the revival of a united Church, and because it is effective.

It is the creation of one person, as almost every other religious community has been before it. He is a short, slim man, with shiny and rather damp eyes and a flat nose that may have seen better days. Those who know him best say that he is a timid man, with an annoying habit of changing arrangements at the last moment. He avoids interviews like the plague and refers people who want more than a few words of spiritual comfort from him to his numerous books and other writings. His name is Roger Schutz and one day it may be listed alongside those of Benedict and Ignatius and the other great reformers of the Christian religious life. As a boy, the Franco-Swiss son of a manse, he had been confronted with the Christian divisions which have made humbug of the faith preached on all sides; while coming from a stoutly Protestant home he had been boarded out during his school terms with a Catholic family in the next village. He sees this now as the start of his vocation. It developed further when he became a theological student in Lausanne, where his licentiate dissertation was on 'The Monastic ideal until St Benedict and its Conformity with the Gospel'. At the age of twenty-four he began to organize his friends into study groups, brought them together for spiritual retreats, and called this fellowship the Great Community. It was this only in a loose sense, for its members lived separately in their own homes. Schutz was bent upon something more permanent and more coherent.

When a student leads a band of friends calling themselves the Great Community and then goes on to found a monastery it seems at least possible that a romantic attachment to the past has been partly responsible; the pattern is not unknown in the history of the religious life. Today he is quite clear on rational grounds alone why the step was taken. 'Living the common life at Taizé,' he has written, 'what do we desire but to unite men pledged to follow the footsteps of Christ? To be an existential sign of the unity of the Church? A community is a microcosm of the Church. It sums up in itself the whole reality of the Church.'

Schutz had made his own retreats with the Carthusian monks of La Grande Chartreuse and with the Trappists. In 1940 he crossed the border to look for a house. In coming to Burgundy he was entering a country richer than most in the monastic tradition. On the road to Macon were the ruins of Cluny, which William the Pious, Duke of Aquitaine, founded in 910, which produced a pope (Gregory VII) and which in the eleventh and twelfth centuries was enormously influential as the headquarters of a reformed Benedictine life. A few miles outside Dijon was Cîteaux, which after nine hundred years is still the base-camp of an extremely

rigorous form of monasticism; a very solid Cistercian bar-
racks which no woman may enter and which, unless they
are making a retreat or doing business, men may visit only
between 2.30 and 4.30 in the afternoon. Schutz found what
he wanted between the two, only just out of sight of Cluny
itself. In 1940, though it was in unoccupied France, Taizé
was almost an abandoned village; the windows of its seventeenth-century manor house, which had once belonged to
the counts of Brie, were shuttered. But a notary in Cluny
had suggested that the manor might be for sale and it was.
Schutz moved in and for the next two years lived there alone
except for the refugees he sheltered. By 1942 the Germans
had taken over unoccupied France and Schutz returned to
Switzerland. In Geneva he met three other students – Max
Thurian and Daniel de Montmollin, who were theologians,
and Pierre Souvairain, who had graduated in agriculture –
and until the European war was over the four men shared
an apartment. Although none had yet vowed himself to
anything, although no rule of life for them was to appear for
another decade, this was the beginning of the Taizé Communauté.

The four moved into Schutz's Burgundian manor in the
summer of 1944. The first thing they did was to take in
twenty orphans. Then they began to organize a retreat house
for adults who wanted to spend a quiet day or two in prayer
and meditation. They were also busy making friends with
the Catholic priests and laymen of the district, which was
not an automatic thing for Protestant clergymen to be doing
in France twenty-five years ago. It paid off astonishingly.
By Easter 1948, with five brothers in Taizé, Prior Schutz
and his community had been given permission to celebrate their first office in that Catholic village church with
the Romanesque tower. This was henceforth to serve both
Protestants and Catholics in the area on the authority of no
lesser dignitaries than the Bishop of Autun and the papal
nuncio in Paris – who in those days was Monsignor Roncalli,
but who afterwards became Pope John XXIII. Given
Schutz's vision of a reconciliation between divided Christian

Churches, which had led him on ever since his student days in Lausanne, it was perhaps the most important breakthrough of his life. It meant that his chosen purpose had some chance of success and that there could now be total commitment to it. On Easter morning of the next year there were seven brothers in Taizé and together they vowed themselves to chastity, to poverty, to obedience and to community for life.

The place has changed a bit since then. The almost abandoned village is now bulging at the seams with people whose lives have become geared to the community's and with people who are just visiting it. There may be only sixty villagers under M. le maire's authority and seventy-odd brethren under M. le prieur's obedience, but except in winter the average floating population of Taizé cannot be much less than two thousand a day. Nuns come plodding up the hill in dozens, clerics go rambling along the ridge road towards the water-tower in foursomes, and coach parties lurch to a standstill on the gravel outside M. Barbier's shop, which does a roaring trade most months of the year in light or heavy refreshments. Neither the manor, the Romanesque church nor the pantiled buildings of Taizé were ever intended to accommodate these numbers, so there have been several structural alterations too. The church is now used by the community only in winter, when few people are about. Most of the time since 1962 worship at Taizé has taken place farther along the ridge in the huge Church of the Reconciliation, which from the outside looks like an aircraft hangar or possibly an electricity generating station; with the water-tower it is almost the only ugly thing for miles around. Beyond that is an encampment of white-walled, rather military-looking huts, which is where the community puts up retreatants and other guests it cannot manage elsewhere. And almost everywhere you look in Taizé construction work is going on all the time. In the village proper cottages are being knocked into more habitable shapes. In the field between the manor and the ugly concrete church five great bells hang from a metal frame and men are creating a moat around them so that the visitors can inspect the bells closely from the roadside and yet be kept out of harm's way when they begin to swing. The men wear dungarees and they handle their shovels, their trowels and their cigarettes as though they have been labourers all their lives. Some of them have been. Most of them belong to the community and are therefore a kind of monk as well.

These have come to Taizé, together with their brethren, from a dozen different countries and an even greater variety of religious backgrounds. There are more French, Swiss, Germans and Dutch in the community than anything else; but there are also Scandinavians, an Australian, an American, a Scot and a Spaniard. Between them they cover about twenty different Protestant denominations but they have sunk these differences in the unity of the life at Taizé. About one in six of them is an ordained minister of religion, the rest are laymen, but apart from the fact that the pastors alone can perform certain sacramental functions like administering communion there is no distinction at all in the way they live and are regarded within the community. They are all Brothers of Taizé together. Apart from that first nucleus they have all come to the community, been accepted by it and settled into it along a common pattern.

When a man believes he has a vocation to Taizé he is told to come and make a retreat there for a start. He is given a room in that white-walled encampment beyond the ugly church. He finds himself in the company of a motley gang of itinerants; young men from half the Christian student organizations of Europe; Catholic priests and Protestant pastors; Presbyterian ordinands passing time in their last long vacation at Cambridge. All of them have come partly, as they would say, for the peace and quiet and right atmosphere in which to recharge their spiritual batteries; partly just to satisfy their curiosity about Taizé itself. With the rest of them the man who thinks he has a vocation will do chores about the place, attend the offices in the church, potter around the district, read a bit and spend a fair amount of his time relaxing on his bed. He will then go home but eventually he will return to live with the community in the manor as a postulant. There is no fixed period for this; for some it lasts a few weeks, for others several months. The criterion is in the postulant himself. Everything depends on how long it takes the rest of the community to decide whether he has the potential to become one of them. One day they vote on him among themselves and if the ballot goes in his favour he becomes a novice. For the next three years he will to some extent be a student – of the Bible, of Church history and of sociology – under the direction of a senior brother. 'In order to be trained in the school of Christ,' says the community's Rule, 'the new Brother has need of sound biblical and humane nurture.' He will also be applying on behalf of the community whatever skills he brought with him from the life outside; he will, to the visiting observer, be indistinguishable from any other member of Taizé Communauté. But his most important function during his novitiate will be to learn how to live in common with his new brethren; how to share everything with them; how to avoid getting on their nerves and how to put up with those who get on his; how to discipline himself to unaccustomed periods of silence; how, most of all, to grow into the particular philosophy of Taizé. Towards the end of his novitiate he will be discussed by the prior with the brothers who have been closest to him for the past three years. And on their advice and on his own assessment Roger Schutz decides whether or not to allow the new man to become a fully professed member of the community.

The profession is the most serious step the man has taken in his life and it is invested with all the weight and significance of a marriage ceremony. One morning, preferably on the first Easter morning after he has passed muster, the new brother is taken to the Church of the Reconciliation. He is dressed, like the rest of the community, in the long white cassock with a hood down the back and a cord around the waist which is worn at Taizé only in church. He is required there to renew his baptismal vows and then, while he lies prostrate on the floor, the community sing Psalm 126.

Then the prior exhorts him to remember that Christ will strengthen his faith, to walk in the footsteps of Christ for the rest of his life, to surrender himself, to maintain himself in simplicity and joy, to be a sign of brotherly love within the Church. The exhortation also reminds the new brother what he is giving up; home, brothers, sisters, mother, father, wife, children and land. 'This is a way opposed to all human reason, but like Abraham you can advance on this path by faith, not by sight, always assured that he who loses his life for Christ's sake shall find it.' And with this thought in his head the brother takes the vows he is expected to keep until the day he dies.

Will you, he is asked, through love of Christ, consecrate yourself with your whole being to him?

Will you, henceforth, fulfil the services of God in our Community, in communion with your Brothers?

Will you, in renouncing all ownership to property, live with your Brothers not only in the community of material goods but also in the community of spiritual goods, while striving for openness of heart?

Will you, in order to be more available to serve with your Brothers and to give yourself completely to the love of Christ, remain celibate?

Will you, in order that we may be but one heart and one soul and that our unity of service may be fully realized, assume the decisions made in Community and as expressed by the Prior?

Will you, while always discerning Christ in your Brothers, be watchful with them on bad days as well as good, in poverty as well as abundance, in suffering as in joy?

A silver ring goes on his wedding finger after that as a reminder of his solemn commitment. And though several men leave Taizé and return to their old lives when they are in the novitiate, finding the existence progressively less to their taste and temperament, in all the years since it was founded only one fully professed brother has renounced his vows and opted out of the community. He left to get married.

This is the way that all the brothers have come to Taizé. And, whatever life any one of them may have left behind, it does not look as if he has exchanged it for something that is harsh or bleak or degrading, though these are some of the world's assumptions about the monastic existence. There is a Rule governing the community's life but it does not read like a series of regimental orders; it is a discursive mixture of humane common sense and high Christian sentiment and it has been described as 'a spiritual document redolent of the Gospel'.

In the manor each brother has a room which is simply furnished but which is also comfortable; the bed is well sprung and so is the armchair, there are shelves for books and an icon to decorate the wall. He takes his meal not in an institutional eating shed but in a more cosy domestic atmosphere with just a few of his brothers, and although no one talks until the soup, the pasta, the salad and *fromage* are done and the fruit is being passed round, the silence is relieved by a Brandenburg Concerto, an Orthodox chant or something else decently classical coming off the record player in the corner. This small gathering is where the brother hears what is going on in the world outside, for someone is deputed to monitor the papers and the wireless and to bring the news in to the rest. They call these groups foyers at Taizé; the community is divided into six of them, and they are there so that brothers can know each other as brothers and not just as matey members of the same religious commando; but they are reshuffled from time to time so that the community will not become a parcel of cliques either. . .

The foyer is one small focal point of the brother's life. Another is his work. There is an accumulation of secular skills in the community and they have not been wasted. Taizé cannot afford to waste them when it is a deeply embedded principle of the monastic life that a community shall be as far as possible self-supporting. Gifts of money do come in from well-wishers but the Rule says that 'the boldness to use in the best possible way all present-day goods and, without fear of possible poverty, to lay up no capital, gives an incalculable strength' and so these are put to other uses, as in the mid sixties they were being devoted to a land-reform scheme in the Catholic diocese of Talca in Chile. So Taizé keeps going by its own efforts and talents. After the rising bell at 7 a.m., after the first office of the day in church and after breakfast, it begins to earn its bread and butter.

Some of the brothers will be out on the building work and others will be coping with the perpetual stream of visitors. But for the theologians, like Roger Schutz himself and Max, it means a day of writing if they are at home. For Dominique it means a day in the printery, turning out the books and tracts the theologians have written, which sell like hot cakes in several languages; turning out, too, much distinctly untheological contract work, like the manual on chicken farming which Taizé published for the Cameroons Government some time back. For Daniel and his assistants it means a day in the pottery, making platters and jugs and urns. For Eric and Mark it means designing stained glass to order for churches throughout Europe. They also do abstract wood engravings, icons and thick brushy drawings of any subject that has taken their fancy. All these pieces, along with those coming out of the pottery, and the records made of the Taizé Communauté singing in choir, keep the tills ringing in the *centre d'exposition* across the road from the workshops, where the tourists rummage for their souvenirs. A lot of monasteries and even more cathedrals have souvenir attachments and usually the only striking thing about them is how a religion which has produced such a beauty of glass at Chartres and masonry at St Peter's could countenance such shoddy junk on its doorsteps today. But the stuff coming out of the Taizé workshops is modern art and has been good enough for exhibition in Tokyo and elsewhere.

There are times, wandering around Taizé, when the visitor might be forgiven for supposing that he had dropped into the centre of a flourishing arts and crafts movement rather than a religious community. The *centre d'exposition* is packed with gorgeous things. On walls down in the village are neo-Romanesque figures in bas-relief, done by Ber-

nard, who was and still is occasionally a sculptor. Every
room in the retreat house contains one of Mark's icons.
Daniel's workshop is not just a place bent on making ends
meet; it is an artist's den, with pieces of crystal, stones cut
across to show their whorling and tinted insides, and many
other utterly uncommercial bits of bric-à-brac. There are
white doves fluttering around the courtyard of the manor
and a cartwheel balanced beautifully but uselessly against
the wall of a workshop. There are even tropical fish tanked
up inside the printery. It is as though the whole place were
dedicated not to the worship of God but to the pursuit of a
very tranquil beauty.

There is, in fact, nothing more beautiful in Taizé than
its chief act of worship and its main expression of the common life of the monks. The community is split into half a
dozen small factories from breakfast time until 6 in the
evening and it eats its meals in separate foyers. But three
times a day, and more frequently on Sundays, it gathers en
masse in church to sing its offices – at 7.30 a.m., at noon and
at 7 in the evening.

The church may look like an aircraft hangar from the
outside but inside Denys, who used to be an architect and
who designed it, has made it into a setting for superb theatre.
It is cavernous, flat-ceilinged, its walls are white and rough.
A little light comes through small windows along one side
and through larger ones around the door, whose stained
glass has been done by Eric and Mark. There is a prome-
nade around two sides of this theatre and then steps down
into the well, where there are rows of chairs for a congregation. In front of them is a low-walled enclosure, where the
community will sit in an arc, and its open side faces a great
slabby and free-standing altar raised to the level of everybody's head. Yellow spotlights sunk into the floor play on
the back wall and throw everything into sharply sculptured
relief.

The office is announced half an hour before it begins by
those moated bells out in the field, which are controlled elec-
trically by a switch in Dominique's printery. People begin to

slip in through the doors, to fill the congregational seats and to squat upon the steps. While they are coming a brother appears from the wings behind the altar, bearing a lighted taper on the end of a long pole. Very slowly he raises this torch to each of the candles on a wide iron circle hanging above the altar; then to a single candle standing alone and high in front of it; then to five others in a row before an icon to the left of it. As he raises his torch the wide sleeves of his white cassock fall away down his arms and his shadow trembles huge against the yellowed backdrop. For a few moments he has this stage all to himself, until other brethren come in. They arrive alone or in twos, but however they come they move with the pace of men who are sure of every step and know they have all the time in the world to make it. They have what any theatrical producer would instantly recognize as presence and the swish and sway of their cassocks only points it up. There is not an old or a fat one among them and so their entrance is like a meeting of athletes. They go each to his place inside the enclosure, remove a mat from their seats and then kneel on the floor with their heads held high. Last of all, in the almost total silence which has been there since the candles were being lit, Jean-Luc crosses the altar from the wings and climbs up to his silver-piped organ in a loft on the other wall. He looks round, plays six fluting chords, his brethren rise with a rustle of robes, and begin to sing the introit. '*Rendez grâce au Seigneur car il est bon, car éternel est son amour, alleluia. . . .*' And if anyone has an ear for sound, for the balance between silence and music, for the tension of the one broken by the other, for the soaring lilt of that opening verse with thin, rather boyish tenor above grounding bass, a shiver goes down his spine at that point.

The office lasts for perhaps half an hour. There are choral psalms in which the congregation joins and there are passages of liturgy sung solo by one of the brothers. There are prayers : for the Church, for the state of the world, for the members of the community who are away from home; for Gérard and Bernard, who are in Africa, for Robert who is in Spain. .... There is a lesson, and the words of the Gospel drift heavy as incense over the church in great rolling French periods and accents. There are also many more silences. The longest silence of all comes near the end when very quietly, almost in a whisper, Roger Schutz says 'Prions-nous'. He says it while everyone is sitting and it would take willpower for a man not to go on his knees with the rest. It is a silence which seems to last a measure of days, in which a man may examine his soul and wonder where on earth he is going, while the candles flicker and the arc of white figures is utterly still and in all that great gathering only the organist sits fidgeting a little at his keyboard. It is a silence which lingers for perhaps five minutes, so that unless a man can pray in it he is towards the end craving a release. It ends to make the heart jump, with a crashing brilliance of chords as Jean-Luc starts his voluntary. The white figures get to their feet and then, in a slow clockwise procession, close behind each other, with cassocks and sleeves undulating in unison, they move away gaunt and long-shadowed against the yellow wall. They have just worshipped their God together, not piously, but with drama and with a rare beauty of sound and stillness and image.

Beautiful as its liturgy is and attractive as so much of the apparatus at Taizé may be, these things are only by-products of its philosophy. They are means being used to achieve a larger end. In worshipping their God the seventy brothers of Taizé have particularly dedicated themselves to unity and reconciliation. The fact that between them they represent two score denominations whose doctrines do not always correspond is itself an expression of this. But within the Christian context the dedication has been carried several stages further at Taizé. In the weird complex of Christian theological differences and Christian political rivalries the unification of several Protestant sects is a comparatively simple matter. The establishment of a bridgehead between Catholic and Protestant until a few years ago had not only been a tougher prospect; for four centuries it had been unthinkable. And a link between these two western camps of

Christianity and the eastern Orthodox one was still not a matter for discussion until two or three years back. Even now it is only a matter for very gingerly conversation between the two sides. Yet at Taizé all these bridgeheads have been established. When Denys designed his church he made most of it a great Protestant theatre. He also built into its crypt a chapel for Catholics and another one for Orthodox. They are being used.

Every Sunday there is an Orthodox mass at 8 a.m. and a Catholic mass at 9, and throughout the week the Catholic chapel is packed with people saying the rosary or just kneeling in prayer. There are also five Franciscan friars of the Catholic Church and five bearded priests of the Orthodox faith permanently attached to the community. At every office the community celebrates in its own part of the church these ten men, whose own doctrines and rituals are so alien to those of Protestantism, make their entrance behind the white-robed brethren and take their places in a swither of brown and black cloaking to the right of the altar. Catholic masses have already been said at the Protestant altar. And on Easter Day 1967, which was not their own, for they go by a different calendar from that of western Christians, the Orthodox priests celebrated their Easter liturgy there too. Ecumenism, the Christian trade name for this settling of differences, cannot go much further than that.

It is one sign of Taizé's achievement so far. That and the Catholic Dominican sisters who help to man the *centre d'acceuil* which copes with the visitors who have come to stay, and the nuns from a Belgian order who help to sell the souvenirs in the *centre d'exposition*. That and the casual throwaway line of a Protestant brother of Taizé : 'We've just lost our bishop,' he said, and he was talking of a Catholic. That and the name given to two of the bells out in the field; one called John XXIII and the other Pacem in Terris, which was the same pope's greatest encyclical. That and the coachloads of nuns and priests who come grinding up the hill from the level crossing by M. le maire's cottage. Nearly two hundred thousand visitors a year come to Taizé now and they aren't all Protestants. Some of them aren't even Christians. 'Haven't we been discovered and recognized by so many agnostics through our liturgical prayer?' asks Schutz. And they have.

This is one part of Taizé's influence. Another is in its interpretation of the religious life. Periodically this has changed and been modified throughout the centuries since it began. Benedict changed it enormously and Francis a little more; Ignatius shifted its direction and so did other men before and after him, with a subtle emphasis on this point and then on that. But of its nature it has tended to become hidebound, with long periods of rigidity between one change and the next. It has been meticulously codified with rules of strict obedience and in varying degrees it has been lived in isolation, which has been death to flexibility. The way of Taizé has gone against this grain. In very small details it has been flexible from the start; so that, although the rising bell goes at 7 in the morning and the community closes down for silence from 10 in the evening, there is at least one brother who gets up at 5 a.m. and goes off to bed early to compensate at the other end of the day; and he is encouraged to do this because he is thus finding the rhythm of days that suits him best. It is not a habit that would be favoured today at Cîteaux. But it is the kind of thing that is being pondered by more and more monks and nuns and other religious all over the world. That and the liturgy, with its great reflective silences which are so alien to the crammed rituals of traditional monasticism. And most of all the religious world is pondering Taizé's attachment to the temporary nature of its life. 'The things that specially distinguish us at Taizé may have to disappear one day ... when visible unity has been achieved.'

This is not a doctrine in the grand tradition of monasticism, whose insistence has been rather on the eternal and the unchanging and the sureness of continuity. It is a doctrine which depends upon the assertion that a religious community must not be reclusive; that instead it must see itself as part of a world which is always changing; that it must always be taking stock of itself and prepared to adapt itself to contemporary needs. The emphasis is clearly seen in everything that Schutz has written. It is reflected in some of his titles: *Living Today for God, A Dynamic of the Provisional*, and so on. Over the past decade this doctrine has more and more been considered and debated and absorbed by the rest of the religious world. The Rule of Taizé has now been translated into German, English, Dutch and Spanish. There is scarcely a conference of religious throughout Europe and in the United States without one of the brothers being present, to whom the Catholics and the Anglicans turn from time to time in their discussions of where the religious life is and ought to be going, to ask what is the interpretation of this or that and the practice of the other at Taizé. This is one reason why there is very rarely anything like the full community of seventy living in Taizé at any one time. Brothers are continually dashing off to conferences and dialogues all over the place.

Another reason is closer to the heart of the Taizé philosophy. For the modernization of the monastic order of things is not very high on the list of its priorities; Schutz, in fact, resists the suggestion that he has founded a school of theology or liturgy or religious behaviour. He stands pat, instead, upon something with wider implications. 'The Christians of today ... know it is not possible to separate spiritual and social progress. There is only one thing to do; to work, in the midst of many opposing influences, for the spiritual and human development of the poorest, in fact of all.' Taizé, in short, is not only to be a sign of Christian faith and a meeting point of Christian factions. It is also to be a centre of missionary work, not so much preaching a Christian faith as acting out what it takes to be Christian principles. 'At this point in human history it is important to give freely and never to look for remuneration as representatives of the Church, to be one who is present rather than one who is working for a particular end.' This is the principle that had Robert running a medical practice in the district, when there was no secular doctor for miles around, though, now that there is, Robert spends most of his time away from home on ecumenical work in Spain. It set Alain to work with the local farmers' cooperative, of which he has been elected a director, not because he is a member of the community – which gets no income from the coop – but because of his agricultural skills. It has put three brothers into a house in Lyons, where one works as a lorry driver, another as a probation officer and the third in a factory. There are six other brothers in Chicago, two in Récif, and six more in three different fraternities in Africa. Not all of them are doing workaday jobs like the men in Lyons. But all of them are, one way and another, spreading the doctrines of Taizé. They are present in the world and not in their monastery. And that is what distinguishes them sharply from the tradition they have followed.

Schutz says that they and their brothers at home are not to work for any particular end. If this is a rejection of the proselytizer, the man who would convert the heathen and the agnostic and the merely lukewarm to a fervent belief in a God-man who walked the earth two thousand years ago, then this too is a departure from the Christian tradition. Yet there is an end-product to Taizé, and Eric with his icons, Dominique with his slugs of type, Clément with his trowel, Daniel with his potter's wheel and all the rest believe they are working towards it. It is an end-product that a Buddhist might hope for, or a Moslem or a Jew, or a man with no faith in anything that is not of the here and now and of this earth. It is proclaimed at Taizé with all the brash technique of the roadside gasoline advertiser. Outside the Church of the Reconciliation there is a gigantic and gaudy hoarding. On it in three languages is written: 'All You Who Enter Here Be Reconciled. The Father With His Son. The Husband With His Wife. The Believer With The Unbeliever. The Christian With His Separated Brother.' This may not be an original injunction. But by any worldly standards it betrays an enormous, almost a monstrous ambition. To hope to change mankind, to shift perhaps the flux of human nature itself, so much and at so many points : this is what the brothers of Taizé have really set their hands to. Men living lives, as their leader himself admits, whose shape and texture and very essence is against all human reason.

THE TRADITION

'So the religious life is a help towards saintliness, because it is a life of burial.' – R. M. BENSON, Founder of the Society of St John the Evangelist, *The Religious Vocation*, p. 229

THE religious life, in its purely technical sense, began with the hermit and was not a Christian invention. Five centuries before Christ, Buddha left home at the age of twenty-nine and spent six years in almost complete solitude sitting under the sacred bo tree at Gaya while seeking salvation. Long before Buddha, holy men of Hinduism had done likewise. In immediately pre-Christian times devout Jews were in the habit of taking themselves off from their fellow men in order to contemplate their God without distraction. Two sects in particular, the Essenes in Palestine and the Therapeutae near Alexandria, were dedicated to an ascetic and eremitical existence, practising poverty, chastity, obedience, contemplation and penance, and setting much store by manual labour.

It has been reckoned on the somewhat shaky evidence offered by St Jerome (who has been described as a stylist rather than an historian) that the first Christian hermit was St Paul of Thebes, who fled from the Decian persecution in A.D. 250 and hid in a desert mountain cave, where he lived till he was 113. After him came St Antony the Hermit, who was born about the time of Paul's flight. He was the son of wealthy parents who died when he was young, whereupon he put his younger sister into a home for Christian virgins, sold his possessions and lived alone, first in his own village, then in an empty tomb some distance away, later still in the ruins of an old fort on the east bank of the Nile. He stayed there for twenty years and his days were spent in weaving mats and praying. He was an illiterate but he had learned most of the Scriptures off by heart and so he attracted disciples. A settlement of huts or cells grew around his fort at Pispir, in which these solitaries emulated Antony and sometimes gathered together to listen to his sermons on the principles that should govern their lives. These would be what have since been known as the evangelical counsels of perfection, which have always been the foundation of Christian religious life. They are the ultimate authority invoked in support of a life vowed to poverty, chastity and obedience. They are drawn from a number of biblical texts and the two most frequently quoted both come from St Matthew's Gospel. Upholding the life of poverty there is this : 'Jesus said unto him, "If thou wilt be perfect go and sell that thou hast and give to the poor and thou shalt have treasure in heaven : and come and follow me."' In support of chastity there is this : 'For there are some eunuchs, which were so born from their mother's womb and there are some eunuchs which were made eunuchs of men; and there be eunuchs, which have made themselves eunuchs for the kingdom of heaven's sake. He that is able to receive it, let him receive it.' The authority for a vow of obedience has always been more debatable. Thomas Aquinas suggested that it lay in Christ's words to the young man quoted above : 'Come and follow me.' Others, particularly in recent years, have argued that the only authority is Christ's declared obedience to the will of God on innumerable occasions, a precept which all Christians must follow and not just those with a vocation to the religious life.

At this time the Emperor Diocletian was trying to put down Christianity, ordering the destruction of churches, the burning of books, and threatening torture and death to adherents. Antony and his hermits set off for Alexandria, looking for martyrdom. For some reason they didn't find it, but they did encounter people clamouring to imitate their way of life. Many other eremitical settlements arose in Egypt and in Palestine as a result, and in each of them one hermit was chosen as a spiritual director, after the fashion of Antony at Pispir. The most famous of these offshoots was Nitria, sixty miles south of Alexandria. There five thousand men lived, according to the historian Palladius, 'each in accordance with his own powers and wishes, so that he is allowed to live alone or with another or with a number of others.' Nitria became so popular with visitors that the very basis of the eremitical life, solitude, was undermined and many of the hermits shifted farther into the desert and built their huts at a greater distance from each other. Apart from solitude the lives of these early desert fathers were characterized by two things. One was a sparse diet. It is said that Antony confined himself to one meal a day, usually of bread, salt and water; and his imitators don't seem to have fared much better. The other was deliberate and penitential discomfort. Macarius the Alexandrian is reckoned to have sat naked for six months in a marsh, while mosquitoes bit him all over; an Ethiopian named Moses was so determined to exist without sleep that for six years he spent the nights standing up in his cell.

In the first years of the fourth century the centre of all this eremitical activity was still Egypt, with a similar movement taking shape in Palestine. And it was in Egypt in A.D. 318 that the first detectable move towards communal religious life, towards the monastery rather than the hermitage, occurred. Three hundred miles south of Pispir, at Tabennisi on the Nile, St Pachomius founded a new kind of community. It was to be followed, before he died twenty-eight years later, by eight others for men and two for women. They had high walls enclosing a number of buildings and some of them accommodated a thousand people. They were, in effect, small religious towns. With them came two other innovations. Pachomius was an ex-soldier and so he produced a Rule which was to be obeyed. He also put in charge of each community a man whose function more nearly resembled that of the subsequent traditional monastic abbot than that of the eremitical leader. The latter had been no more than a spiritual guide and the hermits had to fend for themselves and could come and go as they pleased. Pachomius's leaders looked after the material needs of their communities as well as their spiritual requirements; Abbot Hor planted trees around his establishment to provide timber, not landscape. In the different houses of each community, which contained perhaps thirty monks, there was an oratory for common prayer and a refectory for common meals, while the entire community would gather twice a week in the principal church for worship. The life was still highly individualistic by later standards; Pachomius allowed his monks to choose what penances they would perform, what meals they would attend, what crafts they would take up. But it was an important development towards the totally communal life. It was a pattern rapidly followed elsewhere. Constantine promised religious tolerance with the Edict of Milan in A.D. 313 and so created a climate for expansion; Pachomius provided a model. As a result 'Never in the history of the Christian Church has there been such a stampede towards the monastic life as took place in Egypt between the years 350 and 400.' Monasteries also sprang up in Palestine and Asia Minor, along the North African coast, in Greece, Sicily, Italy, Spain and Gaul.

Hermits did not vanish as communities began to appear. The most celebrated of them all, St Simeon Stylites, did not arrive until early in the fifth century, when he mounted his pillar, gradually increased its height from nine to sixty feet, and stayed put on a three-foot platform for thirty-six years. There were many others like him and the eremitical species has never been extinguished. But a norm of religious life was being fashioned and they did not correspond to it. By the last quarter of the fourth century St Basil had tasted the hermit life himself, turned his back on it, and composed a Rule for monks which pointed the way ahead even more explicitly than Pachomius had done. Basil said that the solitary life was against the law of love because the solitary was bound to be self-centred; that it was bad for the individual to be in a position where his faults could not be corrected; that the solitary was in peril much more than the cenobite – the man living in community – of supposing that at some stage he had attained spiritual perfection.

Basil's Rule was stricter than the one Pachomius had laid down. It set the hours of liturgical prayer and it specified manual labours for its followers. It discouraged the extreme austerities practised by the desert fathers but it was at heart a rigorous code. It became the blueprint of eastern monasticism. The west had to wait nearly two centuries more before it received and adopted a similar statute, and in that time the monastic colony on Egyptian lines had spread across Europe as far north as Ireland. The statute came eventually from the hand of St Benedict some time between 530 and his death in 543. And for the next six hundred years the monastic life based on St Benedict's Rule became the norm in every country of Europe to the north and west of Italy; even in the middle of the twentieth century purists argue that a substantial departure from the Rule is a departure from the monastic life itself. In those six centuries the monasteries were a major force in western civilization, so much so that J. H. Newman was tempted to label them 'the Benedictine centuries'; Benedict is to be seen as much more than the originator of a sub-classification of the Christian life.

There are few men of such influence of whom we know so little. We have no idea what he looked like, for a contemporary portrait does not exist. The Mazzaroppi painting in his old abbey of Montecassino shows him entirely bald, with a squat and square head, a patriarchal beard, a generous mouth. A panel in Perigueux Cathedral has him tonsured, clean-shaven, with two scars on his left cheek, thin lips, small mouth and a huge cranium. We are scarcely better informed about his life. The only record is in the second book of *Dialogues* which St Gregory the Great wrote half a century after his death, and that is sketchy in the extreme. It begins 'From his boyhood he had the wisdom of age, for with a virtue far beyond his years he surrendered his heart to no worldly pleasure ...' Benedict's birthday is generally assumed to be 480. He came of a good family in the province of Nursia, was educated in Rome, but abandoned his school and set off for the wilderness accompanied

by his old nurse. In the village of Enfide she broke someone's sieve, so Benedict prayed and it was mended. Whereupon he fled to a cave at Subiaco, forty miles from Rome,
and lived there for three years. One day 'the devil brought
before his mind's eye the image of a woman he had once
seen and by this imagination inflamed the servant of God
with such a heat of passion that he could scarce control it'.
Control it he did by stripping and jumping into a nettlebed,
saying later in his life that never again was he vexed by lust.
'Soon after this many men began to leave the world and to
put themselves eagerly under his guidance.' In particular the
monks of Vicoravo asked him to take the place of their dead
abbot and when he did, and tried to reform them, they
attempted to poison him. But Benedict blessed the glass of
wine before drinking it and the vessel shattered. He took
the hint, nevertheless, and became a solitary again for a
time. He grew, writes St Gregory, in virtue and miracu-
lous power; once he persuaded a monk to walk upon the
surface of a lake and on another occasion made an iron bill-
hook float to the surface. He cured a man with a mottled
skin and brought a dead child back to life. He also returned
to the monastic existence. He built twelve monasteries before he died, placing an abbot in charge of twelve monks in
each of them. About 525 he moved to the abbey of Montecassino, and it was there that he composed his Rule and
where, six days before his death, he ordered his grave to be
opened. We know nothing else about the patriarch of
western monasticism except what is implied in his Rule.

It is a relatively short document of seventy-five chapters,
some of them no more than a paragraph in length. It was
witten to bring order to a religious situation that had become
chaotic and in some cases scandalous, as Benedict makes
clear in his first chapter by distinguishing four kinds of
monks. The first are the cenobites, who live in monasteries
under a rule and an abbot. The second are hermits who,
after long probation in a monastery, 'having learnt in association with many brethren how to fight against the devil,
go out well-armed from the ranks of the community to the

solitary combat of the desert'. Third are the detestable Sara-baites, living in twos or threes or alone, whose only law is their own pleasure; 'whatever they think or choose to do, that they call holy; what they like not, that they regard as unlawful'. Last are the Gyrovagues, who wander from place to place 'ever roaming and never stable, given up to their own wills and the allurements of gluttony, and worse in all respects than the Sarabaites'.

Benedict was equally clear about what he was proposing for his followers. They were to establish a school of the Lord's service. The abbot was to be the representative of Christ in the monastery and he was to be obeyed as if he were God. Discipline was to be strict but not invariably harsh; gentle characters were to be admonished verbally and only 'bold, hard, proud and disobedient' men given corporal punishment. No monk should have anything he could call his own 'for monks should not even have their bodies and wills at their own disposal.' A Benedictine monastery was to be completely self-contained and self-sufficient. It was to be supported economically by what it grew in its fields and gardens. Its whole life was to be directed towards the wor-ship of God and the sanctification of its individual souls. Nothing that happened inside its walls was for any other purpose than this; nothing, indeed, had any reference to what might be happening outside its walls. The life was to be utterly regular and quite unvarying in its routine. The aver-age day would see the monk spending about four hours in communal prayer, a similar period in private prayer or devo-tional reading, and about six hours in domestic chores, manual work or some craft. And at all points it was meticu-lously planned. The Rule considers how many psalms are to be said at the night offices; at what seasons alleluia is to be said; how the monks are to sleep; how boys – who were offered to the monastery for life by pious parents – are to be corrected; what kind of man the cellarer of the monastery should be; how guests are to be received; whether a monk should receive letters or anything else. It stipulates the amount of food and drink the monks are to take; two cooked dishes at the daily meal with fruit or young vegetables if available, a pound of bread and half a pint of wine a day, no flesh – except for the sick – from quadrupeds. It orders how the monks shall be clothed : a cowl, a belt, shoes and stockings, all to be made from whatever material is locally available and can be bought cheaply. It leaves nothing at all to chance or to the initiative of anyone but the abbot whose responsibility, Benedict warns, is a heavy one. 'And whatever number of brethren he knows he has under his care, let him regard it as certain that he will have to give the Lord an account of all these souls on the Day of Judgement, and certainly of his own soul also.'

This was the charter that brought order to the monastic life in the west. It was carried to England by St Augustine of Canterbury in 597, though there the Benedictine life did not gain a foothold beyond the south-east, until in the middle of the seventh century men like Wilfrid of Lindisfarne and Benedict Biscop returned from Rome and began to build communities at Jarrow, Wearmouth and elsewhere in the north; until then monasticism across the Channel had been an adaptation of the Pachomian way, brought in turn by Patrick from the Continent to Ireland and by Columba from Ireland to Iona and the mainland. And by that time in Italy the Benedictine life was already undergoing subtle changes from the pattern envisaged by its founder. By 643 the abbey of Bobbio, which contained about 150 monks, owned twenty-eight farms and in one year produced for resale 2,100 bushels of corn, 1,600 cartloads of hay, 2,700 litres of oil, 5,000 pigs and cattle, and 800 amphoras of wine. This may not have infringed the letter of the Rule, but it was not in the original spirit of self-containment and absolute separation from the world.

There were other departures from Benedict's precepts and most of them took place gradually over long periods of time. The monastery he planned was entirely for lay brothers (Benedict himself was never ordained) but by the tenth century it was becoming normal for monks to take holy orders. Benedict assumed that his abbots would live the common life with their brethren but by the beginning of the twelfth century in England they had a separate house, chapel and servants. At about the same time the practice of child oblation, under which small boys were taken into the community for the rest of their lives, had ceased. Under the growing patronage of kings, bishops and lesser lords, monasteries like St Martin of Tours, St Philibert of Jumièges and St Denis had enough power and credit to produce their own coinage. During the early Middle Ages the Benedictine monasteries contained the only medical learning to survive in western Europe from the ancient world; Baldwin, who was originally a monk of St Denis, came to Edward the Confessor's court as king's physician and even after being made abbot of Bury St Edmunds was regarded as the leading consultant in the realm. The monasteries produced scholars like Bede and Matthew Paris, a monk of St Albans, whose 'copious chronicles provide a mass of information about contemporary Europe and the Near East which is not to be found elsewhere'. They were the chief repositories of culture and of art; all the greatest examples of book illustration in England before 1220 came out of the cloister. They were so much caught up in the world Benedict had counselled them to avoid that many English abbeys were eventually in the hands of moneylenders, which meant Jews. At Bury in 1180 'matters had reached such a pitch that the tribe had quartered themselves on the abbey, using its strongroom as a bank, lodging their women and children in the offices and wandering about the minster while Mass was being sung.'

The changes that came in defiance of Benedict's teaching were frequently the result of laxity, but as often as not they followed from outside pressure or patronage, either ecclesiastical or secular. The Council of Chalcedon in 451 had ordered that all monks should come under the jurisdiction of the local bishop; in 628 the abbey of Bobbio was exempted from episcopal control and placed directly under the authority of the Holy See. From that date onwards the tide of exemptions ebbed and flowed through history; some popes preferred to regulate the monastic life themselves while others dispensed abbeys freely into the hands of their bishops, which very often meant into the hands of the kings and princelings who had the gift of bishoprics; a movement which did not help the stability of the monastic life. The Rule, moreover, was subject to amendment by subsequent legislation. Benedict of Aniane, a nobleman who fought with Charlemagne and later became a kind of arch-abbot, led a general meeting of abbots at Aachen in 817 which promulgated the *Codex regularum* and the *Concordia regularum*. Among other things these considerably increased the liturgical prayer of the community and saw agricultural labour as an extraordinary activity of monks – which laid the way open for the employment of others to work monastic lands. It was the foundation of a social division within the monastery which has persisted into the twentieth century; the literate or well educated priest-monk responsible for the corporate worship of the monastery in choir, and the illiterate or under-educated lay brother whose particular function has been that of labourer and servant.

A further change of direction came from Cluny in the eleventh and twelfth centuries. Under Abbot Odilo and his successor Hugh the autonomy of the monastery, implicit in Benedict's Rule, was reduced by binding dependent houses to the abbey of Cluny. Cluny appointed their superiors, where Benedict had ruled that the abbot of every community should be elected by his brethren. It required the monks of dependent houses to make their profession of obedience to Cluny through their own superior, rather than to him alone. It exacted an annual tribute. By the middle of the twelfth century Cluny stood at the head of 314 dependent monasteries. Its leading figures came from noble families and they were the confidants of kings and popes. Its life was still based on Benedict's Rule but an emphasis had been shifted. The liturgy of Montecassino had been simple and without ceremony, and it had been balanced in the monastic day by equal periods of contemplation and work. At Cluny everything was relegated behind an almost ceaseless worship in the choir, which took up so much time that study was nearly impossible. It was liturgical worship made more solemn and splendid than anything Benedict imagined, by use of chant, ritual and ornament.

Even before the Clunaic reforms there had been pressure in some quarters for a return to the simplicities of early monasticism, and it came in two places : Cîteaux and La Grande Chartreuse. The first originated with a group of hermits living in a Burgundian wood. Under the influence of an Englishman, Stephen Harding, who was returning from a pilgrimage to Rome, they set up a house where they intended to observe St Benedict's Rule literally, in the strictest poverty and seclusion. They were to wear a habit of white to distinguish them from the black Benedictine monks. The experiment began in 1098, but within a dozen years numbers at Cîteaux had fallen so low that it looked as if it would have to be abandoned. Then St Bernard arrived with thirty companions and from that moment the future of the Cistercian life was assured. Bernard was himself a Burgundian, a nobleman who before his arrival at Cîteaux had done time among solitaries in Britanny and had been abbot of St Cyprian. He was a frail man who suffered from chronic stomach trouble which was not helped by the extreme austerities and mortifications he practised. Within two years of joining Harding he was told to found a new abbey at Clairvaux and it was from there that he was to exert his influence not only on the order but on the Church at large. He denounced the persecution of Jews and he preached the Second Crusade. He was the chief backer of Pope Innocent II in his struggles with the antipope Anacletus. He wrote one of the outstanding books of medieval mysticism. But nothing he did was to have such a lasting effect as his rescue and consolidation of the Cistercian life.

There had been no thought of founding a new order when the hermits started their house at Cîteaux; essentially they were after a communal life more severe and more remote from society than the one Benedictinism had grown into. Bernard built an order but it stuck closely to those first principles. Powerful benefactors, who had left their mark on the Benedictines, were kept away from Cistercian houses. The monks rejected every evidence of luxury and wealth; cloaks, shirts, warm hoods, bedspreads and combs went and crucifixes were made of wood, not precious metal. They abandoned all feudal possessions, like manorial bakeries and mills, and they disdained any income from church possessions such as tithes, altar and burial dues and advowsons. Their lands were to be cultivated only for their own use and by their own labour, and this meant introducing lay brothers to do the bulk of the work so that the priests could get on with the chief function of the monastery, which was prayer in the choir and in the cloister. Literary work was forbidden by statute, and as a result the early Cistercians had the reputation of being illiterates. In church the services and the liturgy were severely trimmed. The offices of the saints, the litanies, the possessions, the visits to the altars all disappeared and the elaborations of chant and ritual which were at that moment reaching greater heights in Cluny and its offshoots disappeared with them. The Cistercian monks were bent on one thing above all others and that was individual sanctification. So they lived sparely and they conducted themselves in silence except when conversation was absolutely necessary.

It was a life of high ideal and it attracted disciples as rapidly as Benedictinism had in its early years. Under Bernard the abbey of Clairvaux housed 700 monks and in England there were 600 at Rievaulx under Abbot Aelred. But, like the Benedictines, the Cistercians were to shed some of their early fervour and strictness as their numbers began to swell. They were never to depart from the Rule as much as the Benedictines, but by 1200 many abbeys took incomes from sources forbidden by statute. About the same time Cistercian abbots began to build libraries and Cistercian monks started to write chronicles. The white monks in England became the biggest wool producers in the country, having started sheep farming to make their own clothes. In 1325 the abbot of Beaulieu was disciplined by the mother house at Cîteaux for drinking with knights, eating off silver plate and having watchdogs tethered to his bed with silver chains.

The simultaneous reform, at La Grande Chartreuse, was to be severer and more lasting. It was the work of St Bruno, who was a canon of Cologne and a teacher at Rheims before joining the same forest hermits who started Cîteaux. He spent a couple of years with them before he left with two companions to make his own community at a place in the Dauphine Alps north of Grenoble. The Carthusians were backtracking to an age before Benedict's. In place of the dormitory, which had been the standard sleeping arrangement since Montecassino, the Carthusian monk inhabited a separate cell. He left it only for lauds, matins and vespers in the church each day and for occasional meals and conversation with his brethren. Otherwise he prayed and read alone, ate alone, and worked alone. A hairshirt was as obligatory as the habit that covered it. Silence was total except for the daily excursions into choir and the weekly periods of relaxation. It was a life for contemplative ascetics and it was to be preserved almost entirely in its original state by the most inflexible observation of its Rule. It is the one form of communal religious life that has, even today, scarcely budged an inch from its origins. Because of its inflexibility and its rigours the Carthusian order was never to attract great numbers. It was never to pull any weight in Church politics. Its communities were never to affect the lives of society around them. It is significant chiefly because it was founded at a particular point in time, as a protest against change and decay. It was an emphatic re-assertion of the need to withdraw from a world which could corrupt and come between a man and his desire to contemplate his God without distraction, which had been the foundation of the religious life so far.

For six hundred years after Benedict this, together with the idea of communal life, had been the standard, and an infectious one. It had led the canons of the Church – the priests who long before Benedict had been grouped around a bishop to sing the offices in the basilican churches of Rome and other cities – to reorganize themselves on a comparable footing, with comparable disciplines. The secular priests alone had been untouched by the spiritual fervour and the intellectual growth which, at different stages, characterized the religious foundations. Planted in isolation in the world most of them were in as wretched a condition, morally, spiritually and materially, as the people they were supposed to be ministering to. There was a need for new forms of religious life whose followers, far from withdrawing from the world as the monks had proposed, would go preaching in secular situations while drawing on the strength of the communal life for stability. The first attempt to do this came with the foundation of the Order of Fontevrault at the end of the eleventh century by Robert of Arbrissel, who was an assistant to the Bishop of Rennes. He set up two houses, one for women and another for men, and when he died in 1117 his successor at the head of them was a married woman, Petronilla of Chemaille; not a novelty, for at Whitby four hundred years earlier St Hilda had become the first abbess of a mixed community. Robert's really original idea was to have two groups of religious, one staying within the enclosure while the other went out preaching, the jobs being interchangeable from time to time. Fontevrault was followed within a few years by another double monastery at Prémontre, set up by Norbert, a kinsman of the Emperor Henry IV, to begin the Premonstratensian order which was also vowed to get out into the world and stimulate parochial life.

The twelfth century saw several other attempts to combine monastic life and secular activity. And because it was a time when the Church was deep in its crusades it also threw up the orders dedicated to fighting the Moslems and to protecting the Christian pilgrims on their way to and from Jerusalem. The Order of the Temple was organized in 1120, so impoverished at first that two knights had to share one horse and one mess tin, but eventually, as a result of Pope Alexander III allowing them to keep whatever treasures they looted from the enemies of the Church, it grew into a corporation of colossal and ostentatious wealth. The Order of St John of Jerusalem began by running its hospital for sick pilgrims but then began to fight for them and eventually ended up as a military threat to Moslem shipping in the Mediterranean from its stronghold on Malta, where it remained until Napoleon dispossessed it. There were other military orders, like the Teutonic Knights and the Knights of the Sword, and there were bargaining foundations like the Trinitarians, who existed to ransom Christian prisoners from the Saracens, normally by money but if that failed by exchanging places with them. Between them they took the religious life an unrecognizable distance from what St Benedict had envisaged. If they could be called monks at all it was only because they were based on community and because they began by taking the vows of poverty, chastity and obedience, though poverty didn't last long in the case of the Templars.

They were, though, a response to the times they were living in. If the twelfth century marked a change in the religious life it was even more a turning-point in the European world as a whole. It was a time when merchants and craftsmen began to form themselves into guilds, when wealth from the east began to flow through the market-place in the wake of the crusaders, when people began to travel more freely than ever before, when the troubadours were on the hoof from Provence, when universities began to appear and when traditional beliefs were being questioned by pedagogues like Peter Abelard in Paris. This was a situation the Church felt a need to control and it led in the thirteenth century to the development of the mendicant orders of friars. It produced the Carmelites and the Augustinians, the Bonshommes, the Friars of the Sack and the Crutched Friars. It also produced the Franciscans and the Dominicans. Of the two the Franciscans were the more radical departure from the norm of religious life, and this was in keeping with the character of their founder. St Francis, son of a rich cloth merchant in Assisi, was a frivolous charmer in his youth, bound for a soldier's life, but with a deep streak of tenderness in him. It was to come out revealingly later in his life in his instructions to the ministers in charge of the Franciscan friaries who were, he said, to be as mothers – not fathers – to their brethren. Francis had been captured in a military skirmish in Perugia and experienced conversion while he was in prison. On his release he abandoned his family, became a hermit and one day in church heard the lesson from Matthew's Gospel : 'As ye go, preach, saying, The kingdom of heaven is at hand. Heal the sick, cleanse the lepers, raise the dead, cast out devils : freely ye have received, freely give. Provide neither gold nor silver, nor brass in your purses, nor scrip for your journey, neither two coats, neither shoes, nor yet staves.' And with that, Francis went barefoot into the world and began to follow the instruction to the letter. Like the first Cistercians he had no intention of founding an order, but from a small group of followers a movement began to spread across Italy. It was distinguished from anything that had gone before because the Friars Minor, as they became known, were to attempt life on Christ's own pattern; living and moving among the people without a livelihood, begging their alms, coming unlettered and unpriested on the same terms as those they were trying to convert. It was an effort to convert by providing an example of simplicity and absolute poverty.

This was not the intention of Dominic, a Spaniard who was a priest and a theologian who discovered his vocation when he encountered the Albigensian heretics – who accused the Church of taking New Testament allegories literally – in the South of France. The Dominican Order of Preachers he founded was to attack ignorance and intellectual error by the application of the trained mind. The Dominicans were to propagate the Catholic truths with every means at their disposal and everything was to be subordinated to this end. In a Dominican house fasts could be broken, offices in church were to be said briskly and without elaboration, manual work was abandoned altogether, all to leave the maximum time for study. They were, in effect, to be schools for intellectual shock troops and for this reason each one contained a doctor of theology, while the friars themselves were frequently dispatched to the new university cities of Bologna, Paris and Oxford to preach and to teach. It was the Dominican Thomas Aquinas who brought Aristotle to the defence of the faith, and it was the anti-heretical bent of the Dominican mind that led to the order being used by the papacy as a chief instrument of the Inquisition.

Both Franciscans and Dominicans were founded at the same time and each was to borrow something of the other's ethos before long. The Dominicans became mendicants, as the Franciscans had begun, while the Franciscans developed from a completely itinerant and unruly body into one with a central organization and a growing taste for study which in time was to produce its own scholars like Roger Bacon and Duns Scotus. And because of their mobility, which monks had never officially enjoyed, they were both to be used by the Church as its first considerable missionary force. 'There was no country in Europe into which the Friar did not penetrate, bringing with him the stir of religious revival. For work in heathen countries no missionary was more available. He was to be found in Morocco and Tunis. He preached to motley crowds in Syrian seaports. He voyaged to India and Persia and to the distant parts of China.' A whole collection of other mendicant orders began to develop to such an extent that in 1274 the Council of Lyons banned all but the Franciscans, the Dominicans, the Carmelites and the Augustinians. These, having the field to themselves, attracted great numbers from then on. By 1303 there were 557 Dominican houses, ranging from Britanny to Russia and Africa, containing 15,000 religious. By 1316 the Franciscans numbered about 35,000 in 1,400 friaries. It has been estimated that at this time there could not have been fewer than 80,000 mendicants roaming Christendom.

Inevitably there was friction both with the secular priests and the older monastic orders. Popes issued several bulls which gave backing to the friars, like the one of Martin IV in 1281 which put them under his jurisdiction and exempted them from both parochial and diocesan authority. They were attacked by the seculars for attracting penitents from the parish priest, and the monks resented them because their idealization of poverty reflected badly on the life of the wealthy monasteries. Not that this lasted very long. The friars were no better than the monks had been at sticking to the concepts of their founders. To the irritation of the monks at the engagement of friars to preach in monastic cathedrals and to lecture the monks on theology, were added quarrels about the appropriation of revenues like burial dues, which had previously gone into other pockets. They watched, moreover, these interlopers progressively acquiring more influence among the hierarchies of the Church. Between 1350 and 1535 no fewer than forty-four Dominicans were made bishops in England. There the friars were subjected to increasing attack. Fitzralph, Archbishop of Armagh, in a series of sermons between 1356 and 1357 criticized the friars for their motives as confessors, for their avarice, their luxurious lives and their sumptuous building. Wycliff not only accused them of immorality but of ruining the nation by begging and sending out of the country a sum he calculated at £40,000 a year.

The truth is that by the end of the fourteenth century the religious life was on the slide everywhere. The mendicants had fallen to the same temptations of acquiring property, benefactors and wealth that had seduced the monastic orders before them. The monasteries themselves were mostly becoming houses of decadence. There were exceptions. There were men like Abbot Thomas de la Mare of St Albans, who would rise before midnight while his brethren still slept, to recite private prayers. He usually ate and drank only once a day and carried out personal fasts and abstinences in excess of those ordained by Church and Rule. He wore a hairshirt and had himself flogged once a week. And though before becoming a monk he had excelled in field sports, at St Albans he refused even to watch hunting or hawking, or to let any of his monks do so. But de la Mare's conduct was no longer the norm. The norm was nearer the practice of William Clowns, Abbot of Leicester, who was said to be the

most skilful runner of greyhounds in the country; Edward
III, the Black Prince and their attendant lords made an
annual trek to the Quorn country specifically to enjoy the
abbot's pursuit of the hare. The most common fault, in England at any rate, was that the monks no longer observed the
monastic enclosure which was intended to prevent them
from coming close to the world and the world encroaching
on them. They went out to consort with the townsfolk and
they encouraged the townsfolk to come in to visit them.
Things became so lax at Daventry by 1433 that the accounts
were neglected, the monks were to be found in local taverns
and all kept hounds of their own. Women came into the
cloisters to do their washing and the prior was charged
with adultery. At Dorchester the monks hunted and
hawked and in the evening after compline invited women in
to help the consumption of ale. The abbot was accused of
keeping five mistresses at the expense of the community. A
century before, an adulterous abbot would have been deposed and any other monk suspected of immorality would
have been punished by close confinement, a restricted diet
and various humiliations in choir and chapter. If it did not
happen now it was because controls over the monasteries
from outside had been relaxed; the diocesan bishop's responsibility for visitation and insistence on at least a tolerable
observation of the Rule had generally passed to a royal servant who was very rarely there to do his job, usually being
too much involved in public affairs or attendance on the
monarch. And for once the fifteenth century failed to produce from within the Church itself anyone with reforming
zeal to restore the religious life to the straight and narrow.

The corruption of the religious life was only a small contri-
butory cause of the Reformation movement, though it undoubtedly helped to give it popular support. Four years after
Luther, the Augustinian friar, had nailed his theses to Wittenberg church door he attacked the life, in *De votis
monasticis judicium*, not on the grounds of decadence but
because the religious implied, by taking vows based on the
evangelical counsels, that his was a superior form of life to

that lived by other Christians. The Reformers, in fact, explicitly allowed for the possibility of religious communities in their order of things. In the Wittenberg Articles of 1536 there is this passage :

If certain men of outstanding character, capable of living a life under a rule, feel a desire to pass their lives in the cloister, we do not wish to forbid them, so long at least as their doctrines and worship remain pure, and, notably, so long as they consider the practices of monastic life as things indifferent. We are persuaded that numerous authentic Christians of irreproachable spirituality have passed their lives in convents. It is even certainly to be wished that such convents will exist, occupied by wise and fervent religious, in which the study of Christian doctrine can be pursued for the greater good of the Church. These might be then a place where, by the practice of pious exercises of religious life, young people would receive not only an intellectual training, but a spiritual one as well.

Although monasticism was quenched in most areas of Reform a number of communities, especially in Germany and Scandinavia, where legislation restricted rather than repressed, survived by adopting Lutheran doctrines in place of Catholic ones. At Mollenbeck, on the Weser, which had been an Augustinian house since 1441, the whole community transferred its allegiance in 1558. Its routine remained the same, but its theology was modified and all references suggesting a cult of saints were erased from the liturgy, and everything smelling of sacrifice from the mass. As a Lutheran community it flourished for over a century, until it foundered in the Thirty Years War, and one of its monks, Conrad Hoyer, published a kind of apologia for monastic life among evangelicals. The Cistercians of Loccum, near Hanover, were another community who made the doctrinal change, practising full monasticism and even saying the offices in Latin till 1658.

The suppression of monasteries was nowhere as thorough as it was in Britain. There the first sign of it came in 1519 when Cardinal Wolsey sent the Austin friars, so far exempt from episcopal control, a set of constitutions he wished them to observe. Two years later he summoned abbots and priors to discuss reform and between 1525 and Wolsey's fall in 1529 a whole stream of royal edicts abolished twenty-nine houses of religious, male and female. This was only a taste of things to come. The Oath of Succession in 1534, which was to secure allegiance to the offspring of Henry VIII and Anne Boleyn as heirs to the crown but which also meant the renunciation of papal authority, let Thomas Cromwell loose on the religious houses, not as Wolsey's henchman but as suppressor in chief. The first tour of Cromwell's commissioners, armed with their questionnaires and injunctions, was made with the intention of disciplining the religious houses rather than bringing them down. It produced, among other things, the *Comperta*, a list of sexual deviations which ran the whole gamut from sodomy to nuns having children. The visitations which followed the 1536 Act of Suppression were made to raise revenue for putting down the Irish and Scots and for fighting abroad the enemies of the king's divorce. Even after they had started the king, oddly enough, was granting exemptions to a number of places like the nunnery at Stixwold, so that the religious in them could offer prayers for himself and his queen. But generally Cromwell's brief was clear and carried out scrupulously well. A few monasteries were converted into colleges or cathedrals. In the rest the plate and jewels were sent to the royal treasury and furniture was auctioned on the spot. At the house of the Austin friars in Stafford a Mr Stamford picked up an alabaster retable, a door and a high altar for 7s. The buildings were stripped of everything movable, while surveyors decided which part of the structure was to be left standing to create a house or a farm for a new tenant. The religious themselves, by the standards of the time, were not treated badly. They were generally given a pension of £5 10s a year for men and £3 for women; and these were paid regularly by successive governments. One of the curiosities of Elizabeth's reign was that, while fines were being collected from Catholic recusants, life pensions were being doled out to ex-Benedictines.

Under Mary there was a brief revival of the religious life in England. The monastery at Westminster was restored in 1556 and by the next year four men's and two women's communities had been refounded. These, however, were the small pious gestures of a queen horrified by her father's sacrilege and they were cut short with her own death. Protestant England was to make its own gestures. In the seventeenth century John Evelyn was to toy with the idea of starting a Charterhouse, but it came to nothing. In 1626 Nicholas Ferrer and his followers at Little Gidding began to practise a form of religious life which was to last for thirty years, under the patronage of Charles I. Ferrer, a fellow of Clare Hall, Cambridge, and later an MP, abandoned a promising career when he moved into the manor at Little Gidding with his mother, brother, married sister and about thirty relatives. They devoted themselves to charitable works, ran an almshouse and a school, did needlework and book-binding, and three times a day walked in procession to the village church to celebrate matins, the litany and evensong. A short service was also held every hour in the house and the family took it in turns to keep watch and recite psalms in church every night from 9 p.m. to 1 a.m. Little Gidding was no more than a curiosity, though, an isolated exception to the general rule of things. From the time Elizabeth came to the throne the religious life virtually disappeared from England for two and a half centuries.

In the European lands which resisted the tide of the Reformation a succession of popes attempted to bring some discipline to the situation in the sixteenth century. The year before Luther rebelled at Wittenberg, Leo X ended all exemptions and put all religious under the authority of the bishops. Paul IV had the vagrant monks of Rome sent off to the galleys. Pius V suppressed a number of orders, compelled 1,500 abbeys to return to the observance of Benedict's Rule, and forbade the Dominicans to receive any new members. Things were tightened up at the Council of Trent, which ruled that entry to a religious community was henceforth to be a matter of free choice only, that no one under the age of forty or with fewer than eight years in profession was to be made superior, and that no one could be professed under the age of sixteen. The Council also circumscribed more rigidly than before the movement of monks and nuns in and out of their monasteries.

Reforms were made in all the established orders and they were most marked among the Carmelites under the influence of two Spaniards. One was Teresa de Ahumada, who had been a nun for twenty-five years before she founded a more primitive Carmelite community in 1562. The other was John de Yepes, a Carmelite whose urge for a more eremitical life would have turned him towards the Carthusians if Teresa had not dissuaded him and invited him to become confessor to her foundling. Together they created the order of Discalced Carmelites, so called because its members went barefoot or wore sandals instead of shoes. Both were to be canonized, one as St Teresa of Avila, the other as St John of the Cross. Both were mystics, whose insights into prayer and commentaries on its techniques were to become part of the spiritual equipment of the Church.

In the processes of the Counter Reformation the sixteenth century produced other new orders. As the Discalced emerged from the regular Carmelites so the Capuchins (who later on were to establish and man Paris's first fire brigade) sprang from the Franciscans. There were original foundations, too. The Theatines were intended to work for the sanctification of the clergy, the Barnabites were to teach the young, the Camillians were to work among the sick. Philip Neri created the Oratorians who were to convert the world and defend the faith not only by conventional preaching and good works but by music and singing as well. If they had anything in common, these new foundations of the sixteenth century, it was that they all dispensed with the old monastic routine of offices in choir for the sake of mobility. Like the Franciscans and the Dominicans before them they were to get out into the world, at home and abroad, as missionaries in one form or another.

The greatest of them was born in 1534, the year that

Henry VIII broke with Rome, when seven students took oaths in the Church of St Mary, Montmartre, and became the first members of the Society of Jesus. Their leader was a crippled Basque called Inigo Lopez de Recalde, whom history was to remember as Ignatius Loyola. Like many religious innovators before him, and since he came from a noble family, he was a soldier before ever he became a Christian zealot. The fusion of the two disciplines, military and religious, was to characterize Loyola's Jesuits in a unique fasion.

Loyola trained his men on the *Spiritual Exercises*, which has been described as 'a little pamphlet of icy dryness and purely administrative appearance', but which is also a means of systematically bending the will to a dedicated life. He drilled them to go anywhere at the drop of a hat and from 1540 onwards, when Paul III recognized the Jesuit constitutions, it was above all to be at the drop of the pope's hat; to the normal three vows of religion were added a fourth, and that was to be always at the pope's personal disposal. The Jesuits thus became a cardinal instrument of the Counter Reformation. They were set to rooting out the Protestant heresies by preaching, by education, by confession. They founded schools throughout Europe to train more young minds in their disciplines. At the Council of Trent they totally opposed any doctrinal modifications and so made sure that there would be no prospect of reconciliation between Catholicism and Reform. They became confessors to the Habsburgs and so contrived a hardening of the Catholic arteries throughout the Austrian Empire. More than any other group of men, they stemmed the tide of Protestantism on the Continent. They were just as vigorous abroad. They went to India and the Far East, they proselytized in Brazil and Peru, and when the French began to explore North America the Jesuits went with them. They were to become so powerful that Catholics were to fear and hate them as much as any Protestant. Before Ignatius died in 1556 his society was already being fought in the Spanish dominions of the New World by the Dominicans, who saw their well established missionary title there threatened by the newcomers. Eventually, however, the Jesuits were virtually in control of almost a quarter of South America. And it was partly because of their autocracy there, because they held the Indians in paternal subjection and prevented white settlers from exploiting them, that the Jesuits were to be persecuted by the Church they had served and by its secular backers. The colonials complained to the kings of Spain and Portugal. The kings took over Jesuit colleges and churches, shipped Jesuit missionaries off to the papal states, imprisoned and executed others at home. In France the Jesuits were attacked for their opposition to the Jansenists and because it was believed they taught that the end always justified the means. Under pressure from the Bourbons, Pope Clement XIV suppressed the society in 1773 and although it was allowed to carry on its work in Germany and Austria, in Prussia and Russia, it was to remain on the windy side of the papacy until 1814.

In their prime, at the start of the seventeenth century, the Jesuits were the Catholic Church's main hope of regaining its hold over Europe. The Thirty Years War put an end to that. And the Age of Reason, which the Jesuit-educated Descartes introduced, put an end to any hopes the Church might have had of holding all its people in unquestioning obedience even in the areas where it remained entrenched. The religious orders in the new climate of lay influence began to appear as remnants of an antique universalism. As the Church became increasingly secularized so the religious were more and more under fire from the parish clergy who had always resented their power and their privileges. The friction was greatest in France, where the Assembly of the Clergy in 1625 tried to bring the orders entirely under episcopal control. If they did not succeed completely it was because Richelieu, who imposed a compromise, had acquired a taste for the government of religious orders; within a year or two he had become, among many other things, Abbot of Cluny and Abbot of Cîteaux and intended to gather all French Benedictine communities under his skirts as Superior-General in chief. The answer of the religious to these secular pressures was once again to attempt reform from within, as the Benedictines of the Maurist Congregation, two hundred communities in all, did by returning to the strict observance of the Rule. The Maurists were outdone by Richelieu's godson, Jean de Rancé, who entered the Cistercian monastery of La Trappe in 1663, after a fairly randy life, notwithstanding the fact that from the age of eleven he had been titular head of several abbeys. Once in La Trappe, however, he reversed gear and proceeded as operative abbot to make the Trappists a sub-order whose asceticism and devotion to silence was second in severity only to that of the Carthusians.

The seventeenth century also saw the arrival of new societies of priests whose object was to stiffen a secular clergy ill equipped to combat bourgeois rationalism and to train a new and better breed of parish priest. By placing themselves at the disposal of the bishops they avoided, from the outset, the exemption controversies that were plaguing the old orders. They lived in community, but they owned personal property and were otherwise generally indistinguishable from secular priests except that they were not encumbered with a parish. France was their biggest breeding ground. It produced Vincent de Paul's Vincentians, who 'went wherever the bishop sent for them, to preach, to hear confessions, teach the catechism to children, minister to the sick, relieve the destitute. They went from deanery to deanery in the diocese, visiting each parish in turn, and when their words and example had touched men's minds and hearts the bishop came to preside over a general Communion.' An Oratorian missionary named Jean Eudes established seminaries for the improved training of clergy and staffed them with his Eudists. A parish priest of Saint-Sulpice named Olier created the Sulpicians with a similar purpose. A canon of Rheims, Jean-Baptiste de la Salle, started the Institute of the Brothers of the Christian Schools, which introduced a new concept of primary education to France, with instruction in the vernacular instead of in Latin, and with pupils tutored individually instead of en masse. By the beginning of the eighteenth century all these societies were flourishing in France. Similar ones, like the Passionists and the Redemptorists, were starting to appear in Italy.

They were not enough to turn the tide of scepticism that was now on the flood throughout continental Europe. What had happened to the Jesuits by 1773 was no more than an extreme example of the treatment that many more religious societies and orders were to experience in the next thirty years. Throughout the Austrian Empire the contemplative orders were suppressed completely and many others turned out of their houses by the Emperor Joseph II. In France, under the Archbishop of Toulouse, a commission of regulars which consisted mainly of laymen suppressed in 1766 nine congregations of religious, over a third of the monks and nuns. Those that were left survived the Revolution in only token numbers. Many nuns went to the guillotine while most of the male religious simply abandoned their community life and allowed themselves to be totally secularized. The only ones Napoleon countenanced were a few charitable or teaching orders of women. Otherwise, and this applied to every land the Napoleonic armies crossed, disbandment or banishment was the rule. The anti-religious process was to continue well into the nineteenth century in what had been Catholic Europe; not even in Spain and Portugal did the religious orders escape general persecution.

Yet while the religious life was declining fast almost everywhere except in Italy itself, it was beginning to revive in England where it had been virtually absent for well over two hundred years. After the dissolution and after the abortive attempt at revival under Mary, most of the English monks, nuns and other religious took the easy way out of their troubles by opting for a pension and a secular life. But a number fled to the Continent, finding refuge in the Italian monasteries of Montecassino and Padua, in the Spanish abbeys of Montserrat, Compostela and Valladolid, in Flanders and in France. A group of English monks led by Blessed John Roberts established St Gregory's priory at Douai, Flanders, in 1605. The monks of Westminster in

1608 founded the priory of St Laurence at Dieulouard in
Lorraine. By 1624 English nuns led by a descendant of Sir
Thomas More had set themselves up at Cambrai. And during the period of Catholic suppression in England these
Benedictines and other exiles formed a kind of underground
movement on the Continent, running seminaries for the
children of people who were keeping their faith secretly at
home, sending missionaries across the Channel to remind
them that they were not abandoned. The Benedictines were
in 1619 united in an English congregation by papal brief,
to strengthen their sense of community against the day when
they might return. They were the first of many Benedictine congregations of abbeys, groups generally formed within
national frontiers.

Two things brought them back to England. One was the
wave of anti-religious feeling that swept the Continent at the
end of the eighteenth century, particularly since the French
Revolution. The other was the relaxation of Catholic penal
laws in England in 1778 and 1791. So back they gradually
came. The monks of St Gregory's and those of St Laurence's
returned in 1791. They were both at first given house room
on the estate of Sir Edward Smythe at Acton Burnell, spent
several years after that in a number of places, and then
found permanent homes. In 1802 the monks of St Laurence
became the monks of Ampleforth. In 1814 the monks of St
Gregory became the monks of Downside. In 1838 the
women of Cambrai became the nuns of Stanbrook Abbey.
By that time the English were well accustomed to refugee
religious from the Continent. At the turn of the century
there were Benedictine nuns in Hampshire, London, Dorset and Lancashire, canonesses of St Augustine in Suffolk,
canonesses of the Holy Sepulchre in Yorkshire, Carmelites
in Cornwall, Durham and London, Dominican nuns in
Gloucester, Poor Clares in Northumberland. There were
even French Trappist monks at Lulworth Cove, set up there
on land owned by a wealthy Catholic gentleman, Mr
Thomas Weld, in 1796, and they were visited by George III
and his family. The spectacle of the monk and nun around
the country was therefore no novelty to the English when

their own national Church took up the religious life for the first time in the nineteenth century.

Took it up seriously, that is. For the one form of religious life that seems not to have been totally extinguished by the Tudors was the hermit's. In the mid-eighteenth century it was fashionable (purely for decorative purposes, it seems) for landed gentry to recruit hermits to their premises, like the Hon. Charles Hamilton of Cobham, who built a cell in his garden and installed a solitary there. The terms of his service were that he would 'continue in the hermitage seven years, where he should be provided with a Bible, optical glasses, a mat for his feet, a hassock for his pillow, an hourglass for his timepiece, water for his beverage, and food from the house. He must wear a camlet robe, and never, under any circumstances, must he cut his hair, beard or nails, stray beyond the limits of Mr Hamilton's grounds for seven years, or exchange one word with the servant.' For this he was to be paid £700. He lasted three weeks and so didn't get a penny. In 1810 the following advertisement appeared in the *Courier*. 'A young man who wishes to retire from the world and live as a hermit, in some convenient spot in England, is willing to arrange with any nobleman or gentleman who may be desirous of having one. Any letter directed to S. Laurence (post paid), to be left at Mr Otton's, No. 6, Coleman Lane, Plymouth, mentioning what gratuity will be given, and all other particulars, will be duly attended.'

These were not even straws in the wind. But the poet Southey's suggestion in 1829 that the Church of England should found sisters of charity on the Catholic model to work among the poor was. This came to nothing. Then on 14 July 1833 John Keble preached his assize sermon in Oxford. It attacked the plan to suppress ten Irish bishoprics, it denounced the spread of liberalism in Anglican theology and it launched the Oxford Movement to restore to the Church of England its High Catholic traditions. It was the crucial step towards the revival of the religious life in the English Church. This was very largely the work of Keble's colleague at the head of the Oxford Movement, Edward

Bouverie Pusey, a fellow of Oriel and canon of Christ Church. The third leader, J. H. Newman, did in fact dabble with an embryonic monastery at Littlemore in 1842, but he was already on his way out of the Anglican Church, which he left for Catholicism three years later. It was Pusey who fostered the Park Village Sisterhood before, during and after its foundation in 1845. In 1839 he had written to the Vicar of Leeds, Dr Hook, of what he had in mind :

I want very much to have one or more societies of Sœurs de la Charité formed; I think them desirable (1) in themselves as belonging to and fostering a high tone in the Church; (2) as giving holy employment to many who yearn for something; (3) as directing zeal, which will otherwise go off in some irregular way, or go over to Rome. ... It seems best that at first they should not be discursive, as those of the Romish Church in Ireland, but be employed in hospitals, lunatic asylums, prisons, among the females. Do you know any who would engage in it on a small scale, quietly, or one who would be a Mother Superior, i.e., one fitted to guide it?

Two years later, on Trinity Sunday 1841, the daughter of a Gloucestershire clergyman, Miss Marian Rebecca Hughes, took a vow of celibacy in Oxford and became the first professed Anglican religious. She then went to France to find out about the religious life from the Ursulines in Bayeux and the Convent of the Visitation in Caen. Pusey took himself off to Romish Ireland to see how they conducted their affairs. Miss Hughes was, in the event, not to join the first Anglican sisterhood because she had parents to look after at home; she was to become the superior of another community a few years later when she was free of domestic duties. But on 26 March 1845 two aspirants to the religious life took up residence as Sisters of Mercy at No. 17, Park Village West, Upper Albany Street, Regent's Park. One was Miss Jane Ellacombe, who, at twenty-six, had broken off an engagement to free herself for the religious life. The other was Miss Mary Bruce, aged thirty-two, 'a lady of Scottish ancestry and Irish birth, who had been known to Dr Pusey for some time'. At their initiation service, conducted by Pusey and the Rev. W. Dodsworth, they both burst into floods of tears. Their superior in religion did not arrive until May. She was Miss Emma Langston, a forty-one-year-old governess, 'a lady of great refinement and goodness, whose very countenance indicated benevolence'; a lady who had never got round to being confirmed until just before she was translated from Miss Langston to Mother Emma. By September there were seven sisters in Park Village. They wore a habit cut in the shape of a sack, of black wool supplied by a merchant who was a good churchgoer in Leeds. They lived under a rule which was basically that of St Augustine, with several other later Catholic regulations grafted on, which stipulated that they were to give six hours a day to works of mercy except on Sundays and holy days, when only the most urgent outside tasks were to be attended to. They were never to retire from a meal without having mortified themselves in some slight way. The superior was to receive all incoming mail and no sister was to speak to any visitor without the superior's permission. They had to be up at 5 a.m., and said four offices, with breakfast in the middle, before they went off to teach in poor schools of the district, and there were more offices in the evening before they got to bed about 10 p.m.

These were genteel Victorian ladies and they were scarcely bred to stand the strain of a pell-mell life of austerity. Miss Bruce was one who had to leave early on. They were also women whose zeal often outran their common sense and their physical capacities, and Pusey from the start saw that if he didn't want to end up as sponsor of a houseful of invalids some of the sisters would have to be restrained from overfasting. This killed off Sister Katherine who one Lent took no food at all except a dish of oatmeal each day after compline. The most zealous postulant of all stayed with the community less than twenty-four hours. She had wanted to imitate St Catherine of Siena by abstaining at all times from all food but the bread and wine of Holy Communion; when the rest of the community sat down to dinner she left in disgust at their self-indulgence.

That was the beginning of the religious life in the Angli-

can Church. Within a dozen years of their foundation the
Park Villagers had amalgamated with another women's
order based in Devonport to form, eventually, the Society
of the Most Holy Trinity. By the end of the nineteenth
century the Anglo-Catholic revival in the Church of England had become strong enough to have produced about
thirty orders of women. There was nothing like the same
growth rate among men, whose starting point was the eccentric venture of Joseph Leycester Lyne, later known as Father
Ignatius. Lyne had been a licensed lay reader and then a
deacon of the Anglican Church when he came under the
influence of Mother Lydia Sellon, superior of the Society of
the Most Holy Trinity. He decided that God wanted him
to introduce the Benedictine life to the Church of England
and on Shrove Tuesday 1863, at the age of twenty-four,
with two companions (neither of whom were priests or had
ever been inside a monastery in their lives) he moved into
part of the rectory at Claydon in Suffolk. Mr Drury, the
rector, celebrated Holy Eucharist for them each morning;
otherwise they conducted their own services from a seventeenth-century Catholic breviary which Ignatius, the only
one who knew Latin, had to translate as they went along.
He also functioned as organist, adapting the Kyrie from
Mendelssohn's *Elijah*, the Sanctus and Benedictus from
Mozart's second and twelfth masses, and taking the Agnus
Dei and O Salutus from 'various composers'. The locals
were scandalized and Ignatius was once badly knocked
about and threatened with burning on a bonfire. He was
reprimanded by the Bishop of Norwich and his request
for ordination as a priest was turned down by the Archbishop of Canterbury. He persevered, bought some land in
Wales, and started to build a monastery near the ruins of
a pre-Reformation priory at Llanthony in the Black Mountains.

The life there was penitential enough to have staggered
a Carthusian. Every day one or other of the brethren was
led into choir with a rope round his neck, was spat upon
and walked over by the rest of the community as he lay

prostrate in the sanctuary, and had to beg for his food until it was someone else's turn the next day. The reading of anything but the Bible was strongly discouraged. 'We never allow ourselves to think,' wrote Ignatius, 'it is all decided for us.' The community lived there for thirty-eight years, what time Ignatius went through a form of ordination by a roving prelate called Vilatte who had been in turn a Catholic, a Methodist, a Congregationalist and a Presbyterian. Ignatius also subscribed to the flat-earth theory, became a Welsh Nationalist, and advertised himself on missionary trips to America as 'the Druid of the Welsh Church'. He died in 1908, and the remnant of his community transferred themselves to the newly founded Benedictines on Caldey Island who were, within a year or two, to convert to Rome.

The first Anglican men's order that lasted was the Society of St John the Evangelist, whose members were to become popularly known as the Cowley Fathers. It was founded by R. M. Benson in 1865 and from the start Benson made it clear that he was not attracted by the picturesque side of the religious life that had so dazzled Joseph Lyne. The men of Cowley were to live simply and unobtrusively. They were to devote themselves to prayer, study and mission work. Benson proposed sending them to the help of any London rector who asked for them; he wanted to start a house in London to be used for proselytizing young people; there was to be a house in Oxford where young Christian men might stay while getting their university education; he thought that eventually Cowley Fathers might take up foreign missionary work. Possibly Benson trod carefully in the early years of the society because he didn't want to rouse the same public antagonism that had followed Lyne's experiments. It was not until 1894 that incense was used in the Cowley church, and not until years later that the sacrament was reserved in the Catholic manner. By then the society had a number of bishops backing it strongly enough to have subscribed a high altar for a new church; a great number of Anglicans still contemplated monkery with the gravest suspicions, but the Church's leaders were at least acquiescent even if they weren't all enthusiastic. By then, too, a couple of other men's orders had been started. Under the influence of Christian Socialism, Charles Gore and five other clergymen had taken vows in the chapel of Pusey House, Oxford, in 1892 and founded the Community of the Resurrection, which before the century ended had established itself in a mill-owner's old mansion on a hillside overlooking Mirfield in Yorkshire. Almost simultaneously, a young curate called Herbert Kelly, with an urge to become a missionary, had been persuaded instead by the bishop in Korea to start training youths who were badly needed out there for secular jobs; and that was the beginning of the Society of the Sacred Mission. The century had started with scarcely any religious life at all in England, and what little existed was fugitive; but by the time it ended the Catholic revival was well established, there was a great proliferation of Anglican women's communities, and a tentative start had been made with Anglican men's communities.

Elsewhere the old orders had been having their ups and downs. The Jesuits returned to papal favour in 1814 but were expelled again from Russia in 1820, from Switzerland in 1848, from Germany in 1872 and from France in 1880, though they were never absent from any area for very long. The Benedictines were similarly bounced in and out of favour all over the place. In Germany a community of Benedictines centred themselvese on the abbey of Beuron in 1868, were ejected after seven years, took refuge first in the Austrian Tyrol, later in Prague, and returned to Beuron in 1887. The community at Solesmes was thrown out by the French Government four times between 1880 and 1903, found sanctuary in the Isle of Wight, and did not get home again until 1922. And because the fourteen Benedictine congregations were tending to make their own individual interpretation of the Rule – sometimes single abbeys within a congregation doing likewise – Leo XIII in 1893 forced all Benedictines to confederate under an Abbot Primate in Rome. He did the same thing with the Cistercians, uniting the nine congregations of the Common Observance with those of the Strict Observance (the Trappists) under an Abbot General.

Yet the second half of the nineteenth century was generally a period of growth. As soon as Napoleon was gone from Europe the teaching orders began to appear again, new ones as well as the old. In a spate, Brothers of Christian Instruction were followed by Brothers of the Sacred Heart, of St Francis Xavier, of the Immaculate Conception, of Our Lady Mother of Mercy, of the Holy Family. They came in France, in Holland, in Belgium, in Italy. With them came new missionary orders, to trail behind the white man who was opening up Africa and the East. There was also a New World to be succoured, as America developed and grew. A monk from Montserrat had been with Columbus. English monks had crossed the Atlantic and returned again to their exile on the Continent. When the Jesuits were suppressed by Pope Clement some of them set out for Maryland, where they founded the University of Georgetown. In 1804, after they had been dismissed from nearly all Europe but Spain, the Dominicans followed the Jesuits and founded three provinces in North America. By the middle of the century reports reached Rome that the Catholic immigrants to the United States were in need of some stiffening against various anti-Catholic pressures there. That is what took the Benedictine monk permanently into the Americas. In September 1846, knowing next to nothing of the language, Dom Boniface Wimmer, from the abbey of Metten, Bavaria, and twenty of his brethren, stepped off the boat in New York. They set up a mission church at Beatty, Pennsylvania, and within six years they were joined there by a group of German Benedictine nuns. These were the earliest of many Benedictine immigrants to the United States. They were a transplantation which was to flourish, grow its own firm roots and become the most abundant of all the offshoots issuing from Montecassino and the patriarch of western monasticism. A hundred years after Dom Boniface made his landfall in the Hudson river there were to be more Benedictine monks between New York and San Francisco, between the Gulf of Mexico and the Forty-ninth Parallel, than in any other one country of the world. And by then they and all the other orders, societies, congregations and institutes, which from the moment of their various foundations had experienced by turns expansion and contraction, regression and reform, were to be on the threshold of yet another critical moment in the history of the religious life.

TOWARDS A NEW DISSOLUTION

'Monasticism in the Church is nothing else than martyrdom reappearing under a new form required by
altered circumstances.' – LOUIS BOUYER, Cong.
Orat., *The Meaning of the Monastic Life*, p. 54.

IN 1967 there were 1,405,931 men and women in the religious communities of the Roman Catholic Church. By far
the majority – 1,072,934 – were women. Most numerous
among the men were the Jesuits, with 36,038. After them
came the Franciscans (Friars Minor) with 26,940, the
Salesians (a teaching society founded in Turin by Don Bosco
in 1859) with 22,626 and the Christian Brothers (another
nineteenth-century teaching order) with 17,787. There were
12,070 Benedictines, 10,003 Dominicans, 3,770 Trappists,
4,018 Discalced Carmelites and 1,665 Cistercians of the
Common Observance. There were about 500 Carthusians. It
is impossible to say how the multitude of women's communities were distributed because the statistical sources which
tabulate the men – like the *Annuario pontificio* – do not
keep the same account of women. They are merely tabu-
lated en masse on a regional basis. In 1967 most of them
(576,814) were located in Europe, but there were 256,350 in
North America. In the same year the Anglican Church had
1,883 women in its religious communities and 328 men.

In spite of its comparatively minute tally the Anglican
Church's figures represent a good half-century of steady
growth. By 1900 the religious communities of women were
firmly established and three years before, the principle of a
religious life in the Church of England had been tacitly
approved by the bishops attending the Lambeth Conference.
Men's communities, though, were scarcely off the ground
and it was not until 1935 that the religious became such a
significant element of Anglicanism as to justify setting up

a central administrative machine in the Advisory Council on
Religious Communities. In those three and a half decades
the development of communities, particularly of men's communities, took place along two distinct paths. One of them,
by far the narrower, meant reproducing as exactly as
Anglican theology would allow the ethos and behaviour of
one or other of the ancient Catholic orders. The other meant
adapting in a specifically Anglican way the basic and traditional principles of the religious life. To an extent the
entire early development of the religious life in the Church
of England involved a lot of backward glancing at the
Middle Ages and the monastic heyday. It was the product
of a movement to reassert within the national Church a
number of Catholic theological principles which had been
eroded by the Reformation; it was also conducted in a period
of romantic nostalgia for the fifteenth century and earlier
which accounted for the popularity of Sir Walter Scott's
chivalrous novels, for the prolific design of neo-Gothic
churches and for the curious infection of manufactured
Gothic ruins on the estates of gentry from one end of the
country to the other.

The Community of the Resurrection is a classic example
of the specifically Anglican strain, which can also be detected in the origins of the Cowley Fathers and of the
Society of the Sacred Mission at Kelham. On its arrival at
Mirfield in 1898 it was easy for the extreme Protestant agita-
tors of the West Riding to mistake the community for a
Catholic fifth column planted in their midst. Pamphlets
were distributed around the district saying 'Christians!
Churchmen! Englishmen! Beware of the Mirfield Monks!
The Community seeks to entrap our wives into the hateful
confessional! There are papers on confession being handed
to young girls which no one with any sense of decency
would dare to read in public!' Easy enough to take that
kind of line when the Community of the Resurrection did
indeed wish to revive the habit of confession and several
other things which had been rejected as papist devices three
hundred years before.

Yet its origins were unmistakably English, not Roman. Charles Gore was that late Victorian oddity, an aristocrat by birth and a socialist by conviction. It is said that he became the latter on hearing a sermon by Bishop Westcott, who was president of the Christian Social Union, when he was a schoolboy at Harrow. Both he and the five other co-founders of the community were members of the Union before the move to Yorkshire, taking part in demonstrations against slum housing, low wages and factory conditions. Once it reached the north, the community used the quarry which stands in its grounds for frequent Labour meetings. Keir Hardie was once a visitor and so was Mrs Pankhurst, who talked for hours and could not be stopped. What Gore was trying to establish was a community of men 'to reproduce the life of the first Christians, of whom it is recorded in the Acts of the Apostles that "they continued steadfast in the Apostles' teaching and the fellowship, in the breaking of bread and the prayers ... and not one of them said that aught of the things which he possessed was his own; but they had all things in common"'. The only slavish copy from traditional monasticism was the saying of the seven-fold office each day – matins and prime, terce and sext, none, evensong and compline. These were, though, said in English, not Latin. At the beginning the brethren's vows were not made for life. They were asked to make an intention to stay in the community for the rest of their days, but actual promises were to be renewed each year. Similarly they were asked to make a life intention but not a promise of celibacy. They were to hand over all possessions and income to the community but they were to keep private capital untouched as long as they remained there. They were to be generally under obedience to the superior but they could appeal against any of his decisions to the General Chapter; in other words, to the whole community. They were required to do nothing that might offend their individual consciences and they were to be free to leave at the end of each year. Their dress was to be the cassock of the ordinary Anglican clergyman, without a cowl.

Gore had detached himself from the community before it moved to Mirfield, on being made a canon of Westminster; he was later to become Bishop of Worcester. But under his successor Walter Frere (who also became a bishop – of Truro) and under subsequent superiors the Rule of the Community of the Resurrection was altered and modified in certain respects – life vows were eventually introduced for one thing – without ever losing its distinctive tolerance of individual conscience. Nor was it to lose the streak of social rebellion and engagement in social and political problems that had marked it from the beginning. It was to open outposts in the West Indies and in Africa. In one of these, at Sophiatown in the coloured shanty area of Johannesburg, Fr Trevor Huddleston conducted between 1944 and 1956 his great battles against the South African Government and its apartheid policy. It is doubtful whether his freelance political activities there would have been tolerated to the same extent by any order embracing in their entirety traditional religious concepts which have included, under the vow of obedience, the need to ask and receive permission from a superior for each separate external action. A Jesuit or a Dominican might have got away with it; scarcely anyone else.

A desire to imitate precisely the Catholic religious traditions was to be seen in the Anglican revival from the start The astonishing progress of Joseph Lyne was the first clear demonstration of this. Two years after he began his version of the Benedictine life a wealthy curate of St Paul's, Knightsbridge, George Nugee, was starting the Anglican Order of St Augustine and it lasted until 1900. It early proved as offensive to local susceptibilities as Lyne's venture had at Claydon Rectory. Not long after Nugee and a dozen others had moved into a house in Hampshire, an aggrieved Admiral of the Fleet, a neighbour of theirs, was writing to the Bishop of Winchester that

in connection with our parish church there has long been something very like conventual life, and now a Priory is added called 'St Augustine's', and from these places are continually issuing forth phantoms, until lately only read of or seen in Roman Catholic countries. Thus our rural population is made accustomed, by the daily procession and perpetual appearance of these 'sisters' and 'brothers', to Romish institutions in connection with our English Protestant religion; and our light and beautiful highways are darkened, and to our English sense rendered loathsome and terrible by these associations of the Inquisition.

The Augustinians survived a number of similar representations to Anglican authority over thirty years, and just before their priory was closed and they dissolved upon the death of their founder they helped a much more serious contender for the traditionalist role. In 1893 Benjamin Fearnley Carlyle was clothed in their chapel as a Benedictine oblate. He was at this time a nineteen-year-old medical student and he had already drawn up detailed plans for an Anglican Benedictine Order with three distinct levels; of oblates observing the Rule but living in the world, of monks on mission work, and of other monks living a strictly enclosed and contemplative régime. All this based on wide reading about monasticism since the age of thirteen and experience as superior of a 'brotherhood' at Blundell's School which horrified the school chaplain when he discovered the boys at Romish devotions before a home-made altar in a rented room.

The clothing ceremony in the Augustinian chapel was a false start for Carlyle. In 1896, taking the name of Brother Aelred, he went through a similar procedure at West Malling Abbey where Anglican nuns had been living according to the Benedictine Rule for several years. This time the ceremony had the approval of the Archbishop of Canterbury. With half a dozen other young men Aelred for the next year or two was constantly on the move from one dwelling to another, as landlords shifted them on or as local Protestants demonstrated against them. But in 1906 they found a permanent refuge on Caldey Island, off the Pembrokeshire coast. They had also, by this time, found a patron in Lord Halifax and it was doubtless due to his intercession that Aelred was first of all confirmed as abbot by Archbishop Temple and then ordained by an American

Episcopalian bishop in Wisconsin on the authority of the Archbishop of York.

Next to the ruins of Caldey's medieval priory the Anglican Benedictines began to build an abbey, with an altar of pink alabaster, with Abbot Aelred's private chapel paved with black and white marble, with a sanctuary lamp hanging from a silver galleon, and with a peacock and two peahens strutting around the cloister garth. The place became the object of Anglo-Catholic pilgrimages from all over Britain. Here one could listen to offices sung in Latin from the *Breviarum monasticum* as well as a dash of plainchant according to the most highly esteemed Catholic Benedictine usage of Solesmes. Here one could actually see monks with pates bared by a deep-shaven tonsure. And all inside the comfortable embrace of the Church of England. It was not to stay that way for much longer. From the start there had always been some doubt among canon lawyers about the exact legal position of the Caldey Benedictines – being offshore islanders – in relation to the see of Canterbury. And from his adolescence Carlyle had periodically cherished the idea that eventually he and his followers would be in communion with Rome.

In 1911 he invited the Archbishop of Canterbury, Randall Davidson, to regularize the canonical status of the community. Davidson's reply was that the monks should receive Bishop Gore – the Gore who had founded the Community of the Resurrection, who had been Bishop of Worcester and was now Bishop of Oxford – as their official visitor so that he could report to the primate on the spirit and observances of Caldey. Gore was shocked by what he found on the island. He told Aelred that before discussions went any further four things must immediately be changed. There must be a legal assurance that the community's property belonged to the Church of England. The communion rite must be taken completely from the Book of Common Prayer and the monks who were also priests must say morning and evening prayer according to the same manual, whatever other offices they sang in choir. The doc-

trines of the Immaculate Conception and the corporal
Assumption of Our Lady and the public observance of these
feasts must be removed from the breviary and the missal.
Exposition and benediction of the Blessed Sacrament must
cease. Gore's own community had been vilified for Romish
practices but it had never gone anything like the way towards traditional monasticism taken by the Caldey
Benedictines. His visitation demonstrated exactly the distance separating the two paths taken by those who wanted
to restore the religious life to the English Church. It also
made it impossible for Caldey to remain even nominally
inside the Anglican Communion. On 5 March 1913 Abbot
Aelred and twenty-two brethren were received into the
Roman Catholic Church and continued as a Benedictine
community on the island until 1928, when they moved to
Prinknash in Gloucestershire, which is where Aelred Carlyle died in 1955. Caldey was to be taken over by a community of Trappists, who migrated from the Abbey of
Chimay in Belgium, who are still there today and who
among other things produce perfumes for sale in that stylish
boutique opposite Brompton Oratory in London.

Yet from the wreckage of Caldey enough survived to
preserve the Benedictine strain of monks in the Church of
England. Three of Aelred's brethren who refused conversion to Rome were taken up by Lord Halifax, who was still
hoping that a permanent place might be found for the senior
monastic order inside Anglicanism. Within a year premises
were found at Pershore, next to the remains of an old Benedictine abbey, and, after the Bishop of Worcester had been
carefully sounded out, the three men of Caldey and a handful of postulants moved in with the blessing of both their
Lordships. By 1926 the new foundation was doing so well
that a larger house was necessary. A suitable one was discovered in Nashdom, a mansion which Lutyens had built
for the Prince and Princess Dolgorouki in Buckingham-
shire, almost within chanting distance of the Cliveden estate
of the Astors. And at Nashdom Abbey Benedictine monks
have remained ever since, with their chapel in what used to

be the ballroom, with the princess's shapely head in bas-relief on a wall now discreetly hidden behind a devotional painting. They have become so secure that since 1939 they have fostered a smaller priory at Three Rivers, Michigan, half way between Chicago and Detroit. Their security demonstrates more than anything else the extreme elasticity of the Church of England now, compared with half a century ago, when even the use of the word mass for communion was regarded by many Anglicans as appallingly tendentious. For the life at Nashdom is virtually indistinguishable from that of any Catholic Benedictine community, except in the minor details that mark one house from another within the Order of St Benedict. The present abbot is reported to have said that if Nashdom went over to Rome tomorrow it would change only one word in its services; the name of the bishop.

Like every other Benedictine the Anglican monks of Nashdom prefix their names with 'Dom' – for dominus or master. Their offices are chanted in Latin from the *Brevarium monasticum*, and their masses are celebrated from the *Missale monasticum*, both of which are also used at Montecassino. Their rituals conform to the decrees of the Vatican's Sacred Congregation of Rites. When a Nashdom monk gets a note or a word wrong during the chanting of the office he at once makes a profound obeisance by way of acknowledging his mistake; a mortification that certainly isn't practised in every Catholic Benedictine community. When a visitor arrives at the abbey he is met at the door by a strong whiff of incense, which pickles the whole building; that doesn't happen in any other Anglican community either, or in many Catholic ones if it comes to that. The incense is manufactured on the spot and occasionally a parcel is sent with Nashdom's greetings to the pope. Yet this is a piece of the Church of England, under some inexplicably vague obedience ultimately to the Archbishop of Canterbury. 'It is,' a Catholic writer has remarked, 'such a *normal* kind of Benedictine community.'

The Church of England has also, since 1921, had its

Franciscans. They sprouted from the now defunct Society of the Divine Compassion, which originated at the end of the nineteenth century in the same Christian Socialism that moulded Mirfield. This society began because a group of Anglican priests decided that the working classes might be better served by the example of men living a poverty-stricken life themselves than by any schemes for social reform that had by then been concocted by either the cooperative movement, the trade unions or socialism. They took themselves off to the East End of London and there they lived among the poor. They were to get their pictures on the front page of the *Daily Mirror* for marching with unemployed dockers, they were to tend smallpox victims during the epidemics of 1901 and 1902 both on the hospital ships moored in the Thames and in the isolation hospital put up specially on Dagenham Marshes, which at one time housed four hundred sick people. One of their number, Fr Andrew, was to write to his mother to say how sad he felt at his catechism class when the children asked God to give them this day their daily bread, and he knew that at home there was nothing for them to eat. They served a small purpose during a bleak half-century of English artisan life and they quietly expired in the 1950s as the original members died off and no new ones came to take their place.

But something like the purpose for which they were founded was by then being served by the Society of St Francis. A novice of SDC, Brother Giles, had decided before the First World War that his vocation was to live among tramps and outcasts. On his return from the army, with two other laymen, he settled in a Dorset farmhouse leased by Lord Sandwich. They did not take the Franciscan Rule in its entirety and live it to the letter, but they aimed to follow its spirit. Others joined them at the Cerne Abbas friary; men like Douglas Downes, who was chaplain of University College, Oxford, and Algy Robertson, who had founded in Poona a hostel in which Christian, Hindu and Moslem students lived in common. The friars in those early days often tramped the roads themselves, sleeping under hedges or in casual wards, looking for genuine tramps (whom they preferred to call wayfarers) they could bring back to the farm for shelter and food. They were, themselves, allowed 2s. a day for expenses while on the road. Gradually they achieved a reputation for genuine help among those who in the years of slump needed it badly. They took in a cat burglar, put him on his feet, and for years after his return to London he would send down to Dorset lads who were beginning to get on the wrong side of the law. They led the agitation for an improvement of the vagrancy laws and the Vagrancy Reform Society, which was founded in the friary, eventually got the Ministry of Health to set up a commission which recommended the need for new homes for young tramps. When the Second World War started they took over a remand home and looked after its occupants, and in the past twenty years there has been a permanently floating population at the friary of men and boys who have been in need of some sort of help; men drying out after a stretch of alcoholism, boys being eased back into normal life after a spell in borstals. It is all consistent with the Franciscan spirit, though the Anglican friars have never attempted a meticulous reproduction of the traditional Franciscan way, as the monks of Nashdom have aimed for with their Benedictinism. The men of Cerne Abbas dress like any other Franciscan, in a brown habit with a thick white rope around the waist, an end of it knotted thrice and dangling to knee level. But their rule since 1937 has been an adaptation of the one written first for the Christa Prema Seva Sangha brotherhood which Fr Algy was once associated with in India. The offices they say in the chapel, which is a whitewashed and converted cowshed, come from the Anglican book *Prime and Hours*, in English, and their communion services are taken from the Book of Common Prayer. They have managed a very Anglican kind of compromise, taking what they will from any tradition that seems to suit their purpose.

If, a century ago, it seemed improbable that by now there

would be nearly fifty women's and seven men's religious communities in the Church of England, the chances were infinitely slimmer of developments in the same direction among the more severely Protestant Churches. Fragments of the religious life had survived the Reformation in the lands which had rejected papal authority. Apart from the handful of Catholic monastic communities which transferred their allegiances after Wittenberg there was the odd experiment in community living like that of the Moravian Church at Herrnhut, in Saxony. This was in no sense a monastery; it was a fraternal village of both sexes which was created early in the eighteenth century by the pietistic Count Nikolaus von Zinzendorf. It was governed at first by twelve elders, eventually by a guardian and his deputy; it was divided into 'choirs' – for married men, for young unmarried men, for small boys, for widows, for married women and for girls – which held separate meetings for prayer and biblical meditation; these were subdivided into 'bands' of three or four members who confessed their sins to each other. There was uninterrupted prayer throughout the twenty-four hours at Herrnhut, taken in rota by everyone in the community. There was communal cultivation of the Zinzendorf estate, but everyone retained his own possessions on joining. A hundred years after the foundation of Herrnhut, Protestantism on the Continent saw a revival of the ancient function of deaconess. In the early Church the deaconess had usually been a middle-aged or elderly woman who cared for the sick and the poor and who also acted as a kind of chaperone when women received adult baptism or when they were interviewed by priests. In 1836, in the Rhineland town of Kaiserswerth, Pastor Theodore Fliedner started a community of deaconesses, who were to be either unmarried or widowed, who were to abandon personal property, and who were to look after the sick and the poor or teach or do miscellaneous parish work. They were, in fact, to be the Protestant equivalent of the many existing Catholic sisterhoods of charity. So were a group of women organized at Echallens, Switzerland, in 1841 by Pastor Louis Germond.

So were the deaconesses of Reuilly, in France, who were established in the next year. But all such innovations were rather freakish movements against the general mind of Protestantism, which ran to parochialism and to a strictly domestic conception of community. In 1847 Kierkegaard wrote, 'There is no doubt that the present time, and Protestantism always, needs the monastery again, or that it should exist. "The Monastery" is an essential dialectical fact in Christianity, and we need to have it there like a lighthouse, in order to gauge where we are – even though I myself should not exactly go into one. But if there is to be true Christianity in every generation there must be individuals with that need.' In 1847 Kierkegaard's was a voice crying in the wilderness, that wasn't to be echoed in the Reformed Churches for the best part of a hundred years.

The twentieth century has been a comparatively luminous one among the Protestants. Taizé is quite the most conspicuous lighthouse but a number of smaller beacons have been lit. In point of time the first of them was the Retreat of Pomeyrol which, though it did not take that name until 1940, began in 1929 when Mlle Antoinette Butte settled in a retreat house at St Germain-en-Laye, just outside Paris. It is primarily a praying community and as such was a Protestant novelty when it began. The sisters meet four times a day for common prayer, they take the threefold vows, and they have recently adopted the Rule of Taizé. Pomeyrol is distinctive in the way that it has shopped for bits and pieces of liturgy from a wide and sometimes curious assortment in the composition of its own.

To the Third Order of Watchers it owes certain meditations and the recitation of the Beatitudes at noon; to the Moravian Brethren the practice of two short scriptural texts and special prayers for each day of the week; to the Federation of Students certain prayers and their manner of intercessions; to the Quakers and to Moral Rearmament silent recollections followed by sharing ... and finally there are borrowed invocations and antiphonal prayers ... also the hymns of the Church of the first centuries from the Roman breviary.

Two years after Mlle Butte opened her doors, a few women met for a three-day retreat at Grandchamp, near Neuchâtel; it was the first time anyone in the Swiss Reformed Church had ever held a retreat. In 1936 one of the women, who was to become Sister Margaret, opened a permanent retreat home in Grandchamp and by the beginning of the war she and two others were permanently settled there. In 1952 the Communauté de Grandchamp was formally constituted and within a year it had aligned itself closely with the Taizé Communauté. It adopted the Taizé Rule and at the same time Grandchamp's superior, Mère Geneviève, and Roger Schutz drafted a joint document in which both communities declared 'their common vocation to the service of Jesus Christ and the unity of their witness within the Churches of the Reform'. There are now about fifty sisters in the community. Those at the mother house are mostly busy receiving guests and organizing retreats which are conducted by local pastors or else by Taizé brothers. Some since 1954 have been running a daughter house at Gelterkinden, in the German-speaking part of Switzerland. A handful have been away on missions in Algeria and the Lebanon. A few have set up an outpost in an industrial suburb of Paris. The pattern of Grandchamp is following very faithfully that of Taizé.

The pattern of the Oekumenische Marienschwestern of Darmstadt – the ecumenical sisterhood of Mary – has been quite unlike anything that has gone before in either Protestant or Catholic Churches. Its preliminaries were commonplace enough; young women attending regular Bible classes given by a Dr Klara Schlink in prewar Germany, though the political situation meant that classes had to function semi-secretly. By the time the war started Dr Schlink and her friend Frl. Erika Madausss were tutoring about a hundred and fifty girls. What transformed this completely orthodox Lutheran activity into a religious community was the flattening of Darmstadt by Allied bombers on the night of 11–12 September 1944. Dr Schlink and her pupils took this to be a sign of divine judgement. They decided that repentance, reparation and unceasing prayer were called for in response and that it was their duty to offer it. As American troops advanced on the blitzed city a few months later, fifteen members of the class went into retreat for three days. The result was that Dr Schlink became Mutter Basilea, Frl. Madauss became Mutter Martyria and that in 1947, under the guidance of a Methodist pastor, they and seven other women began to live together in the attic of Basilea's family home. Within seven years there were over sixty Darmstadt sisters. They had been given a piece of ground on the road to Heidelberg by the father of one of them and there they had themselves built a chapel and a community house out of the rubble of war.

They are, above all, a praying community. Several times a day they meet in the chapel; in the morning for informal prayer in the manner of Quakers, at noon to pray for Christian unity and for the well-being of Israel, in the afternoon for meditation on the sufferings and death of Christ, and at night for vespers and compline in the manner of traditional monasticism. Every sister also spends at least an hour a day praying alone in what is known as a 'conversation of love' on behalf of one of the Christian Churches, and it is her lifelong responsibility to discharge it; in the guest house every room is named after one of the Christian sects and its decorations and the books on its shelves are relevant to that sect alone. Throughout each day and night at least two sisters are at prayer, relieving each other in couples every hour. Beyond the prayer life there is the missionary work. They have an old bus which they drive to poor quarters of the city and hold catechism classes for children aboard it. They preach at railway stations, in women's prisons and in reformatories. They mount a form of medieval mystery play in their home-made 'Jesu Ruf Kapelle' alongside the mother house. They publish tracts on their own printing press and they made crucifixes and devotional figures in their workshop. They run a house for ailing Jews in Israel and this is important to them because they partly exist to make reparation for the evils of Nazism and particularly the injury that Nazi Germany did to the Jews. The Darmstadt sisters are dedicated for life to this existence and each of them wears, on the day of her profession, a bridal wreath and a white gown which is the way a novice in a Roman Catholic convent might make her vows. Someone from the Free Church of Scotland might find it hard to believe, but at that moment too the Darmstadt sister is as Protestant as himself.

Like Taizé and like Grandchamp the Darmstadt sisterhood is superficially, in the basic structure of its daily life, indistinguishable from scores of Catholic communities. It lies, in the total and permanent commitment of its members, at one end of a spectrum which pales off into something as flexible and in a sense sporadic as the Iona Community. Based off the western coast of Scotland, on the route through which the monastic tradition was channelled centuries ago from the Continent of Europe by way of Ireland to the mainland of Great Britain, this is strictly speaking a part-time community. It originated in 1938 when the Rev. George MacLeod of the Presbyterian Church of Scotland and seven other people from the Glasgow district decided to spend their summer on the island rebuilding the ruins of its Benedictine abbey. It was a symbolic gesture to start with. This was a time of industrial depression in the Glasgow area; the eight men who crossed to the island decided that the Church was making too many distinctions between the sacred and the secular, that a spirit of community had to be reawakened to relieve social distress and that Iona, with its ancient tradition of a common life, was as good a place as any to exemplify this. The community of about a hundred and fifty, mostly Presbyterian ministers like MacLeod, lives together at Iona only for the three summer months. For the rest of the year it is divided, living and working individually across Scotland, meeting once a month, observing a Rule which regulates individual prayer, use of time and use of money. It is, one of its members has written, 'a body of men, ministers and craftsmen, who are committed through their life together, and in their own work, to seek the way

of obedience to Jesus Christ, whereby the Church may fulfil her mission in the world today. The members of the
Iona Community are bound together by the common experience of a life shared in work and worship on Iona, by a
common intention in their work on the mainland, and by a
common discipline.' Devoid of strict obedience to a superior,
quite lacking in sanctions for use against the defaulter,
utterly open to the world and for most of the time completely fragmented in the world, Iona has scarcely anything
in common with the religious life practised at a Carthusian
or even a Benedictine level. It is a form of religious life
because it is based on a degree of community and fortified
by a code of self-discipline above and beyond the norms
accepted by any Christian. Its significance is that, in its own
local historical context, it is there at all, part of a very recent
Protestant trend towards something on which the Reformed
Churches had for long turned their backs.

For Protestantism the twentieth century has seen fifty-
odd years of unexpected growth. For Catholicism it began
with some of the familiar old frictions between Church and
State, in which the religious communities bore the brunt of
whatever punitive measures were being taken by secular
governments. The French passed the Laws of Association
in 1901, by which no religious congregations could be formed
without the authority of the State. The following year the
religious were forbidden to carry on any educational work
at all. The result was that most of the men's communities
went into exile – the Benedictines of Solesmes, for example,
migrated to Quarr Abbey in the Isle of Wight and did not
return home until 1922 – while the majority of women's communities transformed themselves into nursing sisterhoods.
The Church in France was finally disestablished in 1905
which meant, among other things, that clerics were as liable
to military service as anyone else : the Abbey of Cîteaux had
forty monks conscripted in the Second World War; the
Abbey of Bellefontaine lost nineteen of its forty-nine monks
in action, collected two Croix de Guerres, and had its abbot,
Dom Gabriel Sortais, wounded at Lille, where he was

fighting with the 25th French Infantry Motorised Division; even a French Benedictine lay brother of Buckfast Abbey in England was mobilized by his government in 1939.

In Portugal, too, the Church was disestablished in 1911, the religious orders were expelled with their property confiscated, and they were not rehabilitated until the early 30s. And while the Catholic Church survived the Nazi régime in Germany and the Fascist era in Italy rather better than might have been expected, it has borne the brunt of anti-clericalism behind the Iron Curtain since the end of the war; though in 1965 there were said to be 28,000 women religious in Poland, where Catholicism still flourishes under Communist government, 5,870 in Yugoslavia and 59 in Hungary.

The most important single event in the Catholic religious world during the first decades of the century was the foundation of yet another variant of the life : the Petits Frères and the Petites Sœurs, the Little Brothers and Sisters of Jesus, who did not appear until several years after the death of the man who inspired them. He was Charles de Foucauld, the son of a French aristocratic family, who was born in 1858 at Strasbourg in a house which is now the Banque de France and which was where Rouget de Lisle first sang the *Marseillaise*. He was trained for an army career, as a cavalry officer, in the military academy at St Cyr and he became the dashing rake of a crack regiment serving in Algeria until his colonel cashiered him for keeping a mistress. De Foucauld retired with her to the shores of Lake Geneva. He was reinstated with his regiment when a rebellion broke out in Africa and when it was put down he asked for leave to explore the southern part of Algeria. It was refused and he dropped his commission again. He was twenty-three and for the next two years he studied Arabic and Hebrew until he was fluent in both. Then, disguised as a rabbi and with his Hebrew tutor as companion, he vanished into the interior of Morocco – at that time virtually a forbidden land to Europeans – for nearly a year. When he emerged he had mapped a thousand miles of previously unrecorded ground;

he wrote a journal of his expedition and it won him the gold medal of the Paris Geographical Society.

But Morocco had given him something of more consequence. It had impressed him with the quality of its religious life. This didn't turn him into a Moslem but it did restore the faith of his fathers. He encountered the Abbé Huvelin in Paris, a priest with a high reputation as a confessor and preacher, and in 1886 he received his first absolution since boyhood in the confessional at St Augustine's church. Temperamentally a whole-hogger, de Foucauld decided that he must live the Christian Gospel to the letter. For the next seven years he was a Trappist monk but found that even Trappist austerities were not enough to satisfy his craving for self-abnegation. He went to Palestine and became handyman to a convent of Poor Clares for three years. That was no good either. So he went back to his Trappist monastery, got himself ordained, and at the age of forty-two set off for the Sahara to live among the Moslems. He did not intend to preach to them or in any recognized sense to convert them to Christianity. He aimed only to live an exemplary Christian life among them in the hope, no doubt, that something would register.

Wearing a white habit with a rough red heart sewn on its left breast de Foucauld called himself Fr Charles of Jesus and settled among the Tuaregs, first at the oasis of Beni-Abbes, later at Tamanrasset, in the middle of the Sahara. The tribesmen accepted him as a benevolent oddity. He lived frugally in a hermitage alongside their camps and didn't meddle in their affairs. But he taught them to cultivate vegetables, he showed the women how to knit and how to make chocolate, and he had medical supplies sent from Europe to treat them with when they were ill. For fifteen years he went on like this until, on a December night in 1916, a band of Senoussite tribesmen raided Tamanrasset. De Foucauld was hauled out of his hut and shot. He appeared to have achieved nothing except to recover his own lost Catholic faith and to have made friends with a crowd of nomadic Arabs. He had built a mud chapel which he called

The Fraternity, he had written a Rule for proposed Little Brothers of Jesus, and he had prayed that others might follow him from Europe. But when he died he didn't have a single disciple. He had left a number of writings behind him, though, and so he was not to be forgotten.

It was seventeen years before his influence began to bite. A handful of imitators had gone off to live a hermit's existence among the tribes of North Africa before then. But in 1933 a Fr René Voillaume and five other priests recently out of the Saint-Sulpice seminary were clothed in the same habit that de Foucauld had worn and settled in an abandoned Arab building at El Abiodh, on the edge of the Sahara. These were the first Petits Frères. They lived a near-Trappist life there, spending long periods at prayer and in silence, working their gardens and running a dispensary for the local sick. It was admirable but it was not what de Foucauld had been working towards during his one and a half decades in the desert. For him a first essential had been to embrace totally the poverty of the most poverty-stricken around him because this was what Christ had advocated to his followers. For anyone likely to join him in his mission de Foucauld had written :

Remembering that our Lord Jesus has said, 'When thou makest a dinner or a supper, call not thy friends, nor thy brethren nor thy kinsmen, nor thy neighbours, who are rich, lest they also invite thee again, and a recompense be made to thee. But when thou makest a feast call the poor, the maimed, the lame, and the blind. And thou shalt be blessed, because they have not wherewith to make thee recompense; for recompense shall be made thee at the resurrection of the just', we shall then direct our efforts towards the conversion of those who are spiritually poorest, the most crippled, the most blind, the infidel people of missionary countries; those who know not the Good News; who have no tabernacle, nor sacrifice, nor priest; the most abandoned souls, those who are most sick, the sheep that are indeed lost.

The Petits Frères at El Abiodh were not quite following this injunction; the very fact that they were practising something close to traditional monasticism separated them from the people they were living among. By the time war started in 1939, fifteen of them were in the community, which promptly broke up because all its members were conscripted into the army.

The war had a salutary effect on the Petits Frères. It thrust most of them into an atheistic environment for the first time in their lives; none of them had to the same extent before been forced to live as a devout Catholic in isolation from others for a protracted period. They saw something of the world as it really was, uninsulated from them by the protective wrappings of the pious society that had reared them. When they reassembled on demobilization they came to the conclusion that they must not literally follow de Foucauld into the desert, but that they must follow his example in any situation where poverty and need was to be found. This meant preserving a tension which was clearly present in de Foucauld's life among the Tuareg; a tension between the hermit's solitude and lengthy periods at prayer, and his personal availability to anyone who sought his help. It meant, in their view, that they must turn their backs on the monastic tradition, that they must whittle themselves down into small fraternities living in the middle of poverty-stricken masses wherever these might be found. This has remained their distinction ever since. There are now about two hundred and fifty Petits Frères and they are scattered throughout twenty-eight different countries. There are about a thousand Little Sisters of Jesus living a similar vocation.

The brothers scarcely ever live in groups of more than five. They possess no property at all. In industrialized areas of the western world they rent working-class accommodation wherever they set up a fraternity; in Africa and other underdeveloped parts of the world they move into whatever is the poorest form of local dwelling. They have one fraternity in Great Britain and its address is 24 Autumn Grove, Leeds 6 – which marks it at once for what it is; just another anonymous-looking house in a long, gas-lit and terraced street, which was put up in the nineteenth century by the cloth barons of the West Riding to quarter their factory fodder in. There are rows and rows of Autumn Groves in that part of the city; a high proportion of their inhabitants are West Indians, Ukrainians and other refugees, for this is a slum area, due for demolition as soon as the city can find the funds to rehouse the people, and so its population is permanently at the bottom of the social pile, however that is composed.

Four Petits Frères live at No. 24, which has two cramped rooms upstairs and two more below. They have contrived a chapel in the space between the sloping slate roof and the ceiling of the upper storey; there is room in it for five people to kneel or for three to stand. And when the brothers have their hour of meditation up there, which they do every night after vespers and compline, the silence is broken by the gurgling of the water tank behind the altar, by the sound of next door's television coming up through the thin walls, and sometimes by tipsy laughter from the street outside. The four men in grey cassocks seem oblivious of it all. The noises off are all part of the world they live in. One of them spends his day labouring in a foundry; another has been bricklaying at a local brewery. There they are indistinguishable from their workmates, in blue one-piece boiler suits and heavy boots, and with dirt slowly growing into the pores of their hands. They talk no religion to their workmates unless someone else raises the topic and they do not honestly think that they have induced anyone to go to church who wasn't already going before they moved into the district. But they hope that their presence among the people will one day have some effect. At the moment the working classes of Leeds who come into contact with the Little Brothers of Jesus probably regard them as benevolent oddities, as the Tuareg did Charles de Foucauld; and in local terms they certainly are odd when the four of them exist on one and a half wage-packets and dispose of the rest either to the seminary for Petits Frères in Toulouse or to various charities. The Leeds fraternity is not exceptional in its condition and way of life. There is the Petit Frère who drives a truck in Hamburg, the one who mans a fishing smack out of Concarneau, the one who blacksmiths in the middle of the soukhs of Marrakesh. There are Little Sisters in a third-floor apartment in the coloured quarter of Chicago, others in an Eskimo village outside Nome, Alaska, more living in caravans at Alice Springs in the middle of Australia.

René Voillaume, Prior of the Little Brothers, who now spends most of his time on the move from one fraternity to another when he isn't exhorting them from headquarters in Toulouse, has put their purpose into a paragraph.

Our Lord has asked us to love men exactly as he loved them, and the Petits Frères's way of life might be summed up by saying that they must do their utmost to ensure that what they feel, what they do, and how they live, forms as perfect an expression as possible of our Lord's own feelings towards mankind. This mission is so absolute that everything must be subordinated to it. ... When a friendship is profound and exclusive, it demands the presence of the person loved and a mutual sharing – as fully as this may be attained – of the particular circumstances of life and especially of any suffering. It must also involve a total and disinterested gift of oneself to the person thus loved for his own sake with a humble respect, in the way God loves each one of us. These demands of Friendship define the essential elements in the constitution of a Brotherhood.

This is not unlike the tone of voice used by Roger Schutz of Taizé. There are considerable differences between the Taizé Communauté and the Petits Frères, quite apart from the fact that one is Protestant and the other Catholic. Oddly, the Protestants here are more in the monastic tradition than the Catholics, simply by being based on a central community. But in common both raise the question of the Christian Church's identification with the masses who are poor materially as well as spiritually; and both urge the necessity of the Christian to give himself and to love without expectation or even hope of a return by way of conversion or any other quid pro quo. Because the Petits Frères have gone out of their way to share poverty wherever they can find it, at its lowest level, they have become a thorn in the conscience of the Catholic Church and particularly of its religious communities, whose notions of poverty once they become well established very rarely coincide with its reality as discovered in the Autumn Groves and worse of this world.

There are diehard Benedictines and Trappists who would scarcely admit to even a tenuous affiliation between their own ethos and life and that of the Little Brothers. At the very least they would argue that whereas they are firmly in the mainstream of the religious life the Petits Frères, by their great preoccupation with the world and existence in it, are in some small pond of their own. History has made a nonsense of such an argument. If the mainstream analogy is to be accepted then Benedictinism will be found issuing from somewhere near the source and the Petits Frères from some tributary nearer an estuary which is teeming with scores of different forms of religious life. From other tributaries come the third orders, the sodalities and the confraternities which have since the twelfth century attached themselves in one way or another to the religious communities proper. They are composed of lay people who for some reason are disinclined or unable – who, in the jargon, have no vocation – to become full-time religious, but who wish to identify themselves with a particular order or religious society. At its strongest this attachment can mean that a Franciscan tertiary (a member of the Secular Third Order of Franciscans) will follow a modified Franciscan Rule in his daily life, will make promises for life which include a profession of celibacy, will support the Franciscan order financially and in every other way possible to him, will wear the scapular (a short cloth yoke covering the shoulders and chest) under his ordinary clothes regularly, and the full Franciscan habit on special occasions when Franciscan tertiaries gather with regular members of the order. At its weakest it will mean following something like the associates' Rule of the Confraternity of the Resurrection, which is a kind of supporters' club of the Anglican Mirfield Fathers. The associates of the fraternity (motto : *Consurrexistis Cum Christo*) can be either men or women who undertake to pray regularly for the Community and the fraternity, to subscribe

10s. a year to the community's work and to interest others in its special aims – the revival of the religious life in the Church of England, mission work at home and abroad, the supply and training of clergy, and the reunion of Christendom.

At about this level 1947 was a momentous year in the history of the religious life. On February 2 Pope Pius XII issued his apostolic constitution *Provida mater ecclesia* which gave official approval at last to the secular institutes. There are well over sixty of these in the Catholic Church today, and they are one of its most significant growth points. A few of them were founded in the nineteenth century, but most have appeared since the First World War. An inclusive definition of them is difficult because while the majority of their members are lay people a few consist only of priests and slightly more include both priests and laity; some are for women only, some for men, others mix the sexes. It is no easier to define their structure and their activity. As one authority has it,

There are some institutes whose members are wholly, or almost wholly, dispersed, living isolated from the others in their own homes or lodgings; there are others whose ideal is to live in small working teams of two or three; there are still others who, through the accidentals of their history and development live entirely in community and are outwardly difficult to distinguish from some religious communities. There can be no question, however, that the present trend is away from the last pattern.

The members of a secular institute make vows which, while they do not carry the same canonical weight and sanctions as those taken by regular religious, are made with virtually the same life intention. The vow of chastity precludes the membership of married people though in some cases these become attached to an institute through an associated fraternity; the vow of poverty means in this case living inexpensively in the world without actually descending to shabbiness; obedience is made to the rules of the institute which may have a hierarchical structure of government similar to that of a regular religious community, or which may merely be under the ultimate authority of the local bishop. The Catholic Church, whose statistical services are not its strongest point, probably doesn't know itself how many of the faithful are involved in the institutes today; but it is conceivably something over 50,000; one of the institutes, the Secular Ursulines, was reckoned in 1962 to have 16,000 adherents.

Provida mater in its first paragraph defined the institutes as 'Societies, whether clerical or lay, whose members profess the evangelical counsels in the world, in order to attain Christian perfection and to exercise a full apostolate.' In other words, their purpose is at once to aim for personal sanctification – which is what the monastic tradition started with – and to live a good and influential Christian life out in the world, which is what monasticism has traditionally been averse to. The significance of 1947 is that it gave the Church's fullest legal approval to the institutes, thus raising them above the level of the many fraternities and other pious organizations of the faithful. In doing this it drew into the mainstream of the religious life a movement whose whole character was in its essentials – ordinary unordained Catholics spending most of their time at secular jobs in a secular milieu – alien to the tradition so far. *Provida mater* and 1947 were yet another great turning-point in the religious life. What began with the solitary whose back was turned completely on the world, and became, first, the community which also hid itself away, later the community which made periodic excursions into the world, later still the community which spent much of its time in the world but always had a bolt-hole for refuge from it, now includes the non-community almost totally committed to the world. And because each successive stage of evolution has had some effect on the forms of religious life which pre-date it, the full importance of 1947 is still to be realized.

It is more than likely that the steady growth of the institutes has had something to do with a decline in the fortunes of the already established religious communities of the

Catholic Church. There is no consistent pattern to this but it is there and it has become a major preoccupation of the Holy See. In the past twenty or thirty years there have been a number of growth points, none more marked than the United States. There the ground was fertile enough for Carthusians to plant themselves for the first time in 1951, when they established a community at Whittingham, Vermont. An even more remarkable phenomenon was the increase in the number of Cistercian and particularly Trappist houses in the decade immediately after the last war. In 1940 there had been three Cistercian communities in the USA, two of which dated from 1848; between 1944 and 1956 nine others appeared. The Benedictines flourished, particularly the American Benedictine nuns, who reckon three hundred to constitute a pretty small convent and a thousand a rather large one. About a quarter of the world total of Jesuits is to be found in North America now.

It is also possible for the Church to take an optimistic view of developments in some of its mission fields, provided the dates are carefully chosen. In Colombia, for example, where in 1921 there were only 38 religious houses for men, by 1962 there were 502; where there were only 31 women's houses in 1912, half a century later there were 1,469. Elsewhere the situation has been unhealthy. By 1964 the Belgian Cardinal Suenens was writing, 'Everywhere one hears complaints that recruitment does not keep pace with needs, nor indeed with the growth of population; that religious houses are closing down one after another; that the average age of communities is increasing. ... Vocations are decreasing everywhere. It is significant that the least affected are the missionary and purely contemplative communities.' Another Belgian, Dom Benedict Heron O S B, Prior of the Monastery of Christ the King at Gelrode, has estimated that the shortage of vocations runs throughout Europe with the exception of Spain.

A major difficulty in plotting the strength of Catholic religious communities is that the figures issued by the Vatican tend to be unreliable : a fact which is tartly acknowledged in the most respectable Catholic quarters. 'It is instructive', writes a contributor to the *New Catholic Encyclopaedia*, 'to compare the ecclesiastical statistics of the Roman Curia in the early 1960s with the system that Baumgarten criticized fifty years earlier. Almost all his criticisms appear to be as valid in 1965 as in 1912.' The Vatican's chief directory, *Annuario pontificio*, appears to paint a more optimistic picture than the current cries of alarm would justify. According to this source, between 1960 and 1966 the number of men in religious communities rose from 311,368 to 332,993; women in religion grew from 999,230 to 1,060,680 in the same period. The authors of the work seem at least to be wrong in their count of Benedictine monks; they suggest a rise from 11,500 to 12,500 in the first six years of the decade. The *Benedictine Catalogue*, which presumably knows its own business rather better, marks a fall of monks over the same period from 12,131 to 12,070 and of monasteries from 236 to 225 – though Benedictine nuns increased from 22,603 in 377 convents to 23,397 in 409 convents.

The position seems to be most serious in those countries – Holland, Belgium, France and Germany – where the Catholic Church generally has been in a state of upheaval, where it has locally been most daring, in the past few years. In the Low Countries, for example, the Church has been conducting experiments in liturgy and in relations with other Christians, and it has been reviewing Catholic social morality virtually in defiance of Vatican ordinances. In France, with half a century of anti-clericalism to combat, it attempted to bridge the gap by launching the worker-priesthood shortly after the war, only to be trodden on by the Vatican when it became apparent that the priests were getting too politically involved on behalf of the workers for Rome's taste.

In Holland, where there were 33,350 women in religion in 1958, there were 32,443 in 1964. In the best recruiting year the Church has had there this century, 1935, about 1,200 girls entered the active communities; by 1958 the figure had fallen to 465 and by 1964 to 231. The real growth period was

in the second half of the nineteenth century; there was
stability in the first decade of the twentieth but by the 1930s
the women's communities were back to the level of the
1900s and today they are back to the level of the years 1860–
70.

In Belgium, where one diocese has had to close 78 out of
522 women's houses in the past thirty years, the worst is yet
to come. The average age of the women is 54 and only 7·4
per cent of them are under 30. In the diocese of Tournai
nearly 30 per cent of the nuns are over 65.

In Germany between the two world wars the number of
sisters increased from 61,236 to 97,516 and novices rose from
5,511 in 1919 to 7,488 in 1935, with a fall under Nazi government to 1,865 in 1941. After the war the number of sisters rose to 93,260 in 1957 but had fallen to 86,279 in 1965;
novices fell from 3,996 in 1950 to 2,101 in 1965.

In France, where a single diocese saw the numbers of
women in teaching and nursing orders fall by 30 per cent in
ten postwar years, the age pyramid of female religious generally indicates that, as in the case of Belgium, the bleakest
years lie ahead. In 1963 only 8·1 per cent of them were under
30; 24·7 per cent were aged between 31 and 45; 32·5 per cent
were between 46 and 60; and 25 per cent were between 61
and 75.

Even in Catholic Ireland the first small signs of a drop-out
among women have appeared. It is true that between 1958
and 1964 the number of sisters professed rose from 10,142 to
10,803; but the number of novices declined slightly from 574
to 541. Paradoxically the manpower situation in Ireland – at
least among unordained lay brothers – appears to be as
healthy as ever. In communities composed entirely of lay
brothers the figures rose from 2,538 in 1958 to 2,874 in 1964;
in clerical communities, where the lay brother has a distinctly inferior role, there was a rise of lay brethren over the
same period from 780 to 836. In England and Wales during
those years the number of lay brothers in completely lay
communities rose by 15 per cent. In Germany, on the other
hand, the number of lay brothers in clerical communities fell

from 3,512 in 1960 to 3,372 in 1964, while novices dropped
from 268 to 133; in entirely lay communities professed brethren fell from 1,057 in 1960 to 1,028 in 1964 (the novice count
here actually rising from 73 to 97). But in Belgium the total
admission of laymen to religious communities of any kind
fell from 126 in 1958 to 58 in 1964.

Head-counting of Catholic religious at present is an ex-
cessively uneven and unsatisfactory business. The *Annuario*
cannot be relied upon for accuracy and in any case makes no
attempt to plot age pyramids or any other factors that might
indicate future movements. Sources which appear to be reliable have so far charted only a fragment of the ground that
has to be covered; apart from the figures quoted above there
are virtually no others available; there is nothing, for instance, to tell us what the situation has been over a ten-year
period among the monasteries of France; or to give us as
useful a picture as the Dutch one of women religious in
Great Britain. But judging by the general reaction of the
Catholic Church's leaders who are most concerned with the
religious life the overall pattern in Europe at least appears to
be one of decline. Bishop Huyghe of Arras, for example, has
said that 'Unless a complete reversal takes place in the present situation, half the convents of religion which now exist
will have disappeared by 1980.' And judging by personal
observation and reliable travellers' tales the condition of
even the most solidly based communities is now a cause for
concern. There are enormous Benedictine monasteries, like
the majestic baroquery of Melk on the Danube, or Montecassino itself, which was extravagantly rebuilt from the
ruins of the last war, which see more tourists than monks;
'both palaces are capable of holding three hundred monks,
and both communities are down to forty, rattling like peas
in a drum.' At Downside Abbey the Benedictines closed
their novitiate in November 1966 for lack of postulants. The
decline among women, moreover, is also visible among the
comparative handful of Anglican communities. Between
1960 and 1966 the number of men in religion rose by 16 per
cent, from 283 to 328; over the same period the women fell

by 5 per cent from 1,941 to 1,883. A survey of 37 women's active communities in 1965 showed that they were 10 per cent below their 1939 strength and that of a total of 1,405 sisters only 120 were under 35 years old. Again, as with the Catholic communities, it seems to be the active ones that are suffering rather more than the contemplatives. The Anglican contemplative Sisters of the Love of God, for example, have had a permanent queue of women waiting for admission to their novitiate over the past few years.

However widespread the Catholic decline in vocations may or may not be the first signs of concern came in 1944, when the Sacred Congregation for Religious – the central administrative machine for this sector of the Church – established a ten-man commission representing various orders to study reform projects. A further straw in the wind came in 1950, when the first international congress of religious sat in Rome. By the following year Pius XII was clear enough about the way things were shaping to observe, astonishingly for a man who was temperamentally disinclined to change the status quo, that 'The nun's task in the world today cannot be accomplished without certain modifications in the customs of the classical type of religious life.'

In the years since then a number of modifications have been made. Some of the women's orders have had their clothing restyled, trimming hemlines here and shortening head-dress there. A decree of 31 May 1957 enabled superiors to interpret more flexibly the rules governing the visits of nuns and sisters to the world outside the convent walls. But these have only been modifications when what the religious life in its classical form has required has been an overhaul of its basic structure. The dearth of vocations in so many of the women's teaching and nursing orders has been attributed to the overwork that has usually been the price of membership; but shrewd observers have noted that this alone cannot be held responsible for their evident lack of appeal to young women in the mid-twentieth century, when equally industrious bodies like the secular institutes – mostly the product of the times we live in – have been flourishing. The really fundamental problem has been that religious orders have never been geared to the need for rapid change; slowly they have developed, slowly they have established their traditions and only very slowly if left to themselves have they ever made adjustments to a way of life that has been sanctified by time. A French bishop has written :

There are 118,000 active nuns in France, including 160 small congregations with less than 200 members founded before 1900. . . . Our colleagues in the episcopate consider they have made very little or no progress in the way of adapting themselves or making things more humane. The bishops are right. But they do not always realize how heavy the machinery is and how hard it is to set in motion. During the frequent congresses, which the nuns are always glad to attend, they hear lectures and exhortations which they receive with enthusiastic applause, but in practice scarcely any progress can be observed. The reason is that they are so often financially attached to their traditions and customs, which are kept in a sort of secret dungeon. Even the ecclesiastical superiors themselves are often denied access to it, especially in the small congregations. Thus, if there are praiseworthy attempts at adaptation, there are also well-defended strongholds. . . . All the nuns mean well and many see what needs to be done, bnt none of them dare make a beginning.

The emphasis placed by critics of the traditional and atrophied life upon the women's orders and congregations may say as much about the Catholic Church's hallowed attitude to women as it does about the area where recruitment has most obviously been failing in the postwar years. When Bishop Huyghe wrote his book *Tensions and Change* he pointed out at the beginning that although it was based upon research into the religious life of women 'if any reader likes to translate it into the masculine he will not be far from the truth'. No distinction between the sexes has been made in the discussions of the standing committee of Superior-Generals of religious orders, which was appointed in 1957. And in those discussions proposals put up at the first congress have come up time and again in the years since; they are about the necessity of adapting religious and ascetical discipline to the physical and psychological capacities of modern religious, more modern methods of relaxation, the provision of modern technical facilities in so far as these can be squared with the vow of poverty, raising the age of entry and extending the novitiate so as to be surer than before that those committing themselves to the life for life do so in greater maturity than many of their predecessors. At that first congress Fr Lombardi, sj, was speaking of the religious life generally when he said :

When we consider the magnitude of the tasks which these critical times have imposed upon the orders we have to confess that a great number of the orders do not come up to expectations. Officially no doubt they are all very worthy, historically they may have a very glorious past, but in point of fact many of them are very ill-equipped to meet the grave responsibilities of today. On the whole, they are perhaps in no way inferior to the average religious of the past. But when we think of the tremendous call of the present hour we cannot help feeling that many of them show little of the ardent readiness of troops on the eve of a death or glory advance. . . . There are too many of these institutes that proceed at the same old sedate trot, with no idea of how urgently the rapidly changing conditions of our time call for new efforts and new methods in apostolic work and spiritual life. They work to rule and follow their routine order of time, which means in fact that they are sleeping through the time for action.

That was in 1957. Nearly ten years later it was possible for Bishop Huyghe to observe that

Some have completely accepted this new world along with its dangers and its hopes. Resolutely detached from the sociological milieu in which former generations lived, they are alert to the needs of the people who now expect a new type of evangelization. Others still cling desperately to the earlier forms of religious and apostolic life which, they declare, have stood the test of the years; and, in the shelter of their institutions which have become for them a sort of artificial Christianity, they do not see that the world is being formed without them and, unfortunately, without the message of Christ which they should be bringing to it.

As an example of the desperately static attitude the bishop cited the congregation of nuns which in ten years lost thirty per cent of its womanpower; it didn't close a single house, but left them all gradually to dwindle and become a faint shadow of what they had been. There have been more realistic responses to change and decay than this. A number of federations have been set up, like the one that soon after the war united forty-six communities of the nursing Canonesses Regular of St Augustine under one Superior-General. As a psychological device federation has its uses. It reduces a feeling of isolation and hopelessness in those houses which are suffering more than most from old age and scanty vocations, and replaces it to some extent with a confidence in being part of a powerful and cohesive organization. Practically it means that a common policy can be worked out for the running of novitiates, that one novitiate for the whole federation can be established and new blood be deployed where it is most needed. Yet while all this is a help it is, in fact, doing no more than tinker with a structure that really needs changes – many of them major ones – from top to bottom.

Not until the Vatican Council finished at the end of 1965 did the Church officially show any signs of recognizing this. But then, in the decree *De accommodata renovatione vitae religiosae,* it put its finger precisely on the place where the log-jam of tradition must first be made to move. The decree ordained that the organization of life, prayer and work of religious must be in keeping with their physical and psychological condition; everywhere it must be adapted to the needs of the apostolate, to cultural requirements, to social and economic circumstances. 'Therefore', it said, 'constitutions, directories, custom-books, books of prayers and ceremonies and other similar volumes must be revised accordingly and brought into line with the documents of this sacred Council, by the suppression of anything obsolete.' In short, the Church saw at last that there was a need for the religious life to change course and that this couldn't be done until the steering orders had been altered.

Which is more than a five-minute job in the most sluggish section of Christian civilization. Slowly and very cumbersomely the religious orders have begun to crank up the machinery that will overhaul the documents governing their lives. By the end of 1967 some of them were still estimating that it would take a year or two longer before this first stage of adaptation was finished. It wasn't until the end of 1966 that the Dominicans took the preliminary step of sending a questionnaire to every member of the order to find out what the troops thought should be done. This came from the Master-General in Rome, it required replies in Latin if possible, and it warned that direct answers should not occupy more than five lines of typescript, with supporting proof or explanation worth another ten lines at the outside. This in response to such questions as : 'What is the special character of the spirit and life of St Dominic, and what was his intention in founding the order?' (on which several hefty volumes have been written); 'Should the traditional type of novitiate be altered? At what stage should it begin and how long should it last? And what of the duration and nature of temporary vows?' At about the same time as the Dominican questionnaire was put into orbit another was circling the earth from Cistercian headquarters and the Jesuits of Great Britain were making their own survey of members' thoughts on renewal. By now most orders and societies will probably have a fair idea of the changes their people would and would not like to see; how long it will take them to codify these and then to enact them is anybody's guess.

But time is scarcely on their side. For the mid sixties introduced a fresh hazard to the stability of the religious life. To the shortage of vocations and the advancing average age of communities was added an increasing number of men (rather more than women, probably, though for obvious reasons no statistics are available) who were abandoning their vows and simply walking out of their communities; sometimes to a marriage but as often as not just to a secular existence. This in the face of an excommunication which is the Church's penalty for those breaking solemn life vows. There have always been some who have accepted the penalty as the price of freedom; but there have never been as many, in the twentieth century at least, as there have been in this past four or five years. The movement, it seems fairly clear, is becoming something more than an ominous trickle. In the United States it has been unofficially estimated that two thousand nuns abandoned their vows in 1967. Another source reckons that the membership of American Trappist monasteries, which grew at an astonishing rate just after the war, was by the beginning of 1968 half of what it had been in the peak years of the previous decade; by then the abbey at Piffard, in New York, had dwindled from seventy-six to thirty-six monks. An American Benedictine has recently written that

> One of the most disturbing phenomena of the last decade in monastic life has been the greater instability of young religious. They come into the novitiate, they take their vows and surprisingly, in a year or two or even earlier, they present themselves to the superior and say that it was all a mistake; they no longer have any inclination to be religious at all. They have no compunction about breaking their vows which apparently have no deep significance for them. This is almost incomprehensible to the older religious, brought up in a different atmosphere.

In Great Britain, according to the local official Catholic directory, there were ten per cent fewer religious at the start of 1968 than there had been five years before; the Franciscans had diminished by twelve and a half per cent to 402, the 883 monks were eight per cent down on 1963's tally; the biggest drop of all – forty per cent – was among the Dominicans, leaving only 143.

Whatever imperturbable face the Catholic Church may present to the world officially when the future of the religious life is questioned, it is well aware now that a crisis exists; the cold truth is that the religious life is now practised by only one Catholic in 1,666, a lower proportion than ever before in the Church's history. Almost the last words of *De accommodata* demonstrate the Church's anxiety for the future. 'Priests and those responsible for Christian education', said the decree, 'must make a serious effort to see that there are religious vocations, chosen with due care, to provide for new growth in response to the needs of the Church.

Even ordinary sermons should deal more often with the evangelical counsels and religious vocations. Parents must nurture and protect religious vocations in their children, by giving them a Christian upbringing.' The decree, moreover, has conceded that prayer and sermons alone will not suffice to repair the breach that has been opened up; not only are constitutions and rules to be revised wholesale, but communities which offer no hope of any further useful life are not to accept any more novices and where possible they are to be amalgamated with more flourishing bodies which have similar aims.

If there is a note of desperation in some parts of the decree it is no more than is warranted by the condition of the religious life in general in the 1960s. An attempt to serve and relate themselves to the world as it really is today has been made by religious in several quarters, both Catholic and Protestant. These people have for some time been asking themselves questions which are fundamental to the life : what exactly constitutes prayer and what balance should be struck between it and activity; what kind of activity should religious be engaged in at the middle of the twentieth century? They have invoked psychiatry to help them decide whether they are individually fitted for the religious life. They have even started to wonder whether they have become religious in order to serve God and his world or just to help themselves. But these are still a minority. For the most part the religious life is still clothed and conducted in habits basically formed in the Middle Ages. It is still regulated by notions and appliances of authority and obedience which the rest of western society would have regarded as high-handed at the end of the nineteenth century. It is still bogged down in a world of its own that in its essentials has not varied much since it was constructed fourteen hundred years ago by a man called Benedict, who once jumped into a nettlebed because he was ashamed of his capacity for erotic love. It is the most remarkable of all the anomalies in our society today.

PART TWO

THE STRUCTURE TODAY

'It is almost as difficult to say what monks do as to say what the human race in general does ...' – DOM DENYS RUTLEDGE OSB, *The Complete Monk*, p. 103

'... only by living for a while in a monastery can one quite grasp its staggering difference from the ordinary life that we lead.' – PATRICK LEIGH FERMOR, *A Time to Keep Silence*, p. 27

HIGH in the mountains east of Florence the Sacro Eremo is perched at the top of a valley bristling with pines. There are about thirty small cottages here, a church, a guest house, a refectory, a kitchen and some other outbuildings. A high wall surrounds the cottages and if it were not for this the whole place would resemble a village. It is a collective hermitage, the home of the long-winded Congregation of the Hermit-Monks of Camaldoli of the Order of St Bene-dict. It is not substantially different from the earliest Chris-tian religious communities founded by St Pachomius, an antique survival and a mark of continuity which has already stretched along sixteen hundred years. Since the eleventh century, when St Romuald founded the congregation, the life at Sacro Eremo has virtually been unchanged and un-touched by reforms from within and pressures from without alike. The hermit-monk of Sacro Eremo is as self-contained as a man can be in this world. He has his cottage with its four rooms; one is nothing more than a lobby leading to a porch, where there is a log on which the hermit can sit and contemplate God and the scenery; another is a bed-sitter, where he eats meals which come to him through a hatch and which have been prepared by more gregarious hands than his in the kitchen; he has a study, with a table and book-shelves; he also has his oratory, with its altar and its prayer desk. He does not often leave his own four walls and his cottage is separated from his next-door neighbour's by a statutory twenty to thirty feet.

There are lay brothers at Sacro Eremo who live a life as communal as that of any other monk; they are the ones who prepare food in the kitchen and push it through the hatches to the hermits : they exist to make it possible for these men to live in solitude, of which there are different degrees among the Camaldolese. Some are so reclusive that they leave their cottage cells only in Holy Week, on the feast of St Martin and on Quinquagesima Sunday, which precede the two long fasts of Advent and Lent, to take part in communal worship in the church, and to dine and speak with their brethren as an act of charity. Otherwise they are quite alone, speaking only to their confessor, spending an hour each day in manual labour, and the rest of their time in utterly private prayer or study. For even the least reclusive hermits the silence and solitude of each day is relieved only by the offices they attend in the church, at intervals between 1.30 a.m. and sunset, and for the walks they are allowed to take together after vespers on the few occasions when the rule of silence is lifted. Unless he has the special permission of his prior the hermit can communicate with no one else, even by writing. There are perhaps a hundred and sixty men living under the Camaldolese régime in a handful of communities strung out across the northern hemisphere. They range from the Sacro Eremo itself, which is headquarters, to the Hermitage of the Immaculate Heart of Mary, whose unlikely sounding address is New Camaldoli, Lucia Ranch, Big Sur PO, California – deep, and even more unlikely, in the Henry Miller country. There are almost as many living within the similar Congregation of the Hermits of Monte Corona. There are those six hundred Carthusians, whose life is virtually in the same pattern. And none of it is representative of the religious life in the twentieth century any more than the existence of the Little Brothers of Autumn Grove, Leeds 6. It is just the most extreme form of the contemplative life entirely given to prayer. The religious life as a whole has only four common denominators, and they are poverty, obedience, chastity and prayer. The rest is infinite variety.

There are religious communities like the Little Brothers (though they aren't unique in this respect) whose premises are stuck in the sleaziest districts of the most industrialized cities. If they are not actually quartered in a slum themselves they will be surrounded by slums and their own building will be wretched-looking on the outside and gloomy within, full of butter-coloured electric light and an odour of sanctity compounded of central heating, floor polish and elbow grease. Others, like the English Jesuits of Farm Street in London, have revamped the insides of their scarcely more attractive uptown houses with pastel-coloured paint, quietly humming lifts, the most contemporary lettering in the signwriter's manual, and executive-style desks complete with dictaphones. Then there are the monasteries which conform, more or less, to the world's image of them. Some are so remote that, like the abbey of Gethsemani which the Trappists built in an empty corner of Kentucky, they have their own postmark. Some have been carefully sited as though their incumbents wanted to feel themselves half-way to heaven before they had actually started, like Montecassino, which sits arrogantly on the peak of its mountain so that you get a pain in the neck looking up at it from the town almost vertically beneath : a great white rambling shrine containing St Benedict's bones (though it doesn't do to say so to the monks of St Benoît sur Loire, who think they guard his remains) which was bombed to rubble during the war and carefully restored with a rapid grant from the Italian Government the moment the shooting stopped. Some, like Melk on the Danube, are baroque palaces with state bedrooms and grand staircases surviving from the days when the Emperor of Austria and his retinue, or another potentate, would call in for a drop of Benedictine hospitality. A few can number themselves still among the world's great treasuries of art and books. At Kremsmünster, the biggest Benedictine community in Austria, the library holds 100,000 volumes, 400 manuscripts, 792 incunabula and the eight-century Codex Millenarius; there is also an art gallery with work from the fifteenth to the nineteenth centuries, an armoury full of weapons dating from the Turkish invasion of 1683, a museum of astronomy in an eighteenth-century observatory, and collections of geology, stuffed animals and birds. But, then, there are monasteries like the Trappist abbey at Ogden, Utah, which was constructed in 1947 from United States Army surplus Quonset huts; and the Trappist community at Nunraw, Scotland, whose monks lived the same way, in Nissen huts, while they built themselves a permanent abbey from stone. There are also monasteries whose premises have at one time or another had curiously unmonastic histories. The Benedictines of Worth Abbey, in Sussex, inhabit a house which once belonged to the man who invented the torpedo and which was taken over by the military to become the headquarters of the Canadian Corps before the invasion of Normandy.

If the religious life can be divided into parts which each have some kind of unity, then the line must be drawn between the contemplatives and the actives; the contemplatives who, in greater or lesser degree, keep themselves apart from the world so as to concentrate on prayer and the actives who have, more or less, embraced the world so as to spread their Christian fervour. The distinction between the two is becoming blurred today, as religious themselves begin to question their ancient definitions and attitudes. But it still makes more sense than one between monks and nuns proper (who alone, in purist language, inhabit monasteries and convents and are subject to varying degrees of enclosure) on the one hand and the remainder of the religious world on the other – the Franciscan and Dominican friars, the Jesuits, the Sisters of Mercy or Charity and all the rest. It is more sensible if only because it cleaves in two the senior monastic order, the Benedictines. There are 225 Benedictine monasteries and 43 of them are contemplative. In these the monks are subject to strict enclosure, which means that they rarely leave the premises. The life is not so strict as that of a Carthusian or even a Trappist, but it follows closely the

Rule which Benedict composed. In effect the contemplative Benedictines have more in common with the Cistercians than they have with active monks of their own order.

These would prefer to say that they are living a mixed régime of contemplation and activity if only because their day traditionally has been punctuated seven times by attendance together in choir for the offices in addition to their times of private prayer; moreover the monastic life at any level is a way apart from that of many religious because it is lived largely in common : even when the average Jesuit occupies a house with several others he does very little in common with them apart from eating meals.

Contemplative actives or active contemplatives as a label for most Benedictine monasteries? It is a very private Benedictine debating point. Whatever you call those 182 remaining communities the fact is that they are scarcely cut off effectively from the world any more. The world has a habit of coming to the monastery, if it is famous enough, irrespective of how it sees its function. There are abbeys like Montecassino and Subiaco in Italy, like Beuron in Germany, like Maria Laach in Austria and like Montserrat in Spain (which, besides owning a painting of Mary reckoned to be by St Luke, and being the place where St Ignatius hung up his sword after conversion, is also a centre of Catalan and therefore anti-Franco patriotism) which count their annual pilgrims in scores of thousands and spend a fair amount of time accommodating them and catering for them. There are others, the eighteen monasteries of the Solesmes congregation, which get many visitors because they have specialized in liturgical prayer and become the great masters of Gregorian chant. Among the actives the greatest activity is in running schools and parishes. St Benedict visualized the education of small boys specifically to populate his monasteries and at Weingarten, Germany, the abbey still runs a school for this purpose. The saint might have taken less kindly to the spectacle of a hundred Benedictine abbeys – like Downside and Ampleforth in England, like St Scholastica's in Kansas, St Leo's in Florida and St Benedict's in Minnesota

—educating children merely to be good Catholics and citizens. While a proportion of boys attending Benedictine schools do end up as monks, this is scarcely seen by an abbot and his teaching staff to be the main point of the exercise. St Benedict's objection would have been based on other grounds, though. The monk who is a teacher cannot function as a monk in the grand tradition. He cannot attend some of the offices in choir, as by St Benedict's Rule he ought, because at those times he is in the classroom instead; and so he has to read his offices alone, compressed into a bunch at the beginning or the end of the day, so as to fulfil his quota of prayer. At a place like Downside – where twenty-five of the forty-seven resident monks are teachers (together with forty-five laymen) in the abbey's public school – this means that only half the community are keeping to its conventional routine during term time. The rest are throwing themselves wholeheartedly into their teaching jobs, extra-curricular activities and all. On Fridays at Ampleforth, which is the day the combined cadet force is on parade, half a dozen variously pipped and crowned figures in battledress turn out not to be officers and gentlemen at all but merely monks of the Order of St Benedict, who have temporarily swapped one uniform for another.

Ampleforth, by far the largest of the English Benedictine abbeys (153 monks compared with Douai's 73, Downside's 65 and smaller numbers descending to Worth's 24) is a good illustration of the parochial taxation of a community's strength that can occur nowadays. Of its total number only seventy-seven monks live in the monastery. The rest are serving singly, in twos, threes and foursomes, twenty-three different parishes from one end of the country to another, from the diocese of Cardiff to the diocese of Middlesbrough. There they live as any other Catholic parish priest does, following their Rule as far as their work allows, catching up with their offices just like the monk-teachers at home. They are not unique; 115 of the 225 Benedictine monasteries in the world are now involved in parish work. This may not coincide with Everyman's assumptions about the monastic life but, then, you find that riddled with anomalies which-ever side of the contemplative–active line you look. Even the most strictly enclosed Trappists – whose Cistercian ancestors were so dedicated to isolation that they forbade members of the order to confess, bury or administer com-munion to anyone unless he happened to be a guest of the monastery, would not educate boys even to become monks, and walled-up doors leading to the tombs of canon-ized Cistercians so that pilgrims should not come – even the Trappists, who have stuck quietly and closely to the letter of their founder's law, have been known to run a public school in the United States. At Mount Melleray, in Ireland, they have a reputation for curing dipsomaniacs, which they do by gradually decreasing a man's consumption of the real stuff until the poor lost soul is drinking unadulterated water.

The activity of Benedictines, however, is nothing com-pared with the works and functions of most religious com-munities. When, in 1965, the Catholic Church mounted a vocations exhibition in London, fifty-seven communities for men and 142 for women advertised their presence in the British Isles. This is a list, avoiding duplication as far as possible, of the ways in which they saw their vocations :

Men's communities
The evangelization of Africa.
To seek God, living a common life under a rule and under obedi-ence to an abbot.
Preaching and hearing confessions, the publication of eucharistic periodicals and giving Fifty Hours, eucharistic weeks and triduums in parishes.
The society seeks to work closely with the laity in reviving the faith in already Catholic countries and spreading it to missionary coun-tries.
Wherever priests are scarce Pallotines strive to establish missions and parishes, schools and retreat centres.
To seek God in a balanced life of prayer, manual labour, reading and study.
Contemplatives intent on prayer and sacred study .
Spreading the knowledge of God as preachers, lecturers, mis-sionaries and writers.

Run parishes, give missions, retreats, teach in schools, organize broadcasting, act as hospital and prison chaplains.

To send members to lowly and difficult fields of the apostolate for which the Holy See has difficulty in finding missionaries.

Especially for the evangelization of pagans and, above all, of the black race.

To make known Mary's apparition and to combat the evils that Mary complained of – violation of the Sunday, blasphemy, religious indifference, etc.

Keeping alive the faith of Italians abroad by means of spiritual and social assistance – builds churches, halls and clubs, opens mass centres, distributes Italian magazines and helps in the long and difficult process of integration with the local community.

To promote the greater glory of God and the personal sanctification of its members through the care of the sick.

Embraces every work of charity for boys; it has schools of all kinds – primary, grammar, agricultural and technical and labours earnestly for vocations and the 'Good Press'.

Tries to provide a homelike atmosphere where priests with problems, physical, mental or spiritual, may rebuild in so far as is necessary health of mind, body and soul.

To serve Mary and spread devotion to her Seven Sorrows.

Essentially missionary; special emphasis is placed upon Africanization and in particular on the creation of African clergy.

Varied works of charity, the education and instruction of children of all classes, especially the poor, the destitute, deaf, dumb and blind – and the care of the sick and mentally afflicted.

Sharing the social conditions and manual work of the poor.

Conducting approved schools for delinquent boys in England.

The practice of holy slavery to Jesus through Mary.

Women's communities

To form a family entirely consecrated to the heart of Jesus, adored especially in the Eucharist.

The sanctification of all its members for the glory of God by prayer and works of mercy which include clinics, helping the aged, social and parish work, including dispensary work.

A contemplative order but undertaking also farming, religious instruction, art work, the teaching of languages and the running of a guest house for ladies as well as printing.

The Christian education of girls in all types of schools and apostolic work connected with it.

To promote the glory of God and the sanctification of its members through the care of the sick in hospitals and homes for convalescents, the chronically ill, children, the aged and maternity. The sisters specialize in all phases of hospital work and may be doctors, nurses, technicians, radiographers, secretaries, dieticians, pharmacists and physical therapists.

To educate young girls, while giving them a good modern education and striving to instil something of old-time courtesy and consideration for others.

To give glory to God by a life of contemplation and penance, seeking God alone for his own sake; all the ordering of the life is but a means to this end.

Saviour-mindedness is the distinctive spirit as each sister aims to become all things to all people.

Work on the missions, teaching, nursing, undertaking catechetical work, the care of the aged, church needlework, child-care work in Salford and Lancaster, including social works of adoption, fostering, family welfare and preventive case work.

The re-education of girls in training homes, approved schools under the Home Office, special schools under the education department, homes and hostels for unmarried mothers and the rehabilitation of children from broken homes.

The practice of Christian charity towards the sick . . . to all classes of sufferers with any kind of infirmity no matter how contagious or repulsive and to all denominations, Catholic and otherwise.

To provide the religious life for girls wishing to care for and educate children from birth to seven years of age, helping unmarried mothers and teaching young girls who wish to become children's nurses.

Provides residential centres for university students, business and working girls, economical restaurants, free evening classes, dispensaries in mission areas, relief centres in slum areas, homes for immigrants, recreational clubs and social service centres.

Nurse the sick in their own homes without fee, preference being given to the poor.

To act as a living link between the Church and the Jewish people. To help our separated brethren back to the true fold.

Spreading the word of God by means of social communication – the press, cinema, radio, television and by any other means that human progress supplies and the necessities and conditions of the times demand.

Benedictine monks and nuns (To seek God, living a common life under a rule and under obedience to an abbot) were represented in that exhibition, of course. So were Franciscans, Dominicans, Trappist nuns, Little Brothers and Sisters of Jesus. So were the Congregation of the Sisters of Jesus Crucified, who are contemplatives founded in Paris in 1930 to make the religious life possible for sick and invalid women, who 'wish to give greater glory to God by accepting their sufferings joyfully and helping other souls to draw benefit from the Cross'. For the list is not a peculiarly English one; almost every community in it originated outside the British Isles; every vocation represented there will be found in any other country where the religious life is practised. It means that there is practically no social situation in which active religious are not involved. Some of them are tasks which few people but religious, with their dedication and their vow of obedience, care to take on. The Anglican sisters of the Community of St Mary the Virgin, for example, run the only hostel in Great Britain which cares for women who are slowly being rehabilitated after drug addiction; the Ministry of Health doesn't provide one yet. The Community of the Sacred Passion, another Anglican sisterhood, staffs óne of the two leprosariums in England, the other being a Ministry establishment.

There are very few skills which are not to be found in one cloister or another, often badly neglected by superiors who do not know how to employ them, but often encouraged to flourish as best they can in the context of a religious life. With a tradition of study so deeply embedded in monasticism it is scarcely surprising that theological journals everywhere are peppered with contributions from religious; some of the best of them are edited and published from religious communities. At the Vatican Council almost all the heavy-weight *periti*, the theological experts whom individual and less scholarly bishops took to Rome to keep them briefed and up to scratch, were religious; Edward Schillebeeckx, Yves Congar, Jerome Hamer and M. D. Chenu were all Dominicans, Karl Rahner and John Courtney Murray were

Jesuits, Gregory Baum was an Augustinian and Bernard Haring a Redemptorist. All of those eight pressed hard for a more liberal Church and between them originated some of the ideas which have been put into effect and changed Catholicism since 1965. Other forms of scholarship, sometimes distinctly untheological, occur here and there. The Jesuit Father Wilson Brown, in London, is a botanist who identified a whole crop of new plants which now bear his name in Guyana, where his society sent him as a missionary a few years back. Dom David Knowles was detached from his abbey (Downside) many years ago to become an academic in Cambridge, where he was at first Professor of Medieval History and then Regius Professor of Modern History. The Abbot Primate of all the Benedictines, the American Dom Rembert Weakland, is a distinguished musicologist. Sister Mary Corita Kent, of the Sisters of the Immaculate Heart of Mary in California, has had paintings hung in the New York Metropolitan Museum of Modern Art. Father Martin Jarrett-Kerr, of the Community of the Resurrection, has written a study of D. H. Lawrence ('a serious piece of criticism of Lawrence', wrote T. S. Eliot when it appeared in 1951, 'of a kind for which the time is now due') and Father Peter Levi, SJ, like Father Manley Hopkins before him, has produced poetry which gets published in the most discriminating anthologies; so does the American Daniel Berrigan, SJ. But the Jesuits, after all, have a reputation for exploiting a man's talents to the full, even if they don't always feel comfortable with the results and deem it necessary to sit on them for a year or two before the world outside gets wind of them and more or less insists on publication. Teilhard de Chardin spent a large portion of his Jesuit vocation as a biologist and palaeontologist, pottering around China (where he was partly responsible for the discovery of Peking Man in 1929) not so much as a religious as a scientist; and because his scientific writings questioned so many fundamental and orthodox Christian beliefs he was an embarrassment to his Society, which forbade him to publish. There is no end to the odd and worldly things in which a man might

be engaged when he has settled for the withdrawn and
obedient life of a monk. There is a monk of Belmont, Dom
Laurence Beers, whose address in his community's directory
is given as c/o Ministry of Defence and who at the moment
is residing in the officers' mess of an RAF station, where he
acts as chaplain. At Buckfast Abbey there is Dom John
Stephan, who has been president of the Devon Association,
and Dom Paul Patterson, who has been chairman of Exeter's
branch of the Association of Superintendent Electrical En-
gineers on the strength of his acquaintance with the monastery's generators. Whole communities can be roped in for
extra-curricular activities. The Anglican Franciscans have
become guardians of a bird sanctuary off the Northumbrian
coast because one of their friaries happens to be the best
placed to do the job. The monks of Nashdom have been
asked, by doctors experimenting with an antidote to german
measles, whether they would allow themselves to be inocu-
lated and then to remain as enclosed as the deepest contemplatives for a fortnight, to help find how to stop women
having deformed babies.

The huge majority of monks, nuns and other religious, of
course, do not enjoy the ups and downs of having a book
suppressed, then published, or even the mild excitement of
presiding over the local historical association. They live, most
of them, a life of interminable similarity; of offices in church
each day, of domestic chores, of private prayer, of whatever
is the particular vocation of their community; if they are
priests their days are more varied with the obligation to hear
confessions, to conduct retreats, to administer sacraments
outside the community, perhaps to act as spiritual director
of nuns. They may enjoy occasional robust relief, like the
Franciscan who defends the faith on a soapbox in Hyde Park
every Sunday afternoon, sandwiched between Lord Soper,
who is preaching an omnibus Christianity, and the gentleman who damns it all with his preference for Black Power.
But the relief is only occasional. Unless they are enclosed
they can and do travel, though.

In the Anglican Community of the Resurrection a monk

is required to be officially in residence at Mirfield for about eight weeks of the year, in company with three others. During that time the four of them must stay at home, to wait on their brethren at meals, to lay tables, to prepare afternoon tea, to answer the telephone and the door. They each have to write a newsy letter to one of the community's overseas houses. Every member of the community in Britain gathers at Mirfield for the General Chapter, at which the community's affairs are discussed and regulated, and this lasts for three and a half weeks in July, nine days after Christmas and a week after Easter. That is a general pattern into which everybody fits. Most men have a special job assigned to them in addition to their general community functions; one will be the custos in charge of the garden, another director of the Fraternity of the Resurrection administering much paper work to keep in touch with the lay friends and supporters of the community, two or three will be teaching theology to ordinands in the College of the Resurrection. This is the year's engagements of the novice-master at Mirfield for 1967; on dates left blank he is at home.

January 31 –February 1		To Chester to hear confession of nuns and to give an address.
February	2	To the women's community at Horbury, of which he is warden.
	3–6	Theological conference in London.
	23–24	Warden's visit to Horbury.
	25–26	A weekend preaching engagement in Nottingham.
March	8–29	To New York to conduct retreats for communities of nuns.
April	17–19	Warden's visit to Horbury.
May	1–3	Chester to hear nuns' confessions and give an address.
	8–12	Conducted a priests' retreat at the community's retreat house in Huntingdonshire.
	13–15	Gave talks and led discussions at a 'holy party' for inquirers at a country house in Surrey.
June	2–19	On holiday (members of the community normally take a month a year, usually with relatives).

June	20–21	Meeting of the Religious Communities' Advisory Council at Oxford.
	22–24	With other members of the community took part in discussions with Methodist theologians at Mirfield.
July	3–6	Attended conference of religious communities at Oxford.
	26–27	Warden's visit to Horbury.
July 29 –August 7		With other members of the community ran a summer school at Wantage, giving lectures and sermons.
September	2–3	Warden's visit to Horbury.
	4–6	Oxford for meeting of Advisory Council.
	12–13	Theological conference in Oxford.
	14–28	On holiday.
October	3–7	Conducted retreat for nuns near London.
	13–16	Another 'holy party' in the Surrey country house.
November	2	Talk to local branch of the Mothers' Union.
	10–13	Conducted retreat for men and women in Huntingdonshire.

That is the year of a fairly senior member of an Anglican community. It probably represents greater mobility, though not all that much, than more junior Mirfield men enjoy; it certainly leaves the average Benedictine standing, or the religious of either sex whose community is almost totally committed to teaching, nursing or local relief work of one kind or another. But a Jesuit or a Dominican or a handful of other religious in Catholic communities might find it comparable to their own routine.

It is from communities such as Mirfield, both Anglican and Catholic, which have never been fully geared to engagement with the secular world on its own terms (as the Sisters of Charity, the Sisters of Mercy and many others have), that in recent years there has been growing talk of greater activity outside the community in ways the world would recognize as useful. Basically it has involved rethinking the meaning of Christian commitment, a process which has been speeded by the example of the Petits Frères and of the French worker-priests. The worker-priesthood was started in 1944 as a means of bridging the gap between the Church and a suspicious and almost completely anti-clerical working-class. It was backed by Cardinal Suhard of Paris and it meant that priests were to live as manual workers, not in an effort to proselytize those around them, but simply to demonstrate that the Church too was prepared to dirty its hands and be on the dole as well as to starch its linen and cash its cheques; what mattered most of all was not conversions but simply *la présence* – just being there. At the height of the movement perhaps a hundred men were involved, some of them secular priests, others religious. The trouble was that they eventually identified themselves so closely with the workers politically that the Church took fright and in 1959 finally banned the worker-priests altogether. Some of them obediently returned to their religious duties; others either abandoned their orders formally in defiance or else just carried on as if nothing had happened. One of them was Henri Perrin, a Jesuit, who left the Society when it became an issue. At the time matters came to a head for him he was working as a navvy on the construction of the Isère-Arc dam. There was a strike over poor pay and bad working conditions, which the men won, and a letter Perrin wrote just after it was settled (March, 1952) indicates clearly the position that he, a Jesuit, had adopted by then :

Dear Everyone, Here's another collective letter, which is a way of avoiding repeating the same things over and over again to individuals. We are now fully out of the strike, and the results regarding my pay are gratifying. I earned 6,000 francs in the last three days; that is to say, for thirty hours' work. But above all what we have gained is that the management has really got going, that the worksite is running better than ever before, that there are constant adjustments in the organization of the work, and that the 'township' is growing under our eyes. Better still, the bosses, far from trying to make reprisals, treat the strike leaders with obvious respect. They consult us and listen to us. In a word, the situation is good. A new fatal accident that occurred four days after our return to work (one of us was crushed by a tractor in the tunnel) served to reinforce the attitude of the workers and the situation I have just described. As far as I am concerned, all is well, and Christ seems to be taking a guiding hand in events. . . . The funeral of our work-mate also marked a new stage for me. Inevitably, I had to officiate at it myself. All the workers were present, when I appeared all dressed up and ornamented, before a great number of workmates who were not yet aware that I was a priest. Half of them came into church; the other half stayed outside. When we emerged, some of them came up to me and said that in the view of all, or nearly all, the ceremony had increased the trust they felt in me . . .

At the Vatican Council the Catholic Church discovered a lot of truths about itself; one was that it had been ill advised to end the worker-priesthood. Quietly the experiment was restarted. By the middle of 1967 there were fifty-one priests working full-time in French factories. Half of them were men from religious orders, including five Jesuits and a couple of Dominicans. Essentially their aim is the same as that of the Petits Frères : identification with the poorest sec-tions of society. Their ultimate effect on the religious life as a whole is so far incalculable, but in the long run it is likely to be enormous. Already some communities have begun to conduct their own tentative experiments. One Anglican sisterhood has closed the workshop in which for several generations it has sewn church vestments, retrained its womanpower, and started a chiropody practice for old people with sore feet. The Sisters of the Church (another Anglican community which has spent most of its time teaching so far) in 1967 sent a clutch of women to Aus-tralia to live in a house in downtown Sydney and get what-ever jobs they could find locally; within a week or two one of them was a kitchen hand in a hospital and another was packing cosmetics on a Max Factor production line.

This reappraisal of function is accompanied in some cases by a searching look at the meaning and practice of religious poverty. St Benedict was quite clear what he meant by it in the sixth century. 'The life of the monk', he wrote, 'should at all times be Lenten in its character.' Not only were the first Benedictines forbidden to receive presents and ordered to share all worldly goods from a communal chest, but the abbot was instructed to make regular searches of mattresses to be sure that no one was concealing private property. And though the saint was, in fact, noncommittal about the extent of communal ownership it is implicit in the Rule that while a monastery would do well to be solvent it had no business to accumulate anything beyond necessity. Like a lot of other things in the religious life, the conceptions of poverty were to be modified by the centuries.

There are communities which still appear to be living the Benedictine Rule to the letter, even though they have no affiliations with the order, and to wear their poverty like a talisman. The Poor Clares, for example, determined to look the part, pad around in bare feet unless they are out of doors or standing on stone floors, when they are allowed to wear sandals. Some of their houses, it is said, never know where next week's budget is coming from; and the Anglican Franciscans make sure that they have no more money in the bank than will see them through the next six months. Cistercians sleep fully dressed, and though poverty is not the motive for that – it has more to do with always being prepared to meet their Maker – it amounts to an economy of sorts. There are monks who lengthen the life of fraying habits by sewing leather on the elbows and the cuffs. But for every Cistercian sleeping rough there is probably another religious somewhere who will not be above slumbering in a pair of silk pyjamas donated by a reverent relative at Christmas. And for every abbot with leather-bound elbows there will certainly be two who permit themselves the odd cigar when they are away from home and on their travels. It all depends which community a man or woman belongs to, how the rules are written and how they are interpreted. There are some communities which give every member a few shillings a week pocket-money, with a bob or two extra for the smokers, and some which give them nothing at all. There are some so flush with money that if a man takes a fancy to a book in a shop window he can walk in and buy it, reimburse himself from the community's general fund, and put the volume in the library when he has read it. There are some which will provide a typewriter or a dictaphone at the first time of asking and others in which a religious reckons he is lucky to have a fountain pen he can call his own. 'We are taught', says a Benedictine of my acquaintance, 'in the novitiate – but don't always remember after – to live simply and not ask for expensive and unnecessary gadgets. There is a danger in letting people have what they ask for. The trouble is that it's all covered by obedience if they've gone through the proper channels.' There are many places where they have to live more austerely than that implies; where every single item has to be wheedled out of the superior, where every member of the community carries a notebook in which he enters to the nearest halfpenny everything he has spent, and where a man is encouraged and even expected to hitch-hike his journeys rather than travel by public transport. There are places apart from Trappist monasteries – where they never eat flesh meat on principle as a penitential gesture and go totally vegetarian during Advent and Lent – whose meals are adequate and only just. The Mother Superior of a contemplative community recalls that the first thing she did on taking over from her unduly ascetic predecessor was to install central heating and make sure that everyone got at least one square meal a day 'because this life is hard enough without fainting from cold and hunger'. She was a sensible woman. More sensible than the abbot of the Benedictine house in which I watched the most staggering display of excessive food I have seen anywhere outside a metropolitan expense-account restaurant. It was Saturday lunch but, I was told, nothing out of the ordinary. There was soup, a meat course, a heavy pudding, cheese and biscuits, fresh fruit, beer and coffee. Everybody, so far as I could see, waded through the lot. Rather more than half the monks accepted two helpings of one or other of the first three courses. They were all offered a third.

An American Benedictine has remarked that it is possible for a monk to be as poor as a church mouse while his community is as sleek as a city cat. And so it is. Kremsmünster Abbey's assets must amount to millions in either dollars or sterling, however its monks may be individually placed, and Montecassino will be worth a penny or two. 'Monasteries and convents', writes Dom Columba Cary-Elwes,

have almost a natural propensity to become wealthy. They pay no taxes; friends lavish upon them gifts of land, buildings, art works. By their very profession their inmates are industrious' and abstemious; as with the early Puritans, riches came unsought but inevitably. Even if these institutions pass through hard times, they have by their corporate nature a better chance of survival to better times than private individuals, farmers or small businessmen, for example. History bears this out; monasteries and convents, particularly the former, accumulate wealth as dams water.

He is writing from a priory seat in Missouri, and American religious institutions doubtless fare as amply, compared with those elsewhere, as anything else in the United States; in England it is only the active communities which go untaxed; the contemplatives, which are not regarded as charities, have to pay up like the rest of us. But Dom Columba's comment will not be a wild generalization whatever the context.

Anyone who in Italy, Spain or Malta has watched religious quartering a town street by street with their mendicant bowls in hand knows cynically well one way the funds are raised, though barefaced begging is probably beginning to wane everywhere. Within the past decade a French inquiry into 150 Carmelite convents showed that the nuns had to earn between sixty and seventy per cent of their income themselves, instead of the twenty-five per cent which had at one time been the custom. Good churchpeople, however, are in the habit of giving alms whether solicited or not and no group of them is more regular in its donations than the churchpeople who attach themselves to the fraternities and other support bodies belonging to religious communities. Gifts roll in not only by cheque, banknote and coin but often in kind as well and sometimes the generosity can be tiresomely misplaced, so that a conscience-stricken

superior has to issue reminders of vocation and planned
giving and other Christian principles. 'We do not', write
the English Benedictine nuns of Burnham Abbey in their
monthly journal,

want to appear ungrateful but we often receive large and beautiful
boxes of chocolates which we have to give away. I am sure this is
not what the donor intended. We are grateful for a limited number
of plain sweets or plain chocolate as we may eat sweets on Feast
days. Otherwise we would be glad of small book tokens ... or garden tokens. ... Or it would give us great pleasure to know that
any money which would have been spent on us was sent to the
fund for refugees.

And then a tactful reminder of real needs : 'For the Mother
House – a few Ancient and Modern hymn books, with or
without music. A garden rake. Teacloths for Guest House.
Old plastic mackintoshes, plastic or polythene bags.' Not
that every women's community turns up its nose at boxes
of chocolates; among the British lately it has become quite
an ecumenical gesture for neighbouring Anglican and
Catholic convents to exchange bumper boxes of Black Magic
or some other brand on each other's patronal festivals.
    Although the Sisters of St Joseph of Cluny, for example,
are careful in their recruiting publicity to point out that no
dowry is required of their postulants, many communities
still set high hopes on what a newcomer can be expected to
bring to the cloister with him or her. In some places they
may still canvass a fixed sum, but in these tight-fisted days
a more common practice is to accept gratefully whatever a
newcomer can offer. There are communities which insist
on acquiring only the income from a member's capital,
which must remain intact in case there are family claims to
be met on his or her death. There are modern-minded communities which would prefer to have nothing at all to do
with the money anyone might have owned before coming
inside. The Community of the Glorious Ascension, an Anglican teaching order for men which is not yet ten years
old, orders this side of its affairs like this :

1 If a postulant or novice has money of his own, or owns property, he should deposit the money in the bank before entering the community, and make arrangements so that his property may be administered with the least possible concern to himself. The income from these sources should also be put into deposit in the bank and may be allowed to accumulate. No one may be received into any grade of the community who is in debt.

2 Before profession (in temporary vows) a novice must make a will. He shall also deal with any money or property he has in the following way:

(a) He shall make arrangements for the disposal of any income from these sources. He is at liberty to do what he likes with this income, though he may not have it for his own personal use, neither may he allow it to accumulate in his own account.

(b) He must inform his superior as to what he has arranged and the superior may make suggestions. Also the superior may order him to appoint an executor if he consider that the administration of the income or property is going to need a considerable amount of work.

(c) He may not rid himself of his money and property.

(d) He may make over the income from the money and property to the community. If, however, he do this, he has no say in the way in which the money is spent, but it shall be put into the community fund in the normal way.

(e) If he has made over the income to the community and later he be released or removed, then he is at liberty to re-adjust the disposal of his income as he wishes. He may not, however, reclaim any money which was paid to the community from these sources while he was a member.

(f) In his will the brother must make quite clear what is to happen to the money and property and the income from these, in the event of his death.

3 Before profession in solemn vows a brother must dispose of all money and property which he owns. If it be in trust he shall make arrangements for the disposal of the income from this trust. In the disposal of this the rules set out in (a), (b), (d) and (f) above apply here also. (e) above also applies here with the addition that if at solemn profession the brother gave all his money and property to the community he may not reclaim it should he be released or removed. The community, however, if it wishes, may return some or all of it to the released or removed person.

A major source of income for any order which teaches, nurses or performs any other recognized social service is the wages its members collect from the state, the local civil authority or the Church itself. Monks can abide by the Burnham scale as much as any grammar-school teacher with a wife and two children to support. For the non-teaching, non-nursing community, for the *real* monks and nuns who don't collect wages from anyone, other shifts must be made as best they can. Happy the community which has a prolific and best-selling author in its house – and there are one or two here and there – whose royalties come in like a benison every six months. Lucky the prioresses who have those singing or guitar-strumming nuns under their care, talent-spotted by the record companies and at the top of the hit parade before you can chant 'Ave Maria'.

The Cistercians are still farmers, taking St Benedict's injunctions about manual labour more seriously than most these days. They always have been more consistent agriculturalists than any other order. They not only fed and clothed themselves off their own lands through the ages, but in their heyday, by developing a system of outlying grange farms manned by peasants, whose sons as often as not ended up in the monastery, they were of considerable economic influence in their localities. The American Trappist Thomas Merton* has remarked that their sheep-rearing, wool-growing activities in the twelfth century were on such a scale that in the north of England the role of the Cistercians was comparable to the role of General Motors in the States today. Their role is much diminished nowadays, though Wilhering and other Austrian abbeys still run the monastic granges which generally disappeared with the Reformation, and they still look to the large farming families who work them for a lot of their vocations. But every Cistercian monastery runs a farm of some kind, both to fulfil its vocation and to pacify the bank manager – and sometimes to clean up the prizes in agricultural shows against the local farmers. Among the big news emerging

* Died December 1968.

from the American monastery of New Melleray in 1966 was this : 'The farm department won the 1965 Dubuque County corngrowing contest (125 bushels per acre); the alfalfa dehydration plant is functioning smoothly; the dairy (Holsteins) and the beef cattle (Angus) departments have improved their stock; the garage department invented a revolutionary alfalfa chopper; and 10,000 lbs of honey and 5,000 lbs of liturgical incense were produced ...'

A Cistercian farm may run to a thousand acres and more, like Nunraw's in Scotland, or it can be two hundred acres and less, like Mount St Bernard's in Leicestershire. It may be so big that it keeps every man in the community busy when he isn't in choir or saying his prayers; it can be small enough to be left mostly to the lay brothers while the choir monks get on with their studies except when harvest time comes and they are required to reinforce the farm workers.

From their two hundred acres, their market garden and their orchard, the seventy-five monks of Mount St Bernard produce almost but not quite all their food. There are vegetables from the garden and fruit from the orchard; there are eggs from the six hundred birds in a deep-litter laying unit; there is milk from the herd of pedigree Ayrshires – 2 bulls, 45 cows, 27 heifers, 14 young stock. Most of the land, 120 acres, is under grass for the cattle; but there are 25 acres of root crops, 55 acres of corn; the Mount St Bernard harvest is mostly kale, potatoes, oats, barley and wheat. There is also a twelve-sow pig unit producing about 215 porkers a year. All this is run very professionally for the monks have become farmers down to the tip of their cowls. They have installed a six-point herringbone milking parlour and their cows are part of the brucellosis eradication scheme. You can't be more professional than that. And although the only newspaper entering the monastery is a single copy of the *Daily Telegraph* (extracts of which are read out to the community during the evening meal), the *Farmer and Stockbreeder* and other journals of the trade press are almost required reading for anyone working on the farm. The monastery's solitary wireless set – in the possession of Father

Abbot, who listens to it to find out what prayers of intercession the world has need of today – was originally acquired not to get the news but to have the BBC weather forecast for the benefit of those two hundred acres. If it were not for those white figures, cassocked and overalled above their muddy gumboots, gesticulating like the deaf and dumb to each other (for these are Cistercians of the Strict Observance, Trappists, who are among the least conversational of men), if it were not for them, and the great crucifix high on the whitewashed wall at one end of the cowshed, you would never dream down on the farm that you were well outside the jurisdiction of the National Farmers' Union and the National Union of Agricultural Workers. But everything around the dungy yard – the tractors, the trailer combine, the baler, the disc harrows, the fertilizer spinner, the corn drill, the spraying machine and the forage harvester – everything here is here for the greater glory of God and no other purpose. Except for those 215 porkers, which are flesh meat, and therefore fated for a less discriminating market in the world outside to bring in revenue to the monastery along with the surplus milk and eggs.

The Cistercians have their farms. They sometimes have more exotic forms of income. The Trappists of Caldey are in the perfume business, retailing anything from Caldey Number One ('a sophisticated perfume in the modern idiom') at 63s. a bottle to Island Rose hand lotion ('incomparable "body" and soothing qualities') at 4s. 3d. a time. They run a mail-order business, as well as one scent shop in London and another in Los Angeles, to keep trade on the move, aided by publicity material that looks as if it has come straight off Madison Avenue ('When the monks began to make perfume they trained in the best schools of perfumery, consulted the leading authorities, and Number One was their first outstanding achievement. ... When the Caldey gorse is in full bloom the evening air is heavy with its fragrance. The monks, repeatedly asked by visitors to capture this scent, offer Island Gorse as a fine fully balanced perfume. ... The matching After Shave and men's Cologne differ from those found on today's market, reflecting the simplicity and ruggedness of island monastic life ...') There are other communities which keep themselves afloat on the liquor business, from the thin red wine produced by the Salesian Convent in Bethlehem off those bony and sand-blasted Judean terraces, to the tonic stuff that comes from gentler slopes in Devon by way of the Benedictine Abbey at Buckfast ('People write : "It is indeed a wonderful tonic and in my estimation incomparable. ... I am so delighted with BUCKFAST that I am recommending it to my many friends ..."') The Benedictines of Nashdom make incense (Tintern at 6s. 6d. a lb., Sherborne at 9s., Rievaulx at 13s., Evesham at 16s., Glastonbury at 19s.) and the Bene-dictines of Prinknash make pottery with trading outlets in dependent houses, in London stores (Harrods, Barkers), and even in the souvenir shop at Upper Canada Village, Ontario, where Prinknash ware lies among the Crockett caps, the Redskin moccasins and the picture postcards of the St Lawrence river. There is a shop in the Boulevard de Tirlemont in Louvain which sells nothing but the varied produce of Benedictine and Cistercian houses in Belgium, whose shelves are loaded with cheese, liqueurs, mustard and mayonnaise as well as missals. And so some-how the monasteries get by. Just occasionally, when the harvest has failed maybe, or when the faithful are laggardly with their alms, an abbot will have to examine his treasures and sadly dispose of some antique rarity, the better to keep his monks in holy poverty. It was so not very long ago at the Abbey of St Rupert in Salzburg, which stripped itself of two twelfth-century prizes, a chalice and a vestment. They were gobbled up expensively by American museums.

The fact is, of course, that a monastery is like any other institution with mouths to feed, bodies to clothe, work to be done and fabric to kept in repair. Even if it found the notion utterly abhorrent, money would have to pass through its hands and a balance sheet would have to be kept. The Petits Frères themselves cannot escape the menace of house-keeping. And the way they live involves the simplest

housekeeping of all. For the Father Bursar of a full-scale
community, keeping the accounts puts him in more or less
the same position as a company secretary. This is what it
amounts to in hard cash at one British monastery :

There are over forty monks at the mother house, another
twenty in dependent British houses, maybe another thirty
in four small communities overseas. The overseas houses
keep their own balance sheets, they get annual allotments
from the mother house, but as the monks in them have
teaching posts they have some local income of their own
from the governments employing them. The only earned
income of the monks in Britain comes from the royalties
on their writings and work done on parish missions or in
conducting retreats, which often brings in a cheque. Individually the monks get 4s. 8d. a week pocket money (a
few shillings a week more if they are smokers) and a £25
allowance for their annual holidays. In 1967 the monastery
in Britain spent £46,724. Provisions cost £7,393, salaries for
the five full-time and odd part-time employees (for whom it
runs a non-contributory pension scheme) £7,527, lighting
and heating £4,108, allotments to overseas dependencies
£6,300, travel overseas by the superior and other brethren
£3,881. The tobacco allowance amounted to £207. The
monastery had a working deficit that year of £7,152. Its
main source of income for 1967 was the £12,605 it collected
in subscriptions and donations from people who support its
work. It did almost as well – £11,565 – in dividends drawn
from the capital brought to the community by brethren
when they joined it. Guests and retreatants left a voluntary
£3,934 in return for monastic hospitality. Royalties came to
£2,038. That was how the monastery's general fund, from
which it attends to its running costs, shaped up.

It also has what it calls a joint fund, from which it takes
the money for capital expenditure. Out of that in 1967 it
spent £9,383 on repairs and renewal of equipment in
Britain and £50,100 on various subsidiary works of the community, mostly overseas. Into it came £12,934 in legacies
to the monastery, £13,299 income from its investments,

£7,623 on the sale of some investments and £10,918 in recoverable income tax. Its investments are put into about 140 different firms and they have a book value of £484,252. The monastery does not play the market itself (even the bursar wouldn't know how to do that) but it has some good friends in the City of London, churchmen all, who buy and sell on its behalf. At the moment it has shares in almost every sector of industry. They run from Associated TV Ltd to John Brown and Co., the shipbuilders; from Woolworths to Allied Breweries; from Thorn Electric to ICI, Imperial Tobacco, the International Publishing Corporation (owner of the *Daily Mirror* and the *People*) and de Beers. What with one thing and another the monastery has half a million pounds in the bank. It sometimes worries about the placing of its investments, about the morality of some concerns whose stock looks good. It searched its heart a long time when its City advisers suggested backing the South African diamond miners de Beers*; in the end it wrote to Bishop Huddleston of Masasi, who belongs to the Anglican Community of the Resurrection, who made his reputation as an opponent of apartheid in South Africa and who would be expected to provide an impeccably Christian judgement of the problem; he said that de Beers were among the best employers in the Republic, and that if they went out of business the people to suffer would be their native workers; so the monastery thanked him and invested in de Beers. It has other problems of high finance. It has to juggle with its joint fund, spending no more than a tenth of its capital a year on capital works because the flow of legacies is uneven; in 1967 £12,934 came in, when in 1966 there had been £32,000. That at least is likely to balance itself out over the years. The income that is certainly running out is the dividends on the money brought to the monastery by newcomers. They are obliged to leave their capital outside the community in case there are family claims on it after death, so the monastery can't bank on more than the interest. This has been pretty handsome in the past but as more families

*Now Bishop of Stepney.

claim the capital of dead monks it is dwindling steadily. In
1967 the interest amounted to £11,565; in 1966 it was
£18,020. It will never be a growth point because wealthy
young bachelors with a vocation to be monks seem to be a
thing of the past. 'It's quite a blessing these days', says the
bursar thoughtfully, 'if a man comes to us with £100 he can
call his own.' So the monastery watches its half-million carefully, wonders how long it will last, spends its four-and-
eightpences with abandon, and remembers to say its prayers.

The economies of the Poor Clares and the Petits Frères are
nearly light years distant from that one, for the spectrum of
the religious life is almost as broad as that of life in the world
outside the convent or the community house walls, and its
breadth can be measured in every particular of the religious
vocation, in every moment of the religious day and night.
Even inside the two divisions of contemplation and activity
there can be strange distances of habit and usage. A Trappist
sleeps in a dormitory which is divided into cubicles with
only a curtain to be drawn across the open end, because St
Benedict ordained community in everything and the Trappist of the twentieth century adheres more strictly to St
Benedict's Rule than any Benedictine does. Yet a Carthusian, who is also contemplative, has a cell which is his very
private retreat from the moment he enters his Charterhouse until the day he dies. A monk or a nun may inhabit
the same room from the beginning to the end of their vocation or they may be constantly flitting from one cell to another, every six weeks or every six months, as an act of
obedience which has been invoked to prevent their becoming too attached to any one set of four walls, to make sure
that there is absolutely nothing in this world that they can
begin to regard as their own. There are monastic and conventual cells which are bereft of anything but a bed, a table,
a hard chair, a hook behind the door, a crucifix on the wall,
a missal and whatever spiritual reading is at the moment
on loan from the community's library. There are others
where the chair may be easy and well sprung, where if the
incumbent's tastes run to Hokusai prints one will be framed

and hanging opposite the crucifix, where there will be photographs of a nephew or a niece or a wedding group on a mantelpiece, where shelves and table will be an untidy sprawl of books, periodicals and papers which have been begged, borrowed or bought from a variety of sources both inside and outside the community. The English Trappist nuns of Stapehill in Dorset sleep on mattresses stuffed with straw. The Anglican nuns of Fairacres in Oxford, whose purpose in life is identically contemplative, lie on boards covered with thin foam-rubber Dunlopillo.

A community sometimes proclaims its flavour the moment the visitor walks through the front door. At this convent the waiting-rooms, where the nuns are allowed to converse with callers, will be named 'Watchful' and 'Faithful' and the rooms where guests are bedded down will be a series of 'St Uriels', 'St Gabriels' and other archangels. In the waiting-rooms there will be volumes of Trollope and Scott behind glass and you can be sure that nothing intellectually more invigorating or disturbing is to be found in the hinterland. The sisters and the atmosphere they make will be gently smiling, a little brisk, a shade pious. But at that monastery across the town, where the rooms are numbered or left entirely anonymous, where there is no waiting-room but a kind of hanging-around space instead, the first thing the visitor encounters is a revolving rack of recent paperbacks. The reading matter will proceed from the Bishop of Woolwich's latest at the threshold to Alex Comfort on *Sex in Society*, and the opaque psychiatric pronouncements – sprinkled, here and there, with four-letter worded case histories – of Dr R. D. Laing further along in the interior. And the fathers will be suitably sophisticated, very knowing about life outside, sometimes just a bit too hearty in their laughter.

A community can usually be depended upon to give itself away in the literature it publishes. This may run to nothing more than a cyclostyled newsletter aimed at a handful of friends and wellwishers; it may go to thickish volumes (in addition to hardback stuff written by individuals and handled by secular publishers) which are intended to be a source of research and argument in the highest intellectual echelons of the Church as a whole. As an example of the former here is an extract from the small magazine circulating from the Community of St Laurence, an English sisterhood which chiefly looks after incurable invalids and old people.

Dear Friend, Again it is time for us to be writing our letter, that is if you are to receive it in time for Easter. How quickly the days and months fly by. What an endless time it seemed, when we were small, from one Christmas to another. But now the seasons seem to follow one on top of another in the twinkling of an eye. By the time you receive this it will be that Queen of all Festivals, Easter Day, and a very happy one indeed to all of you. We hope you have managed to steer clear of the flu. Perhaps it is too much to expect you all to have done this. If you were so unfortunate as to become such a sufferer we hope it is now only an unpleasant memory. We here have been very fortunate. We did not entirely escape, but we only had one or two isolated cases and for this we are very thankful.

In our last letter we were very sorry to forget to tell you about the loss of one of our treasures, old Mrs Gratton, better known as Gran, not that she was the eldest of our little family but she had so many grandchildren that it seemed quite the thing for all of us to refer to her as 'Gran'. . . . One day we were most interested to find Belper had suddenly come possessed of a Washetaire, and what a wonderful and useful place it is too with its lovely pastel shaded washing machines and tumbler dryers. How reasonable the cost. We worked out that we could do the whole of our wash there for the price we now pay for sending our sheets to a laundry in Derby. It's 2s. 6d. for the use of the washing machine and sixpence for the tumbler dryer, more sixpences if you want things bone dry. Several of the community have spent several happy hours there. There is always an audience too, the other side of the window!!! We sometimes wonder whether these people are plucking up courage to come in themselves!! . . . As I write this we have 26 boys and girls staying with us from Whinshill. They are pre-confirmation candidates and what a happy little crowd they are. Some of the girls had a wonderful time in the night, six of them were discovered in one room and four in one bed!! Smothered laughter and suppressed giggles betrayed them. They leave us after dinner today and we hope they take with them memories of their visit which will be of lasting value to them . . .

A religious community can still be one of the last repositories of adult innocence, but it can also be as sophisticated as ever they come in the world outside. In an issue of the Benedictine *Ampleforth Journal* you can light on a ballad by Bob Dylan, alongside some pretty solid theological correspondence and book reviewing. In one copy of the English Dominican monthly *New Blackfriars* you can find articles on Black Power, Rhodesia, French political thought, God and suffering, redemption and revolution. In its issue of October 1967 the Canadian Dominican review *Maintenant* spent itself entirely on the French-Canadian question, and demanded a socialist republic of Quebec with its own president and a special relationship with the rest of Canada. In the September 1967 number of the *American Benedictine Review* the main articles were entitled : 'If St Benedict were alive today . . .'; 'Psychological hazards of young religious and seminarians'; 'Freedom in the age of renewal'; 'Julien Green and his search for truth'; 'The meaning of the term "Father" as applied to Catholic priests'; 'Liturgical symbol and reality in the poetry of George Herbert'; 'The psychology of American foreign policy'; 'Renewal – the key to the vocation crisis'; 'Meeting today's vocation crisis'; 'Pattern of medieval monastic reforms'; 'Aphorisms for a teacher'; 'The gyrovags, or wandering monks'; 'God is friendship – the key to Aelred of Rievaulx's Christian humanism'; 'Unity day at Coventry – Benedictines participate in "Vision of Unity Week" '.

The quality of the paper, however, is not always a guide to the standard of the contents; the English Sisters of the Love of God publish a good deal of tough-minded spirituality with the aid of a stencilling machine and a stapler. Nor do the contents always represent the mood of the order backing them. The English Carmelites sponsor a literary quarterly which mostly reflects the individual preferences of the friar, Fr Brocard Sewell, who edits it; it is strong on Henry Williamson, Colin Wilson and the adventurous sort of poet whose writings are set down like this :

<pre>
I auricle/the wheel sounds
  turn to (turn ovah TURN
  fly a tern corner up out
  TERN to drumz.
</pre>

Even though the tradition of monasticism, and especially of the contemplative life, is one of withdrawal from the world the insularity of a religious community can still astonish when the community is physically not so very remote from the rest of society. It is less of a shock to find a Camaldolese hermitage blissfully unaware of current affairs when it is stuck in isolation high upon an Italian alp than to discover only slightly smaller ignorance in a Trappistine convent situated a few hundred yards from an English main trunk road. But when, in the 1960s, you ask the Abbess of Stapehill just how aware she and her nuns are of what goes on outside their walls, and she replies. 'Oh, we knew when we had a new pope; and we heard about the Coronation', you realize just how much the world is passing them by. At Stapehill they took, said the abbess, just one periodical and that was the Catholic weekly *The Tablet*. No newspapers, no wireless, certainly no television. One or two of the recently professed nuns had been acquainted with TV in their former existences but for the majority of the abbey the device might never have been invented. Yet the device is among the equipment of some contemplative houses which are physically just as enclosed as Stapehill. And the guest-master of a Trappist monastery in the English midlands is so anxious to demonstrate his awareness of what is going on outside that within a few minutes of a visitor's arrival he is artfully steering conversation towards the most recent movements on the pop-record charts. There are communities which pride themselves on their conversational ability in the currency of the times they are living in, just as there are communities which cherish their ability to communicate in Latin. A Benedictine monk borrows a book from one of his superiors and pencils on the flyleaf 'olim Fr Prior nunc ad usum Br A —'. Not that all Benedictines can communicate as deftly as all that. One of the delegates to the

1967 congress of Benedictine abbots in Rome lamented when he got home : 'All the abbots would nevertheless agree that the sessions were sometimes boring. The speeches were mostly in Latin and had to be translated into English (for the benefit of the Americans, so my fellow-Englishmen insisted). Occasionally a speech in French would have to be translated into both Latin and English. I confess I sometimes wrote letters : other abbots admitted to having used the time in the same occupation.'

The insularity of a community does not necessarily correspond to the degree of its enclosure; it depends much more upon the alertness, the open-mindedness and the readiness of the order, the congregation or the superior to assimilate by all means available within its rule the facts of life and the flow of affairs outside its walls. A community can have its mind broadened while it is eating its meals. In monasteries it is customary to have someone reading from a lectern throughout dinner and supper; it happens in a lot of other communities too. But while in one Benedictine house there will be at dinner an excerpt from the Rule, a piece of Old Testament and then an extract from some saintly biography, in another the biography will be supplanted by the latest non-fictional best-seller. The educative process is sometimes continued in the recreation period; and sometimes the period set aside for this purpose is neither educative nor obviously recreational. Recreation can amount to a solid half-hour's gossip over the coffee after lunch in a Jesuit house, with the talk skipping as nimbly from one topic to another as in any university commonroom. It can be three-quarters of an hour in the mid-afternoon with everyone sitting in a prim half-circle around the superior like a lot of third-formers up for special treatment from the head, in a less stimulating climate. The head/superior reads a postcard he has just received from Fr X, who, everyone will recall, visited the community some time back and is now on holiday in Greece; he then describes a visit he himself made to a community of nuns the day before; and then he gives a potted account of what he has read in that morning's newspaper; and no one is much encouraged to get a word in edgeways. The dead hand that lies over many a religious recreational period is nowhere better exemplified than in the Rule drawn up by the founder of the Anglican Society of St John the Evangelist, the Cowley Fathers. In recreation, wrote R. M. Benson, 'controversy and party spirit must be avoided, for party spirit is the bane of conversation.' Yet in the formal daily recreation periods of an enclosed convent not a mile from Cowley, where the nuns are only allowed a free-for-all chatter for three hours on a Sunday, Mother is liable to promote a general and vigorous consideration of anything from the news coming out of Vietnam to Mr Muggeridge's latest televisual perambulations around Christianity. Which is only one more example of the breadth of the religious spectrum. And though that is so broad that it can have a Dominican clambering into bed after a long evening's wrangle with university students, at about the same time that a convent of nuns is rising to chant the night office; that it can contain both Benedictines living in the priceless treasury of Kremsmünster and Petits Frères subsisting in the gas-lit slums of Leeds; that it can embrace Spanish Carthusians to whom the infallibility of the pope is still almost an article of faith and French Protestants of Taizé who have never believed this and to whom it is not even a matter worth debating with Catholics any more – although the religious life is as broad as all those things suggest, there is one element above all others, above the poverty, the chastity and the obedience which all profess, which spans it from side to side and from end to end, which holds it together and gives it a unity. It is as vital to the Capuchin friars who are bearded in imitation of St Francis and Christ himself as it is to the Trappist monks who are tonsured in a symbolic reference to the crown of thorns. It is as central to the life of a Brigittine nun, whose habit is grey, whose shoulders and face are framed in a white linen wimple, whose head is veiled in black with a white linen crown in the form of a cross with five red drops on it, as it is to a Daughter of the Heart of Mary, who does not look like a nun at all because she dresses in ordinary clothes. One thing alone supports those who falter in the religious life and kindles fervour in those who live it confidently to the end of their days. That is prayer.

PRAYER

'Prayer means thinking of our Lord with loving attention.' – RENÉ VOILLAUME, Prior of the Petits Frères,
Brothers of Men, p. 81

'That is the meaning of the contemplative life ... to
remind us of what we are and Who God is – that we
may get sick of the sight of ourselves and turn to Him.'
– FR LOUIS (THOMAS) MERTON OCSO, *The Seven
Storey Mountain*, p. 446

LET nothing, said St Benedict, be put before the Work of
God. The Work of God, the Opus Dei, was the saying of
the divine office in the monastic choir once during the
night and at seven different times during the day; at lauds
and prime, at terce and sext, at none, vespers and compline.
These were the punctuation marks of a monk's existence.
This was when the common life was lived at its most exalted
level, when all gathered together in the monastic church and
devoted themselves to the most solemn and carefully regulated liturgy, which was at first merely a recitation of prayers
but which later was to be ritualized into a pattern of movement and refined into a haunting sound in the intricacies of
the Gregorian chant. The moment the monk heard the signal for divine office he was to abandon whatever he had
been doing and assemble with the greatest speed, yet soberly,
so that no occasion might be given for levity. If he was
late he was to stand in a place set aside by the abbot for careless persons so that all should know him for what he was
and he might not presume to join the choir until he had
done penance. For nothing else was of the least importance
when set beside the Work of God. And though Benedict
defined this strictly as prayer and worship in the choir it
was, by extension, something from which the monk was
never entirely free. The monastery was to be a school of the
Lord's service and the Lord was to be served best by prayer

at all times, in all places and in subtly different forms : in the choir, in the cloister, in the cell and even when a monk was doing some work of God's out in the fields. Fourteen hundred years after Benedict one of his followers was to write :

Underlying all Benedictine structures of life is prayer ... the ground of a monk's life: it is that foundation, those piles which are driven deep into the earth to support the mass of activity above. It is the profoundest act of created man and no prerogative of the monk, except in his perseverance, extension and intensity. Without prayer the rest is straw. Prayer belongs not to monasticism, but to that Christian life which is more generic, the life of the soul seeking the face of God, sharing the Cross and the sufferings of Christ.

Prayer may not be the monk's prerogative, but it is his profession, more than that of any other man, whether he be priest or not. And for any religious it has a theoretical primacy which in magnitude at any rate is scarcely to be expected of any other Christian outside the priesthood. It is the channel of communication between a man and his God; and however much modern apologists for the religious life may insist that theirs is only one of several Christian vocations (the married couple with three children and a very worldly job to attend to being another) the religious is distinguished from any other Christian by the totality of his commitment to God; by what, according to the norms of society, he has dispensed with to make it. Prayer suffuses a monastery for nearly twenty-four hours a day; and at the other end of the religious scale it is seen as the indispensable qualification for the life of the Petit Frère, whose day begins with mass if there is a church remotely at hand, and ends with vespers, compline and an hour of silent prayer before the altar he has contrived in his lodgings. The prior of the Petits Frères, René Voillaume, has asserted that prayer is such an essential to that vocation 'that unless we were convinced that it alone provides a sufficient reason for embracing such a life we should not have the courage to carry on. Is it not the tale of an idiot to embark in this way, in the flower of one's youth, upon a life in which one will do nothing useful by human standards, and very often by the standards of one's own intelligence?' For the Petits Frères one of the justifications of their prayer life, sandwiching, like two pieces of bread, a filling of completely unspiritual industry, is to demonstrate that contemplative prayer is possible even in the most arid and brutalizing conditions of the twentieth century. But its main justification is that it allows them to carry on the work they have taken up; and so every brotherhood is counselled to build itself a hermitage in some lonely place within reach of its house, an equivalent to the desert sought by the early fathers of the Church, to which in turn they can go for a weekend of solitude and undisturbed contemplation.

There are many different definitions of prayer, of what it consists, of its purpose, of how it is executed; possibly the only common ground is an agreement that it is communication with God. A French Oratorian has implied that for the monk it is an antidote to lurking evils that would poison his system.

Obviously the monk's life is a hard one. And perhaps what is hardest about it is the constant presence of these fundamental renunciations ... the renouncement of earthly possessions, of earthly affections, of his own will. If the monk does not want to be tempted to seek shameful and unlawful compensations for these renouncements, one way alone is open to him, and it is precisely to force himself to engage in it with all his being that he has finally blocked up all other ways. This way, which leads him forward to the heights, all horizontal issues being closed to him, is prayer. In prayer he will breathe the supernatural atmosphere which will purify him, which will relieve him of all his weariness. ... His life is no longer anything but prayer – prayer is his life.

The Benedictines of Buckfast Abbey see the monk's devotion to his prayers as an essential social service.

Every man is bound to worship God, both as an individual and in common with his fellow members of society. Worship implies a social act. This obligation of worship arises from the realization that man did not make himself; that he is a creature made and belonging to a superior being which we call God. From the relationship of creature with creator there springs the necessity of praising and giving thanks to God by mankind as a whole. It is clear that a great many people because of their work have got little opportunity and perhaps as many again have little inclination to spend time in the worship that is due to God from his creatures. The monastery, as the Rule says, is a school of divine service and exists for the purpose of carrying out that duty officially as a social act on behalf of society.

Seen as a social service, one of the most easily appreciated forms of prayer, apart from that implying a statutory quota which must somehow and by somebody (monks if everyone else is too lazy or uninterested) be offered to the Almighty by society at large, is the prayer of intercession with its special intention for a person or an event. In every monastery and most houses of religion there is an intercession board hanging on the wall of the sacristy, where the vestments are kept. It is usually a-flutter with pieces of paper bearing the intercessions which people would have the community make for them in its prayers. 'For Agnes S—, lying grievously ill with cancer and afraid of death.' 'For John and Mary P—, whose marriage is going through a difficult time.' 'For Peter J—, who after years of loneliness and despair, has just rediscovered his faith.' And the community remembers these people and their predicaments in its excursions into choir and commends them, one by one, to God's mercy. A contemplative nun, a Sister of the Love of God, explains just what that means to her :

If I am deeply involved, for example, in the pain of a friend who is suffering, in the anxiety of a mother whose son is fighting in Vietnam, then how am I to pray for these needs? Worship and intercession are both founded in perfect trust and this is the meaning of faith. We can trust perfectly in the goodness of God. He wills that all men are to be healed, that is made perfect with him, which is salvation. We can therefore trust through all and every circumstance and in that trust we hand over our care for our loved ones, or for the world in its needs, to his loving will – and this willing our will with his is our intercession. This act of trust will not take away the pain but it uses the pain and turns it into a positive act of love, which is a continuing intercession. It stills the anxiety which is the reflection of the bit of our wills which is not really in union with his will. Let's be honest, when we are caring most deeply so often we would still hold on by our emotions to some bit of possessiveness in our prayer – that beloved son and what we think is best for him – we cannot just completely let go of him into God's purpose. It is so understandable and we are doing it all the time, but really to intercede we must give our wills to be transformed to be one energy with God's creative purpose. As creatures we shall only truly be what he means us to be as we let go of our own human standpoints.

That woman listens to the BBC news at ten o'clock every night, just before she goes to bed, to see if any last-minute prayer of intercession for the world ought to be made.

Prayer can also be an act of reparation for all the sins in the world, as well as an output with a target figure per shift. A Benedictine nun says that 'Behind the grille of my enclosure which protects me exteriorly from many temptations, I am jointly answerable for all the sins of the world, even the most gross and revolting ones. It is this which throws me on my knees to ask pardon of God in the name of the culprit or culprits whenever I hear any crime spoken of.' It can be the vital part of a concentrated personal and implicitly exclusive relationship with God. 'The monk,' said Cardinal Newman, 'proposed to himself no great or systematic work beyond that of saving his own soul. What he did more than that was the accident of the hour.' A century later he is echoed by a monk of Downside : 'Benedictinism stands or falls not as a civilizing influence which brings the Christian culture to mankind but as a means of individual sanctification.' And because prayer is directed towards God, who is a spirit among other things, surrounded by the innumerable good spirits which are the angels, it is also something which must axiomatically find its way to God through the incalculable forces of evil. 'It is', say the Sisters of the Love of God, 'our great joy and privilege to recite the night office at 2 a.m., a time when the powers of darkness are very active and the suffering needs of mankind and the souls departing from this life are specially needing to be held to the Love of God.' They see their contemplative life as an intensely positive and creative one, 'for it seeks to deepen by prayer and offering the will of man to be participant in the will of God in order that the Divine Will may flow back into the World'.

Prayer can be the recitation of psalms by an abbey full of Benedictines in choir. It can be a Jesuit spending his obligatory hour a day of private devotion, lying on his bed in what one of his predecessors, Jerome Nadel, called contemplative inaction. It can be a mental ejaculation, 'All for Jesus', repeated by a Trappist with every forkful of dung he heaves out of his cowshed. It can be the click of a rosary to break the heavy stillness of a cell. It can be a solitary figure kneeling or lying prostrate, utterly fixed, upon the cold stone of an otherwise empty church; and you very rarely go into a monastic or a conventual church without seeing somebody at prayer. It can even, say some wide-minded souls, be a conversation between one of the fathers or the sisters with an outsider in the guest wing; because the talk goes on with God in mind. There is no end to the possibilities of prayer.

There are techniques of prayer, to be pursued in private. Simon Weil once remarked that there was a certain way of writing a Latin prose or solving a mathematical problem which, by training the mind to be attentive, could constitute a preparation for prayer. Most spiritual directors say that the first step is to pacify perfectly the body and mind; to quieten even the rhythm of the breathing. When that point has been reached the moment is ripe for the recitation of the Jesus prayer. This originated among the mystics of Sinai, was much cultivated by the Orthodox monks of Mount Athos, but has since circulated throughout western Christendom. With his breathing coming slowly and quietly the man at prayer murmurs 'Lord Jesus, Son of the living God ...' as he inhales; and then '... be merciful unto me, a sinner' as he releases his breath again. He breathes his Jesus prayer indefinitely until the rhythm of it is something he would find difficult to shake off, so that it promotes a tranquillity in all that he does. He can achieve the same effect by repeating the Hail Mary slowly and fervently. And this, which in its essentials is a technique that either a Buddhist or a Hindu might identify with his own, can be a prelude to meditation proper.

There are written meditations which, the sages argue, are especially suitable for intellectuals accustomed to setting their thoughts down on paper but which, of course, can easily degenerate into mere literature if a man isn't careful. There is the meditation on the rosary, which was first devised to satisfy the groping piety of illiterates who could not join in divine office, but which can also be of use to more sophisticated souls. The rosary devotion in full consists of reciting 'Our Father' fifteen times, the 'Gloria' fifteen times and 'Hail Mary' 150 times. While these formal prayers are being recited the mind dwells in turn on the Five Joyful Mysteries (the annunciation, the visitation, the nativity, the presentation, the discovery of Jesus in the temple), the Five Sorrowful Mysteries (the agony in the garden, the scourging of Christ, the crowning with thorns, Christ carrying the cross, the crucifixion) and the Five Glorious Mysteries (the resurrection, the ascension, the descent of the Holy Ghost, the assumption of the Blessed Virgin Mary, the coronation of Mary and the glory of All Saints). 'The simple recalling', suggests one commentator,

even quite implicit, before each decade and throughout its recitation, of one or other of these mysteries and of all, one after the other, continually charges and recharges the names of Mary and Jesus for us with all their meaning, all their reality. Thus, finally, in the single name of Jesus, united by his mother to our humanity, is concretized everything that makes him the unique but total object of our faith; the living word of God who creates and re-creates us in his image.

There are more complex methods of meditation than that, the beginnings of those spiritual gymnastics in which the true contemplative hopes to achieve utmost proficiency. There is none more celebrated or daunting than the Jesuit chapbook,

the *Spiritual Exercises* of St Ignatius; a very dangerous piece
of literature, as any Jesuit will tell you, which should only be
used under the guidance of a spiritual director who knows
all the ropes the ututored might easily throttle himself on.
It is a slim volume of 370 paragraphs and St Ignatius decided that four weeks were necessary to get the best out of
either it or the user. It starts by establishing some fundamental principles, like the daily examination of conscience.
The moment you get up in the morning, says St Ignatius,
you resolve not to commit a particular fault or sin that day;
after your midday meal you recollect how many times you
have transgressed and you make a mark for each occasion in
a notebook; you do the same thing after supper; and every
time you catch yourself sinful or faulty you lay your hand on
your breast in a token of sorrow. The book ends with a number of tips for the devout – on Three Ways of Praying, Rules
for Distinguishing between Different Spiritual Influences,
About Scruples, and The Mind of the Church. In between
the daily examination of conscience and The Mind of the
Church come the Exercises proper. The four weeks are
divided into four broad subjects of meditation; first one's
own sins, second the life of Christ up to Palm Sunday, third
the sufferings of Christ, and last the resurrection and ascension, with the Three Ways of Praying as an appendix.

The first exercise of the first week is a meditation on the
first three sins – pride, covetousness and lust. It begins with
a prayer asking God to direct one's whole self to his service,
and this is the preparation for every exercise in the book. It
is followed by an imaginative effort to picture the subject
matter; later in the exercises this may be Mary riding towards Bethlehem, nine months pregnant, and the cave
where she will have her child, or it may be Christ leaving
Nazareth to be baptized in the Jordan; but in the first exercise it is necessary to imagine 'that my soul is a prisoner in
this corruptible body and that my whole self, body and soul,
is condemned to live amongst animals on this earth, like some
one in a foreign land'. Then comes a petition appropriate
to the subject matter; if that is the resurrection the prayer

will be for a share in Christ's joy; here 'my prayer will be that I may feel wholly ashamed of myself, thinking how often I have deserved eternal damnation for my frequent sins, whilst many have been lost for a single sin'. There follows the application of memory, reason and will to the subject matter, here dwelling on each of the sins in turn, on their origin, on their results and on their presence in oneself. Finally there is a colloquy with Christ, what an Anglican curate of the caricatures might call a straight talk with God, and a final 'Our Father . . .'.

That is the first exercise. By the end of the first week the whole gamut of sin has been reviewed, winding up with a meditation on hell which is very clearly the starting point of that most hair-raising passage in all English literature, the Jesuit sermon to which Stephen Dedalus is subjected in Joyce's *Portrait of the Artist as a Young Man*. A handful of additional practices are recommended before the second week starts. It is proposed that on going to bed, just before falling asleep, the thoughts be turned, for the length of a 'Hail Mary', to the next day's exercise; it is suggested that all light should be excluded from the room except when reading or taking meals, that the body should be chastized 'by wearing hairshirts or cords or iron chains, by scourging or beating ourselves and by other kinds of harsh treatment'. This is the broad pattern of all the *Spiritual Exercises*, though they become progressively more sophisticated as they consider, besides images and implications from the New Testament, such by-products of the spiritual life as Three Ways of Subjection, The Making of a Decision, Rules for Achieving Self-Control in the Future with regard to Eating, and suchlike. As a manual of self-discipline there will never, in any philosophy, have been anything to improve upon the *Spiritual Exercises* of St Ignatius Loyola. As an instrument for achieving obedience in a subject there is probably nothing to touch it outside the realm of druggery; it is doubtful whether the most cultivated psychological methods of persuasion known to the twentieth century could better this product of the sixteenth. And someone has called it a little pamphlet of icy dryness and purely administrative appearance.

Somewhere there is a frontier to be crossed between meditation and contemplation. The capital difficulty for any stranger to this territory is that those who appear to navigate it with confidence scarcely define it in terms he will understand. 'Meditation, laborious by nature, is the activity of beginners in the spiritual life,' says Fr Bouyer, 'or of those who have not progressed very far in it. But normally one ought to attain a phase of spiritual progress in which meditation no longer adds anything, or even becomes psychologically impossible to carry out. Then, it would seem, contemplation will flower of its own accord.' And without pausing to varnish this cryptic signpost the experts are off on a debate of their own about whether contemplation is infused ('the effect of a pure influx of grace, taking hold of the soul independently of any effort – or at least any conscious one – of the soul's') or acquired ('obtained by the soul itself, progressively simplifying and unifying its meditation and thus entering of its own accord, by a calm effort of concentration, into a state of spiritual tranquillity'). Then, having dropped the name of St John of the Cross into the heavy atmosphere of dim perception, they are away and lost to sight in a rarefied spiritual climate of their own.

St John of the Cross was another product of the Spanish sixteenth century. He was a religious reformer, co-founder with St Teresa of Avila of the Discalced Carmelites. He was a considerable theologian and a poet of some note. He was also a great ascetic. But he was canonized and finally named a Mystical Doctor of the Church, because of his contemplative insights; and for this he is remembered best. His reputation rests almost wholly on three major treatises: *The Ascent of Mount Carmel and the Dark Night of the Soul, The Spiritual Canticle* and *The Living Flame of Love.* And of these it is the first, the *Ascent-Night,* which is most widely used as a manual of contemplation.

It begins with a poem of eight stanzas, each with five lines to it. The first of them is

> One dark night
> Fired with love's urgent longings
> – Ah, the sheer grace! –
> I went out unseen
> My house being now all stilled;

The whole poem is allegorical, a woman singing her good luck on having gone to her love one dark night, and of their rapturous union. It ends :

> Upon my flowering breast
> Which I kept wholly for Him alone,
> There He lay sleeping,
> And I caressing Him
> There in a breeze from the fanning cedars
>
> When the breeze blew from the turret
> Parting His hair,
> He wounded my neck
> With His gentle hand
> Suspending all my senses
>
> I abandoned and forgot myself,
> Laying my face on my Beloved;
> All things ceased; I went out from myself,
> Leaving my cares
> Forgotten among the lilies.

Carmel then consists of ninety-two chapters of commentary elucidating the spiritual matters buried in the poem; it is followed by a similar treatment of the poem in *Dark Night*, which runs to a further thirty-nine chapters.

St John's thesis is that the aim of the spiritual life is the state of perfect union with God through love, not obedience; this is the summit of Mount Carmel. And though on one short line of verse he builds a mountain of ambiguous meaning, hanging whole chapters on the significance of a single word, the poetic images alone are insufficient for his purpose. He uses others. He likens God to the sun and the soul to a window; when the sun shines upon a smeared or grimy window its full light cannot penetrate; so God cannot fully benefit the soul smeared with inordinate affection for

creatures and worldly things. The soul, argues St John, is
divided into sensory and spiritual parts, each with its own
faculties and powers; to the first belong sight, hearing,
smell, taste, touch, fantasy and imagination; to the second
the intellect, the memory and the will. In passing from the
initial stages of the spiritual life to perfect union with God
the soul must deny its appetites by the purification of its two
parts and by advancing in faith alone. To advance towards
God a man 'must lean on dark faith, take it for his guide
and light and rest on nothing of what he understands, tastes,
feels or imagines'.

In *Carmel* St John instructs the beginner in the ways the
soul must purify itself at its own instigation, why it must
do so, the recognizable stages of progress and the methods
of proof. In *The Night* he describes how God purifies the
passive soul and brings its faith and love to perfection. He
makes it plain that the whole progress of the soul towards
God is a hard and at times a terrible one. There are moments
of illumination which are followed by periods of black despair. There are dark nights when the soul imagines itself in
purgatory or hell. But at the end of it all the soul in blind
faith has ascended the steps of a ladder of love. On taking the
first step 'As a sick person changes colour and loses his appetite for all foods, so on this step of love the soul changes the
colour of its past life and loses its appetite for all things.' On
the second and third step the soul is regaining its strength
and slowly making progress, but on the fourth it is again
seized with a weariness; if it can overcome that then the
soul is well on its way to God. At the fifth it experiences an
impatient longing for God, at the sixth it runs swiftly to
him, at the seventh it becomes bolder in its affection and at
the eighth it lays hold of him without letting him go. The
ninth step is reached only by the perfect and on leaving it
the soul departs from the body. On the tenth and final step
it is assimilated completely with God.

St John of the Cross is not the only spiritual guide engaged by religious to lead them into the intricate ways
of contemplation; the list is a long one, starting with St

Clement of Alexandria who lived within two hundred years of Christ, taking in St Teresa of Avila, St Augustine of Hippo, St Bernard and Charles de Foucauld among others. But no single manual has greater currency, perhaps, than the *Ascent-Night*. And if the non-contemplative, with his alien concepts, his limited vision and his temporal inhibitions can make nothing of the spiritual life at this elevated level, then he must hold on to any simpler signpost he discovers in the hope that this will point to a glimmer of intelligence in it all. He can turn, for example, to the indispensable Fr Bouyer again.

> Our personal assimilation of the gift of God, our personal association with the prayer of all in unity, can take many forms. . . . It may be nothing more than the appropriation of a word, of a phrase of the liturgical prayer; it may give free rein to an outpouring all our own, set in motion by this phrase but overflowing it; it may lose itself in the simple gaze of mystical contemplation. This matters little; what matters essentially is that not only our mind – our intellectual attentiveness – be engaged, but also our heart; that core of our whole personality, that centre not only (nor primarily) of our emotions and our feelings, but of our most intimate decisions, those most thoroughly involving our whole being. . . . While such a prayer normally needs silence for its birth or at least its development it should also normally end in silence. As with all conversation between persons in whom mutual affection, knowledge and comprehension have attained a certain depth, so in such an exchange there must soon come a moment when no word can suffice to express what is in our hearts, a moment when all words are by the same token unnecessary, being both inadequate and superfluous. It is this moment in prayer which we usually call 'mystical'. And there is no true prayer which does not tend towards it . . .

Even for the man or woman who has accepted a contemplative vocation neither St John of the Cross nor any other mystic is a touchstone to the summit of Carmel. The reputation of some convents as places whose nuns are so jolly and joyful, put about by pious retreatants on their return from a weekend in the guest wing, is not always reliable propaganda; what is evident from the guest house and from the side chapel of the conventual church does not always tally with what might be seen in the cloister garth or the refectory, much less in the privacy of the cell. It is perfectly true that a contemplative convent can radiate, even in its inner recesses, a happiness and calm which seems unaccountable to the outsider who is preoccupied with the physical restrictions and monotony imposed upon the nuns. But it is also a fact that there can be islands of despair which have resulted not from the bleak routines of the conventual environment but from that same spiritual journey which St John of the Cross and others promise shall end in the glory of God and perfect union with him.

This is what has become of a Carmelite nun of sixty-six years old:

When Père B became my spiritual director he encouraged me to study the *Treatise on God*. When I reached the chapters on predestination and the smallness of number of the elect they were really a stunning blow from which it took me a long time to recover. It was not that the question of my own personal salvation troubled me, but it seemed to me that up till then I had regarded the loss of souls as solely due to their own perverse will, I was nearly saying as if God could do nothing to prevent them. Aquinas focused the matter for me in a way that was terrible because it was the source of temptation to me no longer to believe in love in the same way. Nevertheless, I have never regretted having been led in this fashion to a more correct idea of the transcendence of God; of his inaccessible mystery. I got over this crisis by adoration, but I feel that the naïve audacities of a child who feels she may ask what she likes of her Father are a thing of the past with me. In fact, I can hardly bring myself to ask God, either for others or myself, even for what he wishes to give us. No doubt this attitude is more authentic, but there is no longer the same spontaneity; and I must admit that, on coming back to those texts of the Gospel such as: 'Ask and you shall receive, that your joy may be full' which used to be the whole ground of my confidence, I feel tempted to say to myself: 'That is no longer true for me.' Now I am old, and everything that could have been a light to me is extinguished; it is in total darkness that I see my contemplative life – or what that should be – alternated by periods of doubt which make it very painful. Having no feeling at all of the presence of God or of the reality of the divine life in us, which demands an act of positive faith of me, I am confronted mostly with this mystery of evil which pervades everything and seems to submerge all the rest. It is the most habitual suffering and nothing comes to counteract it.

That is a woman who has spent most of her life struggling with St John of the Cross up the slopes of Carmel.

Anyone who imagines that to be a religious, especially to be a holy monk or nun – as some reverent outsiders do – is automatically to be possessed beyond doubt of all the blinding truths of the Christian faith, is living in hope of the impossible. Among the inhabitants of the religious world are to be found very nearly all the shades of belief and disbelief – ranging from pure Vaticanism to near-agnosticism – as occur these days among Christians generally, though doubtless not in the same proportions. A religious is not even much likelier to have a standardized impression of God than the man in the street or the Bishop of Woolwich. When, a few years ago, some Dominicans canvassed practically every contemplative convent in France – houses, that is, of the most rigorous spirituality within the religious life – they obtained an impression of God-imagery that might just as well have come from the market place. A fifty-two-year-old Dominican said : 'I have neither an "idea" nor a "mental picture" of God. He is God, someone undefinable, of unimaginable beauty. When I hear God spoken of I feel I must drown myself, get out of my depth, not even try to understand any more. ... Then I am satisfied because completely overwhelmed, I say to myself that I am too stupid to understand but that it must all be true.' Another nun reported that

between the ages of four and seven the presentiment became impressed on my mind that one day the world would come to an end when God would appear in the clouds and that we would all go to meet him. ... Since then the vision of God-Man coming in majesty on the clouds of heaven has always been with me, and I have never ceased ardently to desire the end of the world and the coming of our Lord. This impression, this expectation was so strong that I had got into the habit of looking at the sky whence our deliverance was to come, and one familiar corner of the sky has remained engraved on my memory as the ideal place from which our Lord should reappear. Even now, when I think of God, I see this patch of sky.

For a Dominican nun of eight years' standing 'The image of God which comes most readily to my mind is the image of light or of water.' A Carmelite for thirty years replied : 'How does the face of God present itself to me now? The same as it has always done; no face at all – only love, that is all. If, however, I should wish to picture God to myself, I would think of him as fire and flame, life overflowing, an ocean of peace.' And a sixty-year-old Carthusian said, 'I can find no other (image) than that of my father, a man as wise as he was good and as just as he was wise. ... I have only to extend this portrait to ultimate perfection and add the omnipotent and creative intelligence of a God to have the most beautiful image I can have of God.' Oddly, not one of the people questioned, nearly two thousand of them, saw Michelangelo's God, aquiline and limber, supported by angels as he creates Adam with a casually imperative finger in the middle of the Sistine Chapel ceiling; or the God of any other painter.

The only thing that can be said about the spiritual life of the religious with any assurance is that he or she spends more time and effort in trying to develop it than the Christian living out in the world. That is part of the profession. And nowhere is it professed as thoroughly as among the contemplative orders, the Cistercians and the stricter Trappists, the Carthusians and the Carmelites, the second order of Dominican nuns and the Benedictines who are relatively inactive, plus those dozen or so communities in the Church of England, the Society of the Precious Blood, the Order of St Anne, the Sisters of the Love of God and the rest. These are the monks and nuns proper, papally defined as such as far as the Catholics are concerned, and apart from the active Benedictines there are few outside their number who may lay claim to the same purist title unchallenged. Of the million

or so women in religion in the Catholic Church today it has
been estimated that about 60,000 are contemplatives; and of
the 332,000 men there will not be more than perhaps 16,000
in the contemplative life. These are the people living the
life of strict enclosure, though there can be and are degrees
of strictness. Among the men there is nothing more confined
than the life of the Carthusians, who properly speaking are
hermit-monks like the Camaldolese. They, too, live in separate small cottage cells which they leave only three times in
the average twenty-four hours, first for the office of vigils at
10.30 p.m. in the church, later for conventual mass in the
early morning and finally for vespers, which are said com-
munally in the middle of the afternoon. There is also, once
a week, a communal walk lasting three hours, complete
with the only conversation the Carthusian has except with
his confessor. It is taken in the country around the Charterhouse and everyone is obliged to join in. In a wayward exception to the general rule of such things the Carthusian nun
– all a hundred and fifty of them, in two French and two
Italian houses – are less confined than the monks of the
order. They eat in common and have a daily recreation
together.

Generally enclosure for a man is far less rigid than for a
woman. It means scarcely ever leaving the monastic
grounds, except in emergency or as a senior member attending a conference. But places are provided where visitors may
be received and talk freely to the monks at certain periods.
There is nothing resembling the grille, which is still more
than a talisman of most contemplative convents. There is at
least one convent in this world where it has been abandoned; where the only thing resembling it is the barred
peephole in the front door with the notice underneath,
'Please do not ring unless expecting an answer'; where, if
you do pass muster with the custodian of the peephole,
you may converse with Mother or one of her sisters in an
anteroom, in easy chairs, with chrysanthemums on the tables
and a lingering flavour of furniture polish. There may conceivably be other convents which have also felt winds of

change. But generally the grille is still there; an appliance introduced, it is said, by St Dominic after the family of Diana D'Andolo had tried to abduct her from her thirteenth-century convent, breaking one of her ribs in the scuffle to extract her.

A formidable thing it can be, too, a heavy wooden grating running the width of the only room an outsider is allowed to enter; he sits on one side, the nun sits on the other, and so thick is the wooden latticework, so comparatively small the openings in it, that the pair of them can have a little difficulty in the first few minutes agreeing on a position from which they can look each other in the eye. There is another one in the church, cutting off the community from the sight of any visitors who may be joining them in worship from a side chapel. And this is the reality of a nun's enclosure; a barrier which very often not even the parents of nuns are allowed to pass; so that when parents visit their daughter on her birthday or the anniversary of her profession they must hold conversation through the grille, unable even to touch each other and certainly prevented from exchanging anything so improper as a kiss. There are even some communities where it is forbidden that other nuns below the rank of superior shall cross the grilled frontier. And the Catholic penalty for breaching the enclosure, for a nun stepping outside the grille without permission, for an outsider breaking in, is excommunication.

Grilles are still being installed. One community of nuns in the South of England felt it necessary in 1964 to explain to the world at large why, when certain structural alterations were being made to their premises, they had decided to ask the architect to provide them with a grille in the new parlour:

A grille is a symbol of our voluntary withdrawal from the world, in response to a particular call from God, in order the more effectively to pray for it. No suggestion is intended of protection from the world represented by our guests nor any idea that the community is imprisoned and physically unable to get out. But a grille means more than this. There is always the danger that we put love of man before love of God and that the ties of personal affection will take priority over our consecration to God. Our dedication to intercessary prayer, our love for people which grows as one prays, our close contact chiefly through letters with those for whom we pray all increase this pull and it is so easy for it to undermine our primary consecration. The grille symbolizes the priority over all things of our consecration to God (our having been set apart by him). It prevents physical contact and expressions of affection without involving rudeness or coldness or withdrawal. It helps us to give ourselves wholly in the way God means us to and emphasizes the fact that all we have to give to others is God, not our persons, which are wholly given to him to use. ... It reminds us that we have only what God gives us to give others and keeps our face to face encounter with people in its proper, second, place. Our real meeting with people and our real work for them is in our prayer.

The other cachet of the contemplatives is the almost ever-lasting silence. Precious thing though it is – and no one from outside a religious community can ever value it properly until he has experienced the blessed relaxation of eating his first monastic breakfast, where the only sounds are those made by a few elderly dentures and milk being poured over the cornflakes – it is here carried to almost punishing lengths to the normal ear. Silence is rated highly in any community, not only as a necessary accompaniment to private devotion. It is generally unbroken in every religious house, except in case of the most urgent communication, from after compline in the evening until after breakfast the following day. Among contemplatives it tends to stretch through most of the twenty-four hours, a practice followed elsewhere only on particularly solemn occasions such as the period between Maundy Thursday and Easter Day. In some of the strictest contemplative communities a monk or a nun is forbidden to speak to anyone at any time, unless it is to the superior, or unless special permission has been granted. The Trappists, who were the first to adopt a rule of total silence, were also the ones to devise a system for getting round it, holding conversation without breaking the rule. They have developed to a dexterous art their own variation on the deaf and dumb language. If the first finger and thumb of each hand are touching with the knuckles of the little fingers joined you mean 'mass'; if only the first fingers and thumbs are making a diamond shape the word is 'God'; 'coffee' is the first two fingers of the right hand placed on the left pulse; 'food' is all right-hand fingers on the mouth; and so on. A Benedictine has circulated the story of the Trappist who, wanting to tell a brother that some mutual acquaintance had found his vocation in a Spanish Charterhouse, did so by turning a pirouette and striking an imaginary tambourine; he might, suggested the Benedictine, have conveyed the message less energetically and with more decorum simply by hissing the word *'Burgos'*. Which was rather naughty of the tell-tale, for Benedictines too have been known to employ sign language to get the bread passed in refectory during the silence of their dinner.

It is a Trappist, Thomas Merton, who has outlined in realistic terms the cardinal burden placed upon the monk of his order.

It is after profession that the Cistercian really begins his training as a mature monk. He is simply thrown more or less on his own in the community. . . . He sees his abbot once a week or so, speaks to his confessor once or twice a week, and he might sometimes open his conscience to the Father Prior as well. But on the whole he is left face to face with a huge, inscrutable, and perhaps terrifying force which surrounds him on all sides and which is the community, the common will. This can develop into a terrifying trial to a young monk who does not realize what it is all about. To live in a house full of a hundred or a hundred and fifty completely silent men who are always together yet never speak to one another; to move about in this amorphous yet vital mass which stirs into action at the sound of bells rung at precise intervals of the day and applies itself with a mysterious energy to all its communal activities. . . . If you do not acquire deep faith and supernatural common sense, a couple of years in a Trappist monastery will do strange things to you.

The contemplative life can be hard enough at a less rigorous level than that of the Trappists. A nun says that it is literally hard on the body for a start, with a hard stool to sit on in the refectory, a hard chair and a hard bed in your cell, hard stone or wood for you to kneel on at prayer. And her convent is lenient enough to allow the nuns to cast their votes outside at elections or to visit the oculist in town; to give the young sisters a fortnight's holiday a year, which they spend in bungalows in the convent grounds, where they can gossip with relatives for two hours each day and with friends for one hour; to pack the holidaymaking old ladies and anyone recovering from an illness off to a cottage by the sea at the other end of the country. But except during a holiday, when you are obliged only to attend mass on Sundays and first-class feasts, and vespers every day, says the nun, there is so little time to do what you would choose to. You're either at work or prayer or spiritual reading all day from 5.30 in the morning to nine o'clock at night (as well as being up from 2 a.m. to 3.30 a.m. for the night office) except from 3 p.m. till 4 p.m., when you get a cup of tea; but even in that time you've to put in half an hour's gardening. That hour is the day's formal recreation period and just before it ends you may be asked by another nun to walk with her round the garden. 'She may be the last person you want to walk with but you go in charity.' Then back to work, which means either the kitchen, an office, cleaning, sewing or the sacristy, where the vestments and the vessels and all the other paraphernalia of liturgy is kept. But work isn't nearly as trying as the fact that with the silence and the enclosure, modified as both these are by Cistercian standards, 'you have nothing in the convent which allows you to get away from facing yourself and God. You can't coax away a depression with a cup of tea just when you feel like it, or by taking a night out at the pictures. You just have to stumble through it.' The hardest thing of all, though, is the praying. 'One of the bad times is when you say I'll pray for an hour and nothing happens, your mind keeps wandering and you have to pull it back but it won't stay put. A consciousness of evil or suffering or intense pain is when I know that something's happening. It's a very simple and exhaust-

ing thing. I get nothing out of praying verbally at all. I
might just as well talk to myself.' She doesn't know what
her sisters recognize as something happening in their prayer
life. The nuns, she says, don't talk to each other about that
sort of thing.

A hard life and a very remote one from the patterns which
have been established by the world outside the conventual or
the monastic walls. This is where the hard fasting takes
place. A plain and not overfilling diet is the best that a contemplative can expect; until recently, when the rule was
modified very slightly, a Trappist would never taste fish or
meat from the day he was accepted as a novice till the day he
died unless he was very ill or weak; a Carthusian will still
see no eggs or milk foods either in Advent or Lent and will
eat only one cooked meal a day from 14 September, which is
Holy Cross Day, until the following Easter; and though an
active Benedictine may well enjoy a measure of beer or cider
with his dinner his contemplative brother will probably have
to make the best of water. This is where the silence and the
restriction and the small discomfort of it all are fervently
embraced in penance for the injury done to God by man and
in some mysterious, supernatural and utterly contemplative
way to heal the souls of poor sinners aware of neither God
nor monk.

There is a compelling attractiveness to it which is partly
romantic, partly aesthetic. There never was an occasion
when time and place and event were more spellbindingly
fused than when a column of Cistercians come pacing two
by two along their Gothic cloister, their feet hidden in a
swirl of white hems, their hands concealed within the deep
envelope of their sleeves, their faces lost in the shade of their
pointed hoods. That movement by those men in that setting
makes a myth of the passage of centuries. St Bernard may be
broken into a multitude of holy relics scattered across the
face of a faithless earth, but nothing has really changed. The
Opus Dei still goes on according to the precepts of St Benedict. Seven times a day is God to be praised in choir, for
that, the saint reminded his monks, was how the psalmist

ordered it; and once in the night as well. And every week
every one of the 150 psalms is to be said, beginning with
the twentieth at the night office every Sunday. And so it
mostly still is. And though a conventual mass has its own
gorgeous beauty, when the church is vivid with its seasonal
colours, on altar cloth and cope – white for the great festivals, red for Whitsunday and the commemoration of
martyrs and apostles, purple in Lent and Advent, green at
other times; when it is stained aromatically with its eddying
incense, it is not *then* that you catch the peculiar essence of
the monastic or the conventual life. That comes during the
periods of the divine office at the seven different hours, when
all colour is muted and sound is almost the only perceptible
sensation. When the monks sit in their stalls and recite the
psalms across the choir to each other, *cantores* answering
decani verse by alternate verse, in a murmuration that
quietly rises above misericord and corbel, triforium and
clerestory, to lose itself in the vaulting of the roof. When the
Benedictines of Beuron, who are unexcelled in the art of
plainchant, move in long, drifting Gregorian phrases,
crescendo and diminuendo, from Gloria to Credo to Te
Deum; and it is unthinkable that they should chant in any
tongue other than Latin, the dead language that is quite
palpably bridging the interval between the living and the
dead. When the monks of La Pierre Qui Vire sing compline
by heart from the blackness of the choir, for the only light
floods the altar in the middle of the church and night is
everywhere around it. Or when at any night office the
candles seem to flicker more erratically than during the day,
the great wooden covers of the office books seem to squeak
louder, and noses have to be blown and throats cleared more
frequently. At any of these times the religious life is translated from a philosophy or a strategy or a profession into an
unfathomable mystery, and faith is almost tangible in its
presence. And every day of his life a Cistercian monk will
spend between five and six hours at this numinous Work
of God.

So will a Cistercian nun, whose day begins when a bell

rings in her dormitory at a quarter to three in the morning, summoning her to the night office of vigils. In the church the cantor breaks the silence of the night with the salutation '*Ave Maria, gratia plena, Dominus tecum*' in the commemoration of Mary which precedes every portion of the divine office; and while she does so her sisters kneel and bow with their knuckles on the ground, in a peculiarly Cistercian devotion made especially to the Mother of Christ. The office is sung, there is half an hour of silent prayer, then lauds and the angelus follow one after the other. Twenty minutes later there is a low mass and holy communion. This is dispensed by a priest through a square hole in the grille, the sisters moving up to it one by one and bowing to the knuckles before lifting their heads to receive the Host. Then, in turn, they bow profoundly and move back to their stalls for more quiet prayer before they go to the refectory for the breakfast which Cistercians call mixt.

At 6.15 a.m. they are back in choir to sing prime and when that is done they move into the Chapter room, where the Abbess reads from the Rule of St Benedict, gives a commentary on it, and then proceeds to the business of the day. First the Chapter of Faults, where the nuns accuse themselves publicly and sometimes (in charity, of course) each other of infringements of the Rule or customs of the community. They receive penances for this; so many 'Hail Marys' for Sister A, who failed to keep proper custody of the eyes in the garden yesterday, having looked up instead when an aircraft passed overhead; an extra term of waiting at table in the refectory for Sister B, who allowed the door of the library to close behind her with a bang. There is a space for spiritual reading after the Chapter before terce and conventual mass are sung at eight o'clock. Then comes the manual labour; a squad doing the weekly wash if it is Monday; household and garden chores any day of the week for some; handicrafts which range from weaving to book-binding for others, who will thus bring income to the convent. At 11.15 there is sext to be sung, with an examination of conscience at the end of it. Then comes dinner, with a

prayer before and after the eating and some spiritual reading
by a sister in a pulpit during the meal. Grace, which is said
when the last piece of pudding has been consumed and the
last napkin tightly rolled up in front of each place, is so
long and so fondly intoned that it is broken into two parts;
one in the refectory, the other in the church, with the
Miserere chanted en route from one place to the other.
Washing up then, followed by reading or prayer, or just a
stroll round the garden or anywhere else within the enclosure; except for the novices and the lay sisters who at this
time must receive instruction in the Rule or the usages of
the house, or some spiritual exercises from the Mother Mistresses. At 1.20 p.m. it is back to the choir for ten minutes
of none, and then work again until 3.30 in the afternoon.

There is an hour after this for *lectio divina*, the spiritual
reading which St Benedict placed high in priority after the
Opus Dei. Before vespers are sung, fifteen minutes of silent
prayer are spent, and supper is taken at 5.15. In another
hour there is a public spiritual reading in the Chapter room
before compline, the final office of the day. It ends with the
evening angelus, with a last few moments of silent prayer,
and a sprinkling of holy water upon each nun as she leaves
the church, from her abbess standing by the door. Then the
nuns return to their dormitory to sleep as they have worked
and prayed, fully dressed, on their mattresses of straw.

This is the life they have chosen and it is the life they are
obliged to live unvarying except in its seasonal changes of
liturgy, its professions of novices and its burials of the dead.
A life of communication with no one but God and the two
superiors of the convent, the abbess and the prioress. There
is no such thing for the Cistercian nun as general conversation for the order does not approve of even stilted recreation;
no Cistercian nun knows anything about the background
of her sisters, whence they came and why, even after a lifetime of standing and kneeling alongside them in choir,
washing dishes with them in the kitchen, pottering round
the garden with them in a subsidiary work of God. There
is no reason to know such things for all is directed towards

God alone and everything is a preparation for death. And when death comes the nun lies on a bier in the choir, clothed in her habit, crowned with flowers as she was at her profession, without benefit of coffin, while two of her sisters kneel beside her, reciting the psalms in turn. Without coffin she is committed to her grave, and as the earth covers her body her sisters in God kneel and put their knuckles to the ground and cry three times on her behalf for mercy: *'Domine miserere super peccatrice!'* There are religious in this world who will take the visitor into their community's cemetery, where the crosses with their triangular tops stand like rows of gable ends, and flippantly refer to it as the parking place. No Cistercian ever took such a liberty; nor Carthusian, whose end is chillingly anonymous. Just a piece of earth without even a cross to mark that anyone had ever been. But then the Carthusians are so fiercely concentrated on God to the absolute exclusion of all else that they will make no special intention in their intercessions lest these defile the purity of their prayer.

A Cistercian's represents the most extended pattern of worship among all religious but the hermit's, whose time-table is the one most curiously at odds with that of the world outside. For the monk or nun of a less rigorous order like the Benedictines, the devotions will be similar but the chronology will be more of a piece with the times we live in. Instead of a night office, matins will start the day at 5 a.m. and compline may occur any time between 8 p.m. and 9 p.m., for there tend to be small differences of routine from one house to another within the same order. Basically the structure of all monasticism has not changed in any essential since Benedict composed his Rule. For the severest contemplatives even the timing of the offices, the *lectio divina* and the other periods of the day coincides almost exactly with that of the Middle Ages. This, for example, was the monastic timetable according to the *Regularis Concordia Anglicae*, a document promulgated by abbots meeting at Winchester in A.D. 970 in an attempt to bring stability to an English situation which was threatening schism at the time;

it was the schedule for summer, the winter one starting an hour later and finishing one and threequarter hours earlier :

1.30 a.m.: Rise, trina oratio, gradual psalms. *2.0 a.m.:* Nocturns, psalms for the royal house, vigils and lauds for the dead. Short interval. *3.30 a.m.* or *4.0 a.m.:* Matins, miserere, psalms for the royal house, anthems of the Cross, the Blessed Virgin Mary and the patron saint of the church. Matins of All Saints. Change and wash. *5.0 a.m.:* Trina oratio, reading. *6.0 a.m.:* Prime, psalms and prayer, morrow mass, Chapter, five psalms for the dead. *7.30 a.m.:* Work. *8.0 a.m.:* Terce, sung mass. *9.30 a.m.:* Reading. *11.30 a.m.:* Sext, psalms for the royal house. *12.00 noon:* Dinner. *1.0 p.m.:* Siesta. *2.30 p.m.:* None, psalms, for the royal house, drink. *3.0 p.m.:* Work. *5.30 p.m.:* Supper. *6.0 p.m.:* Vespers, psalms for the royal house, anthems as in the morning, vespers and matins of All Saints, vespers, vigils and lauds of the dead. *7.30 p.m.:* Change into night shoes, collation (a snack). *8.0 p.m.:* Compline, trina oratio. *8.15 p.m.:* Retire.

The Church has traditionally regarded the contemplatives as an élite compared with the actives, has seen them, in modern terms, as a sort of religious Brigade of Guards or United States Marine Corps. To some extent it is because the contemplatives have clung closest to the origins of the religious life, have maintained after a fashion the purity of the line. But at bottom it derives from St Augustine of Hippo's theology of perfection (of which more must be said later on) which he applied to the Church as a whole. Contemporary exponents of the view point in justification to five verses in St Luke's Gospel :

Now it came to pass as they went that he entered into a certain village : and a certain woman named Martha received him into her house. And she had a sister called Mary, which also sat at Jesus' feet and heard his word. But Martha was cumbered about much serving, and came to him and said : 'Lord, dost thou not care that my sister hath left me to serve alone? Bid her therefore that she help me.' And Jesus answered and said unto her : 'Martha, Martha, thou art careful and troubled about many things. But one thing is needful : and Mary hath chosen that good part which shall not be taken away from her.'

The contemplatives have tended to be equated with Mary, while the actives have become identified with the industrious but plaintive Martha. Pius XI was much given to discriminating between the two forms of religious life. 'It is not hard,' he said in his apostolic constitution of 8 July 1924, 'to understand that a much greater contribution to the growth of the Church and the salvation of mankind is made by those who are constantly occupied with the duty of prayer and mortification, than by the workers who till the fields of the Lord; for if they did not bring down from heaven an abundant rain of divine graces, the evangelical labourers would gather but a meagre harvest from their toil'. Even Pope John XXIII, who has been reckoned to have had broader vision than most of his predecessors by people both inside and outside the Church, even he on one occasion quoted a contemplative puff of Pius's and added, 'There is the guarantee of the value of the contemplative life in the eyes of the Church. Let others like Martha give themselves to the work of the external ministry. But it was Mary who received from the Saviour's lips the assurance that she had chosen the best part. That part is yours.' Perhaps the fact that he was addressing the Abbot General and the Reformed Cistercians on their home ground had something to do with it; possibly the speech had been written for him by some contemplative member of the Curia. It is conceivable, of course, that if you are enduring a Cistercian existence your morale needs such flattering boosts from time to time and that popes are sensitive enough to be aware of it. Nevertheless, the perils of taking the Martha–Mary implications for granted – not least the spiritual peril of pride – seem to be considerable.

The possibility of a developing arrogance has been pointed out most vigorously by one who is himself a Cistercian, Fr Thomas Merton. He has considered the Vatican Council's injunction that the Church should nurture greater 'openness to the world' and particularly what this might mean for religious living the most enclosed régime :

To some contemplatives the idea of 'openness to the world' is incomprehensible. It contradicts what they believe is fundamental to their vocation. The essence of the cloistered life consists in their being 'enclosed'. They argue that the cloistered life cannot be open in any real sense without ceasing to be cloistered. This seems to them a matter of simple logic. When you embrace the contemplative cloistered life you turn your back on the world, you renounce the world, you forget the problems and concerns, you pray for it without needing to know what you are praying for. You turn away from the world to God, because the world is opposed to God. The cloistered ideal then becomes an ideal of 'pure contemplation' in which everything is organized in view of a state of perfect recollection; everything is arranged so that one will be entirely purified not only of attachment to the world but even of all interest in it, all concern for it, all memory of it.

But 'openness to the world' means involvement in the affairs of people outside the cloister, identification with them in their desires, problems, struggles, dangers; it means vital concern about a world of total war, genocide, race riots, social injustice, misery, poverty, violence, lust, every kind of disorder. All this is wicked and ungodly. Far from divine, it is diabolical. How can one think of such things and maintain the inner peace, the purity of recollection, the serenity of spirit in which one will hear the sweet, ineffable call to divine union? 'Rejection of the world', 'contempt for the world', then results in a crudely automatic polarization; everything that happens inside the cloister and according to the sacrosanct rules of the cloistered life is wise, pleasing to God, full of redemptive power and supremely significant. The God who is nauseated by the actions of worldlings outside the cloister is consoled and delighted by the actions of observant religious within the cloister. This distorted interpretation of the gospel texts about renouncing the world in our own hearts becomes an excuse for pharisaical complacency. Contemplatives despise the world because they imagine themselves to be superior to it in every way. The cloister is the guarantee of that superiority. If they resume contact with the world they lose their superiority and become like everybody else. The beautiful image is tarnished. They no longer feel secure in the thought that God loves them better than anyone else. Obviously this is a caricature. But this distortion has been made positive by a valid traditional concept of the contemplative life – one which has been taken for granted for sixteen hundred years. Yet

there are many things which have been taken for granted longer
than that which the Church is now questioning.

This obviously *is* a caricature of some contemplatives. It
will scarcely fit the image of the Mother Superior who
listens to the 10 o'clock news before she goes to bed, whose
convent takes a couple of daily papers and a sheaf of serious
periodicals, and who illustrates the meaning of intercessory
prayer by referring to the Vietnam war. It tallies rather
better with the abbess to whom current affairs means first
and foremost papal and royal coronations. Or with the
Anglican contemplative monk who writes :

The conditioning to which modern man is subjected, in the
subtle brainwashing technique of advertising or political propaganda, or the latest craze for distortion in art and literature, cannot
touch the mature contemplative. He is an adopted son of God
through his baptism, and now knows by experience that he is free
to claim the paternity and fellowship of his heavenly Father, and
to be a servant for the redemption of all God's children.

Elite or not, the contemplative has accepted a vocation
which is less common than any other and which can be as
much of a puzzle to some active religious as to any agnostic
who has been brainwashed by admass. It is possible for a
religious who says his offices every day, who is in much demand as a lecturer on various forms of the new Christianity,
and who has a respectable amount in print both periodically
and in paperback, to declare that he just doesn't see what
the contemplatives are getting at. Such a man has told me
so. For many more actives it is a matter of temperamental
unsuitability to the enclosure and the pressing silence. A
friar of my acquaintance was sent during his novitiate to
his order's retreat house for a concentrated period of
spiritual instruction and formation. Except for the offices
and the confrontations with his spiritual director, the course
was wrapped in total silence so unbearable to him that he
would go for long walks in the woods far from the retreat
house, and there bellow every ribald song he had learned in

the army, merely to relieve the tension that had built up in him.

Yet it is not at all uncommon for active religious of many years' standing to experience a strong attraction to the contemplative life at about the age of thirty-five. It is possible for some that by then their spiritual development has taken them to the threshold of true contemplation and that they want to give themselves to this more completely than their first vocation will allow. For others it is almost certainly a reaction against overwork which has pushed them to the point where what they need most of all is peace and quiet for an extended period if they are not to break down. The first thing to suffer in any thoroughly active community dedicated to teaching or nursing is the time to pray, whether that is interpreted as a prostration in front of the altar in church or merely an hour spent torpidly on a bed. In some congregations of active sisters the only form of divine office each day is the recitation of the complete rosary; and, as Bishop Huyghe has pointed out, 'there is no prayer that so easily becomes mechanical when fatigue prevents concentration and control of the imagination.' It is also possible for the liturgy in choir to become mechanical, for the monk or nun to tick off their five or six hours of office a day, their hundred and fifty psalms per week, with the blank steadiness of a metronome. There is a monastic joke about an abbot who was reciting divine office in choir with his community when a violent thunderstorm broke outside. He shut his breviary with a snap and said, 'Brethren, let us pray.' Religious are apt not to laugh too much at that one nowadays because it cuts a bit too near the bone for many of them. It is even on record that some, when asked why they practise daily prayer, have replied, 'We do not know' or 'It is advantageous to us.' There are superiors who distrust any form of prayer life other than the simplest forms of meditations and the verbal formularies of the office books, presumably out of a nagging anxiety of quietism – a seventeenth-century French heresy which held that for perfection man must become so passively 'given' to God that he was indifferent to heaven, hell or his own salvation, and that once he had reached this state of mystical perfection it was impossible for him to sin any more, whatever he did.

There are others, growing in number, who are restlessly reviewing prayer, its techniques and its possibilities, its bases and its applications. They are reacting most of all against a quota of prayer in choir being crammed into a fixed time-table which leaves little space for reflection on what is being chanted or said. They are introducing silences in which there is time to think between the prayers of intercession, between the epistle and the gospel, between the Sanctus and the Agnus Dei. They are beginning to wonder whether it is vital that a nun should have to make her mental prayer in church with her sisters, where she can too easily be distracted by their presence, rather than in the privacy of her cell. The monks of the Maurist Congregation of Bene-dictines are now allowed a week of solitude every few months, free from divine office in choir, in which they can find their own rhythm of prayer and return to their brethren glowing with spiritual health.

The most radical departure of all from the established systems of prayer in western Christendom has been taken in Africa by Benedictine monks and others. There they are now accepting the local dance as a form of worship.

If some night you were able to get into the convent which the Poor Clares have recently founded in the Cameroons, you would be present at a form of adoration which is completely novel to us Europeans. With the Blessed Sacrament exposed, the sisters sing the Divine Office to the lively rhythms of the local music and accompany their prayers with sacred dances of equal originality. With the exception of the prioress the forty members of the com-munity are all native vocations and have invented this new way of praying precisely in order to be able to praise and adore God with their whole being. In fact, music and dancing are for the African the essential means of expression. How could these young women who wanted to consecrate their whole life to God in an enclosed convent, forget this simple fact? Their decision has led to a sharp increase in vocations. Many young women were hesitant about entering a contemplative convent, for they knew of the life only in its European form and did not feel that this was in harmony with their own spiritual needs. But now that the contemplation has in some way become 'African' they have brushed aside their doubts and the number of applications is growing daily.

Which only adds to the enormous and bewildering complexity of prayer, though this is said by the prayerful to be such a simple thing. One commentator will say that it is possible for a highly consecrated person to meditate faithfully every day of his life without making the slightest spiritual progress. Another will claim that the most spiritually advanced can derive much benefit merely from turning the Lord's Prayer over in his mind. Prayer is the ecstasy of the mystic who has reached the summit of Mount Carmel and it is the dark night of the poor soul who is still slogging up its slopes in despair. To some it is thinking of Christ with loving attention; to others it is being so sick of the sight of ourselves that we turn to God. In a multitude of conceptions, Christ-God is its only common denominator and its threshold, so they say, is when God becomes 'you' and not 'him'. No one but a man of prayer can possibly say how that happens. Sometimes not even he can.

AUTHORITY AND
OBEDIENCE

'The monastery is a school – a school in which we learn
from God how to be happy.' – FR LOUIS (THOMAS)
MERTON OCSO, *The Seven Storey Mountain*, p. 446

IN the *Codex iuris canonici*, the Catholic Church's code of
canon law, some lengthy consideration is given to the religious life. At the outset the three evangelical counsels of
perfection are noted as obligatory for all religious. Significantly, obedience is given priority over poverty and
chastity. It could hardly be otherwise when God himself is
to be obeyed before, and as well as, being loved and worshipped. His Church has grown upon the assumptions of
authority and obedience. In no part of the Church are these
assumptions taken more seriously or savoured more carefully than among the religious. Prayer may be the element
that binds their spirits to the Lord but it is obedience, with
all its subtle implications, with all its variety of practices,
with all its thoughtful penalties, that orders the pattern of
their lives and sometimes holds their bodies in fee until the
moment they die. It was by invoking obedience that St
Benedict brought order out of chaos. It is only by snubbing
it in carefully chosen places and at artfully picked moments
that the religious of today can begin to change the shape of
the society he fostered. And the pressures against their doing
so are greater than any others in Christendom.

For a start there is the weight of canon law itself, binding
on all Catholics at various perils to their souls. There are
2,414 canons all told and nearly 200 of them – canons 487
to 681 – are devoted to the religious life. These begin with
some definitions. Canon 488 points out that :

an institute is a society approved by legitimate ecclesiastical authority, the members of which, in accordance with its laws, make public vows, either perpetual or temporary, provided they intend to renew the latter after their expiration and through these means tend to evangelical perfection. An institute whose members profess solemn vows is an order. Vows are solemn when they are recognized as such by the Church with definite juridical effects. A group of independent monasteries united under one superior constitutes a monastic congregation. ... The union of several of these monasteries into a monastic congregation, although establishing a mutual bond among the various houses, leaves them all independent.

Canon 489 notes that strictly speaking a 'rule' refers to one of the ancient Rules – of St Benedict, St Basil, St Augustine, St Francis and others, while constitutions in the strict sense mean particular statutes added by various orders or congregations to the ancient Rules.

After the definitions, every avenue of the religious life is explored. According to Canon 504 no one can become the superior of an order or a congregation unless he has been professed for ten years, was born in lawful wedlock and is at least forty years old. He can become a local superior at thirty. According to Canon 531 there are only two exceptions to the general rule of common ownership of goods; the property used by the Friars Minor of the Observance and the Capuchins belongs not to them but to the Holy See. Canons 547 and 549 declare that in monasteries of nuns, postulants shall bring in a dowry fixed by the constitutions 'or determined by legitimate custom' but that it is absolutely forbidden for a community to spend more than the interest on a dowry until the nun has died. Canon 551 lets a religious take her dowry outside if she leaves her convent, even if she is dismissed or decamps and 'if the day on which the semi-annual interest is due be June 15 and the religious leaves on June 14 the interest for those six months is hers; if she goes on June 16 it is the institute's.' Canon 559 decrees that a novice-master or mistress shall be at least thirty-five, professed ten years and 'distinguished for prudence, charity, piety and faithful observance of the Rule'. Canon 598 positively forbids any woman, even a relative, to enter the enclosure of monks under any pretext unless she is the wife of a king, regent or president. As for the major enclosure of contemplative nuns, Canon 600 is full of safeguards. The only people allowed in without the Holy See's special permit are the local bishop or the regional superior on his visitation, the confessor to administer sacraments to the sick or dying, 'the highest actual ruler of states ... with their wives and their retinues', cardinals and, 'with due precaution' at the Mother Superior's discretion, physicians, surgeons 'and others whose services are needed'. The bishop making a visitation 'must be accompanied by one and preferably two clerics ... of mature age. The companion or companions must not leave the visitor during the entire time he is in the monastery.' If the confessor is admitted 'two nuns must accompany him to the cell of the sick nun and after confession directly to the exit of the enclosure'. A footnote to the canon observes that 'should a consecrated Host be dropped within the major enclosure the priest may enter to pick it up; or a nun may pick it up and consume it or, if she has already received, give it to the priest'. Canon 601 says that after profession no nun may leave her major enclosure even for a short time unless she has special permission from the Holy See or unless she is in danger of 'death or other very serious evil'. According to Canon 602 'by general law nuns are not forbidden to see the altar. This may be forbidden them by their own constitutions, however. In any case the nuns must not be seen by the faithful.' Canon 624 states the rules for women religious collecting alms. They must go in twos, not remaining away from their house for more than a month. They must travel by rail and make sure they arrive and depart during daylight. They must try to find lodgings with other women religious, or at least with some charitable benefactress. 'The modesty owing their state undoubtedly requires not only their avoiding taverns, but also their staying away from sporting events, particularly horse races.'

The Church is an obedient society if it is to live in the image of its founder. It is also a hierarchical society and this is nowhere a greater imperative than among the religious. Standing just below the pope, as far as they are concerned, is the Vatican's Sacred Congregation for Religious and Secular Institutes which (under various titles) since 1586 has been the chief agent of religious government, the penultimate arbiter and court of appeal. At the last count it consisted of a Cardinal Prefect and 29 other cardinals, a secretary and an under-secretary, 48 consultors, 13 commissioners, a treasurer, an archivist, three writers, 22 assistants, 93 experts on ecclesiastical affairs and seven counsellors on civil matters. The entire congregation meets on occasions so special that no one is sure of the last, but once a week the Cardinal Prefect, the secretary, the under-secretary and the commissioners get together. The Anglicans have nothing comparable to this organization any more than they have any rule book as heavy as the *Codex* – they can only muster 151 canons to cover the whole of their Church government; and their Advisory Council on Religious Communities, consisting of a bishop appointed by the primates, six people appointed by the bishops at large and six by the religious communities, is exactly what its title suggests, without any coercive powers. In fact, on all but the very gravest matters of discipline or unless the Church as a whole has an interest in the point at issue the religious, either Catholic or Anglican, are left to run their own affairs without interference from above, though they can never be free from superior influences.

There are some religious institutes with a central command post which directs policy in every one of its houses throughout the world. There are others which offer their houses virtual autonomy and erect a pyramid of central authority more as a token of unity than anything else. There are some orders who elect their superiors for life and others who offer them only limited periods of authority. There is nothing more centralized than the structure of the Jesuits. Sitting in Rome is the Superior-General of the Society, at the moment a Basque, Fr Pedro Arrupe, who is after the pope himself possibly the single most powerful man in the Catholic Church. He rules without any internal counters to his authority other than those imposed by the Jesuit constitutions and the general congregation of Jesuit superiors, which meets in effect only on the General's death to elect a successor. Otherwise he has an absolute right of decision on all issues within the Society. He appoints personally the superior of nearly every Jesuit house and as these are changed every six years this means about 150 appointments a year. He has an advisory 'cabinet' of four men to reduce the amount of work he is faced with; the monthly account of local affairs that each Jesuit provincial has to submit to the General, the similar report that every superior must send from his house twice a year, and the ones that come annually from the four 'consultors' in every house. There is a further buffer of eleven assistants, one to keep an eye on each of the Jesuit regions throughout the world. But though the general congregation appoints the men of cabinet rank, while the General chooses his own regional assistants, all of them are disposed only for his consultation. His word is final on any matter under the Jesuit sun.

They order things differently for Benedictines. The oldest monastic foundation has coagulated into a confederation since Leo XIII in the nineteenth century decided that there was a danger of too many local interpretations made in isolation fragmenting the Order of St Benedict beyond repair. Every twelve years every Benedictine abbot in the world gathers in a confederal congress to elect an Abbot Primate, who is now the American Dom Rembert Weakland, from Latrobe, Pennsylvania. Half way through his term they meet again for a general conference about the order's affairs. It can never be more than that because much more power is invested in the individual congregations and even in individual abbots than ever resides in the congress or the Abbot Primate. This is no more than following the spirit if not the letter of St Benedict, who never visualized anything but individual monasteries looking after their own affairs and nobody else's. Below the confederation come the congregations; the Cassinese and the English, the Bavarian and the Brazilian, the Beuron and the Subiaco and the rest;

eighteen of them altogether, with their strings of related monasteries and dependent priories and their subtly different emphasis on individual aspects of the Benedictine life.

Subiaco with thirty-five has more monasteries than any other, the American-Cassinese the most monks with 2,045. The twenty-one monasteries and 1,078 monks of the (Solesmes) Congregation de France specialize in the liturgy and the Gregorian chant. The twelve monasteries and 599 monks of the English have a reputation for running fine schools for the sons of gentlemen. And although the congregations mostly follow national boundaries this is not invariably the case; a small handful of Benedictine houses in the British Isles do not belong to the English congregation, which is the oldest in the Benedictine Order. It is also one of those which submits its abbots to periodic elections, every eight years here; Subiaco puts a man in for life.

The English run their congregational business by means of a Chapter which meets every four years to elect a new Abbot President if it wishes. To this come all the abbots in the congregation, together with one delegate from every abbey. In a religious world that is once again beginning to change these Chapters will have had more really thoughtful work to get through in the 1960s than for a long time. Normally they haven't exercised themselves much more than was needed to make minute alterations in the local style, or to bestow titular abbacies and priories upon the various monks of long service and good conduct. Dom Herbert Byrne, monk of Ampleforth, is also Titular Abbot of Westminster; Dom Sigebert Trafford, monk of Downside, is Titular Abbot of St Albans; Dom Oswald Dorman, monk of Douai, is Prior of Peterborough; and Dom Vincent Fogarty, monk of Belmont, is Prior of Worcester. And though each title refers to an unimpeachably Anglican see, it is also a reminder, to take a perfectly wholesome Catholic view, that the premises were pinched from the original owners by Thomas Cromwell and Henry VIII.

The infrequency of the congregational Chapters points to where Benedictine power really lies. It is with each abbot sitting on his own throne in his own abbey church with St Benedict's Rule to support him and to remind his brethren that he is the representative of Christ himself in the monastery. He has all the power of a sea captain who may have to answer to his company when he is ashore but who commands as he pleases when his ship is afloat. He has his own brethren in Chapter to refer to and a Chapter meeting can be conducted with the studied formality of the Buckfast Benedictines, who use a ballot box with white beans for 'yes' and black beans for 'no' when they are voting on anything important. It can be as informal as sometimes it is with the Trappists of Caldey, who, it is said, are apt to hold Chapters on the spur of the moment, merely sending the novices out of the room after mass and getting down to their discussion. In some places a Chapter can be so democratic that it goes on for hours so that anyone who might possibly want to speak has had every chance to say his piece. But however democratic the processes of Chapter may seem to be it is in the end the Benedictine abbot, and most other superiors too, who pass judgement and who, if they are careless and determined enough, can ignore that sometimes nebulous but otherwise latently powerful force they call the mind of the community. Fortified by tradition and with the constitution or the Rule behind him a superior can hold a religious in obedience as strictly or as leniently as he pleases.

Exemption from this chain of command only comes when a man is made a bishop or a cardinal and is answerable only to the pope. This happens, but not very often. A handful of religious have been plucked from their vowed life and exalted in some Curial capacity. The Jesuit Cardinal Bea* is in the Curia, and the Benedictine Cardinal Gut and the old Master-General of Dominicans, the Irish Cardinal Browne, and one or two others. About sixty bishops from the orders were mustered at the Vatican Council, with about two hundred Superior-Generals who were there in their own right to have a finger in ordering the general affairs of the Church. But the way to preferment for the monk or the friar is a

* Died November 1968.

very narrow one indeed. And for the nun or the sister it
does not exist at all.

There is a weight of canon law above the religious state
and there is a pyramid of power. There are also vows, which
hold the individual to the life. A Catholic parish priest takes
a vow of celibacy and a promise of obedience to his bishop,
the one being virtually irrevocable with the highest penalties,
the other being of some smaller account and with sanctions
well short of excommunication. The religious is much more
involved than that. He has to obey, besides canon law, the
Rule and constitutions of his order, which lay down the
larger principles of its life; he also has to keep his eye on the
customary (sometimes called the usages or Consuetudines)
of his community, which details the minutiae of his timetable. If he is a monk proper this will tell him when and
where he is to sit or stand with his cowl up or down in
choir; in what order he shall process to the divine office;
what response he is to give the brother who wakens him in
the morning – '*Deo gratias*' as often as not in exchange for
'*Benedicamus Domino*' but with longer variations on particular days like Good Friday, when the knocker-up does his
rounds murmuring '*Christus factus est pro nobis obediens
usque ad mortem*' and expects the sleepy voice to answer
'*Mortem autem crucis*'.

Religious obedience is mostly made not by a promise but
by the much more serious vow. There are several different
varieties. The temporary vow is the one taken during the
novitiate, which is binding only for that period. Simple
vows and solemn vows are then taken for life, the difference
between them being a very fine juridical one that only canon
lawyers can appreciate properly; it concerns degrees of
poverty and the obligations of the divine office more than
anything; it means, in effect, that the strictly enclosed life
of the monks and nuns proper obliges them to take solemn
vows, while less rigidly circumscribed souls are put under
simple vows. But there are also societies holding to a common life, mostly products of the seventeenth century, like
the Oratorians, the Sulpicians, the Sisters of Charity of St

Vincent de Paul and a few others, which take no public vows at all but instead make promises with a life intention, in much the fashion of the parish priest making his promise of obedience. To anyone outside the religious life these may sound artificially fine distinctions. To anyone inside they may mean the difference between eventual dispensation into the secular world again with nothing more than a few hurt feelings all round, and a life sentence which cannot be reduced by one minute – unless the circumstances are so pressing that the pope issues a special dispensation – except by the soul brave enough to face excommunication and the Church's promise of eternal damnation.

Religious vows and promises are generally to the three principles of poverty, chastity and obedience but there are exceptions. Neither the Benedictine nor the Cistercian makes them in that form. They vow themselves first to stability, which means that they will stay in the same monastery all their lives; although occasional exceptions are made today, a Benedictine monk is generally expected to remain a monk of Downside or Bec, or wherever he was professed, to the end of his days – unlike a Jesuit or a Dominican, who is liable to have dropped anchor in a dozen or more communities of his order by the time he is through. The Benedictine secondly vows himself to *conversatio morum,* or a serious attempt at progress in virtue, which implicitly means both poverty and chastity. His third vow is one of plain obedience to his abbot. And while three vows are the general rule some religious have to take a fourth. The most famous of these is the Jesuit vow of instant obedience to the pope's personal wishes; in recent years this has been invoked to put Jesuit missionaries into Japan close behind General MacArthur's conquering Americans at the end of the Second World War, and to staff most of the positions in the Vatican radio station. The canonesses of St Augustine vow never to let the education of girls be neglected.

The religious is also living under a caste system infinitely more artful and complex than that devised for the general rank and file of the Church. It has many more ramifications

than a simple division between the contemplative Marys and
the active Marthas, the celestial doves and the plodding
mules. Canon 491, to start with, declares that while all
religious enjoy an undefined precedence over laymen, within the religious world itself there is further stratification.
Canons regular – Premonstratensians, Lateran Canons and
the like – take precedence over Benedictines and other
monks. Monks take precedence over other regulars –
Dominicans, Franciscans, Jesuits, Barnabites and so on.
Regulars take precedence over all other religious – Redem-
torists, Passionists, Oratorians, Brothers of the Christian
Schools and the rest. Only women in religion are spared the
embarrassment of knowing their place and trying to keep
it in this class-conscious society; they aren't even considered
for membership. They have their own hierarchy within their
own orders and congregations, though, just like the men.
Canon 564 codifies part of it. The novitiate, it says, shall be
separated as far as possible from that part of the house inhabited by the professed brethren so that the novices shall
not be brought into contact with them. 'Separate quarters
shall also be assigned the novices preparing to be lay
brothers, that is separate even from the quarters of the other
novices.'

At the very bottom of the religious pile, just below the
novice who will eventually be a priest as well as a monk, is
the monastic lay brother. Though monasticism started without benefit of priests, within three hundred years of St Benedict monks were taking orders as a rule, concentrating more
and more on worship in choir and less upon the necessary
chores around the establishment. The way for a servant
population was opened by Benedict of Aniane at Aachen in
817 and the practice was generally adopted by the Cistercians two centuries later. Since then a cornerstone of the
monastic life has been the recruitment of men (and in convents, of women) insufficiently educated to have a hope of
becoming priests (or in convents, to keep up intellectually
and vocally with the choir nuns) but perfectly suitable to
toil away at the less cerebral monastic exercises, like stew-

ards in an officers' mess. With a few exceptions the lay brothers have traditionally found themselves excused not only from the full divine office, in place of which they have had a modified liturgy of their own, but also from meetings of Chapter – which has deprived them of any say in the government of their houses. There are, of course, many religious congregations which were built from their beginnings in the nineteenth century specifically for the unordained who wanted to take up the life; it is, for example, laid down in the constitutions of the Marists and the Brothers of St John of God that the superiors shall not be chosen from among priests.

One of the changes starting to creep into the religious life is the status and function of the monastic lay brother and sister. The current position was perfectly expressed by the Benedictine Abbot of Prinknash at the end of 1965 :

In July we held a Chapter of the English Province of our Subiaco Congregation. Among other decisions made then there is one of special interest, namely, that our Brothers be admitted to solemn vows; moreover, we hope that at the General Chapter next year they will be given full Chapter rights and the same monastic habit as the choir monks. The aim of course is to integrate the Brothers completely with the community so that they share fully in its life and have just as much say in the running of the monastery as the clerics. For too long the Brother has been looked upon as a kind of lesser Religious whose main duty is domestic work. This is far from true. Here at Prinknash most of our Brothers hold responsible offices; they head the various industries and in fact often enough the choir-monks work under them. Of course in a monastery domestic chores have to be done as in any other house, but all alike, priests and Brothers, share them. The Brother's vocation is a very special one. He comes to the monastery because he feels drawn to the monastic life but he does not feel called either to the priesthood or to choral duties; and there is surely a place in monastic life for such vocations. There are many young men who would like to dedicate their lives to the service of God in this way; craftsmen and artisans and men who wish to work on the land. And, thank God, we have been greatly blessed in our Brothers. It must be admitted, however, that in recent years there has been a falling off in vocations, due no doubt to the general turmoil of these present days. I should, however, point out that it is an altogether mistaken idea that those unfortunates who are backward, mentally retarded and the like, are suitable candidates for the Brothers; for such is not the case. The Religious life is so completely unsuited for neurotics; when such people are accepted, the usual result is disaster. Monastic life can never be looked upon as an *escape*.

Though the notion of obedience has been implicit ever since the teachings of Christ it was not specifically invoked as a distinctive trade mark of the religious life until Pachomius established his Egyptian communities at the beginning of the fourth century. It was not regarded as an essential until St Benedict compiled his Rule. For his monks there was not only to be obedience to the abbot who represented Christ in the house; there was also to be a complete resignation to its corollary, humility. In chapter seven of the Rule Benedict distinguishes carefully the twelve different degrees of humility he wants to see in his followers. The first degree of humility, he writes, is always to keep the fear of God in mind. After that the monk is to renounce his own will; he is to subject himself to his superior for love of God; he is to bear with patience all the difficulties, contradictions and injustices arising from obedience; he is to confess humbly to his abbot any evil thoughts or secret sins; he is to be content with the meanest and humblest in everything; he should not only talk of himself as the lowest of the low, but he should believe it too; he must do nothing but what is exemplified in the Rule and his superiors; he is to keep his mouth shut until spoken to; he must not be ready or prompt in laughter; when he speaks it must be gently, seriously, sensibly and briefly; and he should not only be humble but take care to show it, by always bowing his head, casting down his eyes, pondering his sins and considering that sooner or later he must be judged by God.

This was to serve as a rule of thumb for religious for the next seven hundred years. It wasn't until the thirteenth century that a more sophisticated, fully developed theology of obedience appeared from the hand of the Dominican

Thomas Aquinas. It was Aquinas who first gave priority to obedience over the other evangelical counsels of chastity and poverty because, he argued, 'great is poverty, greater is chastity but the greatest good is obedience if it is observed inviolably. For the first rises superior to material things, the second to the flesh, but the third to one's own mind and will.' To Aquinas obedience induced subjection, striking at the heart of the ego, beating down the pride which survives when all other vices have been vanquished. It also liberated the individual from the anxieties of independence. It sacrificed man's greatest treasure, free will, and thus became the most handsome gift a man could make to his God. And the Thomist doctrine has been accepted, woven into the fabric of the Church and embroidered by the zealous ever since.

It is recognized, of course, that there are limits even to religious obedience. 'It would not', according to a recent commentator,

be disobedience to refuse to keep a fast to death imposed by an imprudent superior ... the sphere of religious obedience ... does not extend to acts contrary to the rule or unrelated to it. A religious who fulfils his voting obligations has not to go to his superior for guidance on the way he is to vote. A superior may not ... give orders on technical points to nursing sisters or social workers who depend in this respect on a professional authority.

And then, in one of those delightfully vague Christian loopholes,

there can be no culpability in a breach of the religious rule whose motive proceeds from the pursuit of a greater good; it would be culpable if it proceeded from some ill disposition, idleness, gluttony, negligence, for example, but it would not of itself imply an offence against obedience in particular. ... It goes without saying that a religious who gives practically no heed to the rule he is vowed to is on the downward grade towards contempt and is liable to commit actual sins at least against the requirements of the common good and the respect due to superiors.

Basically, though, obedience still means what Aquinas meant it to mean.

The perfection of obedience consists in entering totally into the will of the superior, that is to say, in conforming oneself in all that is licit in his will, forestalling his commands, seizing with predilection on painful occasions of obedience because in them the will has less likelihood of its self-seeking, and because a maximum contract is thus guaranteed with the superior's will and this, in the last resort, means with God's.

This is an important piece of every novice's inheritance when he or she first attempts the religious life. Canon 542 says that no one may enter a novitiate until he or she is at least fifteen years old; but before anyone takes the temporary vows of a novice he will have done time as a postulant, to see if even the limited period of the novitiate is something he can cope with. The Carmelite friars will accept boys of twelve for their juniorate, allowing them into the novitiate at seventeen; a child of eleven can begin the long life of a Scalabrini Father under certain conditions. On the other hand, the Benedictines of Downside try to discourage anyone from even tentatively trying out his vocation until after he has been to university; and there are not many Anglican orders who will take in anyone under twenty-odd. Most orders are not prepared to start making a religious out of anyone older than about thirty-five, though some accept what they call late vocations. Curiosities, of course, tend to crop up all over the place; the English Fr Laurence Bright was an atomic physicist before becoming a Dominican. According to Canon 542, the only people positively disbarred from starting the religious life are bishops, people in debt and people whose parents or grandparents are in dire need; widows and widowers are normally welcome as long as they can fulfil the general conditions of the institute.

The qualifications sought most of all tend not to be educational ones. Look through any directory of the religious life and the same requirements are made over and over again by institute after institute : a sincere desire to serve God as a priest and a religious; good health; a good moral character; a deep personal love of God that manifests itself in great love of our neighbour; a supernatural motive; good common sense and an ability to live happily with others; a sense of vocation and a well-balanced character; a spirit of generosity and courage; a zeal for souls and a cheerful disposition. But the Sisters of Notre Dame de Bon Secours de Troyes require postulants to have 'normal appearance and legitimate birth' among other things. The Missionary Sisters of Our Lady of Apostles, who sound as if they've had their troubles, are on the look-out for females between fifteen and thirty 'of legitimate birth, belonging to an honourable family; having an unblemished reputation; good health; no remarkable deformities; an upright mind; sound judgement; sufficient knowledge, good disposition and qualities suitable to give assurance of service to the congregation; not to have been sent away from another novitiate or any other religious or lay establishment whatsoever'. Inevitably Carthusian nuns must be virgins.

When the postulant arrives at a community's doorstep he is usually given what in the more unsophisticated circles they call a guardian angel; a novice experienced enough to guide the newcomer round the premises and introduce him to the routine and the rules. The postulancy may last a few weeks or a few months; unless a child has been taken in very young indeed it will scarcely last longer. At the end, if the aspirant is to join the novitiate, there is a clothing ceremony. For a girl joining the Franciscan Missionaries of the Divine Motherhood it means walking to the altar in something much like a wedding dress, complete with veil, and there, having made her temporary vows, having a few symbolic locks of her hair cut off; this is later cropped short enough to be comfortable under a tight-fitting guimp, when she is dressed in her novice's habit; and there is an iced cake to be cut and a party to be enjoyed. For men the structure of the temporary profession is more or less the same, though the party trimmings are less decorative. Novitiate periods vary. They cannot be less than one year and in some institutes the novice is in for life after that. Two years is more common. At Ampleforth the budding monk makes a temporary vow for a year and simple vows for three more before committing himself to solemn vows. And at some

time in the period leading up to those final vows he is sent
to university partly, as one of the brethren puts it, 'so that
he can see what a skirt looks like again'. It costs them something in lost vocations at that point but they take the view
that it is better to discover a worldly streak in a man then
than later on. They reckon to keep for life about half the
people who enter the novitiate.

The Jesuit training period is notoriously longest of all. It
is not true that a man cannot become an ordained Jesuit
until he is thirty-three, though he rarely manages it before
then. The curriculum varies from province to province in
some details but in general the pattern begins with two
years' novitiate, in which the man's character is probed,
while he is subjected to those daunting Ignatian Exercises
in all their sidelong complexity, and while he himself
weighs up the society. After that, three years hard labour in
philosophy. Then three years at university for a degree in
almost anything and as often as not in what the man himself wants to read. During those six years he will have been
given his first few crumbs of theology but no more; and
before he is allowed to make a meal of it he is dispatched,
straight from university, for another three years as a teacher
in a Jesuit school. Then he gets his main course of theology,
four years of it; and after that he spends what the society
comically calls the 'third year of probation', in which he
grapples with the Exercises once again and takes part in
various 'experiments', which may mean anything from acting as a prison chaplain to giving retreats to schoolgirls.
Then, and not before, the Jesuit is considered fit for ordination. A moment, as someone has remarked, which 'could
seem like a reward of a well-spent life, rather than the beginning of a priestly career.'

The Benedictine will have long since committed himself
to his monastery for life. At Buckfast Abbey the novice will
have gone through his initial year on temporary vows and
will have assumed the name by which he will be known for
the rest of his life if he is to remain a monk. Not everyone
is obliged to change his or her Christian name on becoming

a religious; it very often depends upon whether the same name is already installed in the community. But the changes that do occur are strongly in favour of the saints, and particularly the monastic saints. Every Catholic monastery on earth has its ration of Benedicts, Cyprians, Mauruses, Aidans, Dunstans and Dominics; most convents will be sprinkled with a Scholastica, a Teresa, a Hildegard, a Mechtilde. After his first twelve months the Buckfast novice is required to take simple vows for three years. And for the next three years he will be studying more closely than before St Benedict's Rule and all its implications; he will be receiving instruction in the fundamentals of spirituality; he will be learning the rituals and chants of the divine office. He will also be learning to strip himself of all the things that formerly expressed his personality; he will have long since lost his civilian clothes and his way of wearing them; he will take longer to learn the alien but now approved ways of moving his body, of greeting his companions, of having nothing that he can call his own.

And at the end of the three years, while the aspiring Jesuit is still only a quarter of the way to his ambition, the young Benedictine, having been accepted by the vote of the professed monks, will be led one morning during mass to where his abbot sits enthroned below the altar steps. He will take with him a sheet of parchment on which his vows are written and he will read these aloud. He will show the script to each of the monks in turn and then he will lay it on the altar and sign it. His abbot will bless him then, and each of his brothers will give him the kiss of peace before they continue with the mass. All but he, who will now lie prostrate before the altar with a black funeral pall covering him, with a candle at his head and another at his feet, while high above in the abbey tower a bell tolls to signify his death to the world. 'Let him understand', says St Benedict, 'that according to the law of the Rule he is no longer free to leave the monastery, or to withdraw his neck from under the yoke of the Rule, which it was open to him, during that prolonged deliberation, either to refuse or to accept.'

Neither he, nor the Carmelite nun who promises 'obedience, chastity and poverty to our Lord God, to the most Holy Virgin Mary of Mount Carmel and to you, reverend Mother Prioress, and to those who shall succeed you, according to the primitive rule of the Order of Barefooted Carmelites and our constitutions', nor the Jesuit still plodding through his studies can ever decently, in the eyes of the Church, have a will to call their own again after they have reached that point. Nor can anyone vowed to the religious life. They have given it away and a terrible weight of law and authority has been accumulated over the ages to see that the Church exacts every jot of their obedience from them. And this great weight is the rock on which the religious life stands.

It is an Anglican superior who has said that 'There is undoubtedly a Jansenist strain in the spirituality of some religious communities which dies hard, and under its influence the vow of poverty can be made to appear grim and joyless and austere, the vow of chastity cold and loveless and inhuman, the vow of obedience tyrannical and unreasonable and opposed to human dignity and responsibility.' It is a Catholic abbot who has written that 'a novice-master or novice-mistress who can and dares to enjoy things, or who can and dares to love someone, is practically unknown'. Fairly swingeing indictments, both of them, and though neither could be sustained as absolute generalizations to be applied to every community in the world both speak of a tradition that once was universal and that today is still widespread, even though erosion has recently set in. The tradition is clear enough in documents such as the *Manual for Novices*, which was published in 1921 for use by the Discalced Carmelites, and which may still be seen in Carmelite library shelves. Chapter 3 is devoted to mortification, and under Section II – Mortification of the Exterior Senses, there are these admonitions:

ARTICLE I *The Sight*

1 Do not raise your eyes more than is necessary even in your cell.

2 In passing the cells of others or on entering them, also the sacristy, the church, the garden and the various offices, repress all

notions of curiosity; do not seek to find out who or what is there, or what is going on.

3 In the streets especially, and in the houses of seculars, be particularly careful to observe modesty of the eyes, and do not examine curiously the buildings or the persons you meet on the way.

4 When you are speaking to any person do not look at him fixedly in the face, at least without a serious cause, especially if he is a superior or a man of dignity.

5 Never allow yourself to be drawn from your solitude in order to see the palaces of the great, public gardens, exhibitions, pictures or other objects remarkable for art, antiquity or novelty, or in general those things that serve for the vain display and amusement of seculars. Our Lord Jesus Christ had nothing but contempt for these worldly vanities . . .

ARTICLE II *The hearing*

2 Do not give ear to profane music or to worldly songs, however artistic their style may be.

3 You should pay no attention to news of current events, much less seek for it, not even what is going on in the Convent or Order, unless it contributes to your edification or regards your particular duty.

4 Avoid as poison of the religious spirit news and accounts of wars, treaties etc. between earthly princes . . .

ARTICLE III *Smell*

1 Do not smell fragrant herbs, fruits or flowers etc., much less bring them into your cell, or keep them for their pleasant odour . . .

ARTICLE IV *Taste*

4 When you eat or drink, think of something unsavoury in order to mortify the taste, especially if you take things agreeable to the palate.

8 Sometimes mingle a little water or bitter flavouring with your food.

9 At intervals put the body to some inconvenience, such as keeping one foot raised etc., in order that the discomfort of the body may impede the gratification of the taste or moderate it, that so each morsel may be dipped in the gall and vinegar of Jesus Crucified . . .

ARTICLE V *Touch*

6 In summer do not seek the refreshments of air, water, cold

drinks, shade or change of garments etc. Be very careful, however, to shake off the heaviness caused by the heat.

7 When an occasion of suffering occurs, seize it eagerly as a jewel from heaven . . .

Section III concerns the Cultivation of Chastity on which, among other things, the manual offers this advice :

10 Touch no one, and do not allow yourself to be touched by anyone without necessity or evident reason, however innocent . . .

11 Repress and fly from as a mortal plague, even though spiritual in their origin, particular friendships and familiar conversations arising from an attractive appearance, pleasing manner, or an agreeable disposition in which you feel a certain sensual gratification; avoid with the greatest care the occasion of being in company with those who are the object of such friendships.

There is, finally, advice on what to do when retiring to rest, in which this direction appears :

12 Sprinkle your bed with holy water on all sides as if it were your tomb and lie with crucifix in hand and your arms folded in the form of a cross, as if you were never to rise again.

That tradition is not yet dead. Mortification is much older than the organized religious life; it was as much a distinguishing mark of the first hermits as solitude; and it was as much an instrument of self-abnegation as a device to quieten sensuality in order to develop and release the Spirit for a flight towards God. Religious are still apt to rationalize it on the same grounds. Over thirty years after the appearance of the *Manual for Novices* it is possible to find someone arguing that mortification should mean a refusal to satisfy nature and what is natural, should mean forcing the body to remain in the world as though it were out of place there because 'the nature of present-day man is a nature which has been vitiated. If we do not wound it, it wounds itself. . . . It should be noted that the three essential mortifications, in food, in comfort, in sleep, are aimed at the same thing under different forms. They attack peaceful and satisfying accommodation, installation and enjoyment in the world.' And this because 'the material privations which lie at the root of the monastic life ... presuppose that the life we call natural, if it is not bad in itself, in its substance, for this was created by God, is in any case bad in its actual exercise, for which we are responsible.' So the mortifications continue in the 1960s under obedience. And though one English Mother Superior reports that before Lent in 1967 she was getting letters from people asking if her convent supplied disciplines, because they had tried half a dozen monasteries up and down the country without success for the first time, this doesn't mean that the discipline has suddenly vanished from the religious life. The discipline is a small whip with which penitents scourge themselves. 'I was', Mother recalls, 'brought up on the discipline myself but I hadn't been superior ten minutes before I realized that it didn't mean a thing to the novices we were getting. And, after all, I should have thought it a pretty well established fact by now that there's a distinct correlation between self-inflicted pain and sexual gratification.' That brisk dismissal will not be common yet, even if the discipline is beginning to wane – which is about all one dare say of it at present. The Trappistine nuns of Holy Cross in Dorset still apply it to themselves once a day. And, according to a Madrid newspaper, two thousand hairshirts and a thousand disciplines had been supplied to the faithful of the Spanish capital by local religious shops and monasteries within five days of Ash Wednesday 1967. At a more ludicrous level there is still in the English midlands a convent whose constitutions forbid the use of anything other than soda for washing either pots or clothes.

There is one kind of penitential gesture required, so the argument goes, to purify the spirit. There is another demanded by a superior merely to break the will and test the obedience of a religious. The precedents for many of these have an honourable place in Church history. The desert fathers used to weave rush baskets in the morning and undo them again in the evening to provide themselves with a virtuous occupation. St Antony obliged one Paul the Simple to empty a well and pour the water on the ground for the

sake of obedience and nothing else. St Teresa of Avila used
to recount with pride how once in refectory she was served
with a small cucumber which was rotten at the core. 'Un-
perturbed I called one of the sisters, one who had most discretion and intelligence, and in order to prove her obedience
I told her to plant it in the little garden we had there. She
asked if she were to place it upright or on its side. I replied
she was to place it on its side. ... I once happened to give a
sister six or seven incompatible offices simultaneously. She
accepted them all without a word, ready to believe she could
fulfil them.' These have their counterparts today when, according to the religious grapevine, instead of rush baskets, it
is sewing that is done and undone; instead of water emptied
from a well, it is dry leaves to be swept from the priory path
in a howling gale; instead of planting rotten cucumbers, the
fashion is now for planting walking sticks or cabbages up-
side down. Much of this sort of thing, where it happens at
all, takes place in the novitiate. But the breaking-in process
there can be a good deal subtler than that.

This is a novice-mistress giving an account of her steward-
ship:

To accustom them to submission in the practice of obedience they
are not allowed to question an order as soon as they receive it; if
they do they are cut short; they must do their best and leave
explanations till later. We avoid demanding anything seemingly
unreasonable or, when correction is required, discouraging penances. These penalties vary according to the subject and the state
of her soul. We send them sometimes to kneel at the communion
rail with arms outstretched, or to make the first part of the morning meditation there; it is clearly a public humiliation, but the
sister can retain her composure from her proximity to our Lord.
Sometimes they have to listen on their knees to the spiritual reading in the refectory, or something of that sort.

And this is a novice who has been on the receiving end of
a similar process:

My stumbling block and battleground were my confidence in
myself and my own judgement. I found no great difficulty in obey-

ing, in doing this or that, or conforming to observances. But not to give my opinion when I considered things went a little awry or would be better otherwise, was too much for me. ... Humiliation in every form came as an almost completely daily trial: humiliating penances to be performed in the middle of the refectory, being proclaimed by others. ... I ought to have been the life and soul of recreation, but I was rarely allowed to finish anything I had begun. On the contrary, our mistress encouraged others whom she found dull or uninterested to take the lead in conversation. Her one objective all the time was to mortify private judgement and self-will, the ego in fact, in every form.

The attitude of the mistress in question would have been moulded not only by her own training and experience but by a conditioning process which has been preserved carefully for centuries in the tablets of the *lectio divina*. 'There is', a superior protests, 'a class of ascetical literature, not intrinsically contemptible, and in its day effective, which speaks of us as worms, refuse and other such flattering terms. This only upsets the young people of today. Why should we persist in maintaining this obsolete and repulsive vocabulary?' There is also a class of literature that would persuade the religious to imitate the sufferings of Christ by almost all means short of actual crucifixion. And so in the period before Easter Day not only are long and heavy fasts undertaken and greater periods of silence than normal observed, both of them commonplace mortifications and doubtless useful ones, but the zealous individual may go so far as to slash his wrists with a razor blade so that he, too, may bleed freely with his dying Lord. 'Excess', a Benedictine has remarked, 'is never very far, as it is never very far from intensity in other fields, from religious enthusiasm.'

Strictness may relax a little when someone has left the novitiate, but obedience is still to be observed. It is a rule among Jesuits that a man must be given a humble job after filling an exalted position, in order to control his pride; the superior of a house thus finds himself drafted to an uncomfortable mission station when his term of office is up and the head of a province can be demoted to the third curacy in

one of the thousand parishes he has just commanded. The
Benedictines too have been known to adopt the same procedure; the last abbot of Ampleforth, Dom Herbert Byrne,
is now a parish priest on the outskirts of Preston. More ante-
diluvian symptoms of obedience than those, though, are also
to be seen outside novitiates. The woman who for two and a
half years was not allowed outside her own section of the
community without asking the superior's permission and
explaining exactly where she wanted to go and why may have
been a novice in a French teaching order. But the women
who after acquiring a degree or any other qualification from
an outside body are quite deliberately sent to work in the
kitchen for the next twelve months to prevent them from
getting too much above themselves, are the fully professed
sisters of an American community. In some monastic orders
there is a ceremony called the mandatum, a form of liturgy
in choir accompanied by the washing of feet. Among some
Benedictines the tradition is that the abbot washes the feet
of his brethren, as Christ washed his disciples' at the Last
Supper; in some Cistercian houses the monks go through
the ritual in pairs in the cloister every Saturday. At Holy
Cross Abbey it is used as yet another opportunity to emphasize the lowliness of the individual. There, where the abbess
is saluted by her nuns with a profound bow every time they
encounter her, the sister who has waited on the rest at table
finishes her week's service by washing their feet as well.
Life at Holy Cross is not by any means the most abject to
be found in the religious life. The Bishop of Arras reports
that there are Continental congregations where the sisters
still kneel before the superior as vassals once knelt before
their sovereign. These are the places of which St Teresa,
perhaps, might have approved most of all; places where obedience consists in the first instance of 'a bias, a voluntary
inclination to accept reasons which favour the superior's decision, which is to be seen in its best light. Then if in good
faith, despite the most sincere good will, these reasons seem
to have but little weight, and are overpowered by arguments
of considerable validity, one must have recourse to blind

obedience.' That is a voice from the middle of the twentieth century.

Obedience is to be summoned for every conceivable reason and applied to every imaginable situation at that level. It is invoked to preserve the chastity of the religious, sometimes by means of the most astonishing precautions. There are houses where the nuns have been forbidden to pass each other on the stairs in case they touched, as this would be against chastity. There are houses where a nun is never allowed to be alone with a visitor in the parlour for fear of some indiscretion, verbal or tactile, passing between them. There are houses which insist that if a nun has to go to the doctor for a physical check-up she must be accompanied every inch of the way by one of her sisters. There are houses which still prohibit their nuns from visiting art galleries, lest their eyes fall on some immodest painting. There are houses where, if a sister is attending university or some other establishment of higher education, she must take someone else from the community with her as chaperone, to spend the day knitting alongside the struggling intellectual. It was at the turn of the century that in Teilhard de Chardin's novitiate young Jesuits had to step into their baths in a blue serge robe, which they then removed under cover of a white linen tent; but it was in 1965 that a novice-mistress replied, when a postulant asked her some question about sex, 'I do not speak of such things. I am a virgin.'

While some nuns have acquired such a horror of the opposite sex that they will not even speak to a man on the telephone, let alone in person; while generally the most stringent precautions against besmirching religious chastity are taken in the case of nuns, authority also keeps a careful eye on what the men are up to. It sometimes forbids the monk or other male religious to enter anyone else's room. It invariably in the novitiate issues vague but very definite warnings against forming what in the vernacular is always referred to as the 'particular friendship'. It rationalizes this as a potential serpent in the breast of the community life; as something that will prevent the individual from sharing his affections equally among his brethren, as in charity he is bound to do. It is, in fact, born of nothing less than a quaking fear that active homosexuality will break out in every corner if two men are given the slightest chance to get on better terms with each other than with any of their fellows.

Homosexual relationships are certainly not unknown in the religious life; within the past few years one English men's community has lost many of its members because of the chaotic tensions that arose when the superior decided that the traditional restrictions had been ridiculous and that henceforth love was to be the watchword of the house; from one extreme of behaviour the community swung conclusively to the other, a number of people paired off in and out of bed, jealousies formed almost as fast as fond relationships, and the whole thing became a caricature of what the well-meaning superior had intended. On that scale homosexuality is doubtless rare; the rules are generally too restrictive to let it develop to anything like the extent a cynical outsider might imagine.

What the rules are doing to individual insiders is another matter. It has been held by one religious authority that the staggering prudery which envelops most communities is nothing less than an inducement to the thing they fear most of all. 'It is easy to see', writes the dean of students at the Catholic Notre Dame University in the United States, 'how the superior, subjects and the individuals themselves create an atmosphere which forces them to take consolation in one another because no one else "understands". The fear of homosexuality has ironically created an atmosphere in which any hint of homosexuality will readily grow.' Not that the topic is very often discussed as bluntly as that by religious anywhere outside a university; homosexuality is still such a dirty word that it has to be diluted to 'particular friendship'. And obedience has been recruited so massively to subdue any thoughtful consideration even of the euphemism that when advice is given as often as not it is so inadequate that it would be comical if individual tensions and worse were not at stake. 'Beware, however,' suggests a Dominican,

of those doting and obsessive enthusiasms, often called forth by external or superficial qualities, called particular friendships. They are bad, and if you entertain them they will separate you from God. If you find anything of the sort rising involuntarily within you, withstand it from the beginning; do not give it any voluntary gratification, and entrust your heart humbly to God. Quiet resistance, relying on grace, will usually drive it away quickly enough. A few words about it with your confessor or superior will help.

If only the good Father had also provided sound advice for the confessor to pass on that might be of some value; but he didn't.

Obedience is also invoked to preserve the security of the order or the community against the world outside, to prevent mere seculars, incapable of understanding, from knowing what goes on in the small world inside. In recent years this side of religious obedience has been flouted perhaps more than any other, both in print and out of it; if it had not been so, this book could never have been written. But censorship is still vigorously applied in places. A Jesuit writes that

It is common to find among the regulations of religious communities, often as part of their constitutions, a provision which limits the reception and sending of mail at the discretion of superiors. Religious superiors or persons delegated by them are thus entitled to read letters addressed to or by their subjects and to decide on the basis of their reading whether or not to transmit these letters to their addresses.

Another Jesuit talks of telephone conversations being tapped by inquisitive superiors. There is certainly one community, and there are probably others, where no novice is allowed to write to anyone – fellow novice or fully professed brother – who has opted out and returned to the secular life, for fear that he will be unsettled by the contact. Essentially censorship is carried out in the spirit outlined by R. M. Benson, the founder of the Anglican Cowley Fathers, towards the end of the nineteenth century. 'The brethren', he wrote, 'must not speak to strangers of any matter relating to the state or condition of the community, nor to one another without serious reason, unless it be to the Superior-General, the Assistant General, or the Provincial Superior. ... People are often anxious to know the numbers of the society and what works are being undertaken. It is no concern of people at large to know these things.'

Under obedience it is possible, it may even be common, for women in nursing and teaching orders to be grossly overworked. There is the case of the nun who, in an understaffed school, already simultaneously teaching two classes with eighty children in each, was told to take on a third class. There is the exhausted cry of the nursing sister who after twenty-five years' hard labour wrote that 'Our life is not one of service but of bondage. Since we can no longer dominate our work we have become slaves to it. What should have proved a source of daily spiritual strength has become a cause of daily dying.' It is easy enough to exact that price from a religious who under obedience is on call at any time, when there are not enough secular nurses – who in any case have regular negotiated hours – to fill the staff rotas. It is also easy for a superior whose mind is so blanketed by tradition and the habit of obedience herself, not only to suppose that her sisters can do tasks which may be quite beyond some of their capacities, in the belief that anyone acting under obedience can even perform miracles, but also to misuse the talents that are actually available to her. Like the provincial replacing a sister who, for six years, had been warden of a girls' hostel with excellent results; the Mother Superior deplored the difficulty of finding a successor who would be half as good. When asked why, then, was she putting the sister in another post, she replied that Sister had finished the two triennial terms permitted by custom of the congregation.

The largest indictment that can be made out against religious obedience as it has so far been generally practised is that it encourages the passivity of a babe in arms in those to whom it is applied unconditionally. This is particularly marked in the case of nuns. There are strong grounds for arguing that the Catholic Church must bear a heavy responsibility for the inferior status of women generally in western civilization, which in the most under-educated areas of society still continues. The influence of Tertullian is seen by some to be at the bottom of this. This early Father of the Church could neither forget nor forgive the mythology of a paradise lost through Eve. Addressing womanhood in general in the third century he cried : 'Do you not know that you are Eve? You are the devil's doorway. It was you who profaned the Tree of Life, you who dragged down with you him whom the devil dared not attack directly. It was you who thus disfigured the image of God which is man.' But St Paul must bear at least some of the blame and it is in Pauline tones that religious commentators sometimes today address women in general and religious women in particular. 'The place of women in the Church, then,' says one,

is not at the altar with the priest and the clergy, but among the faithful. The function of woman is not to govern, at least not primarily. Even if she is a superior, she remains in subjection to the priesthood, to the canonical visitations made by men. She is expected to listen with docility to the conferences she ought regularly to attend. The function of woman in the Church includes no right of speech, but she must listen in silence, as St Paul says.

It is after centuries of similar injunctions that infantilism among religious women has become widespread enough to constitute a problem so big that even a pope can recognize it : significantly, most of the books which in the last few years have started to look critically at the religious life and most of the papers which have been read at one conference after another have concentrated on this problem almost to the exclusion of every other one.

Various attitudes encourage it, some of them trifles; for example the names of individuals in a men's community frequently appear in published lists of one kind or another; in almanacs of the order or in intercession leaflets for the commendation of the faithful. I have never yet seen a similar list of women, and whatever purpose is served by this discrimination it cannot help the sister or the nun to maintain a feeling of individual identity. It may be, as some argue, that woman is psychologically disposed to obedience and submission; certainly the majority of women who think they have a vocation are built this way. The methods of the convent would generally induce the characteristic if it were not there already. For when the novice arrives she is in a state of uncertainty about every new thing she encounters; she is also likely to be nervous about her eventual acceptance or rejection by the community; she feels clumsy and helpless for the first few months in this alien environment. She is confronted in the persons of her superior and novice-mistress with people who are older than she, whose titles, positions and experience make them utterly maternal figures. If they are benevolent and attractive they will, within a system that does everything possible to discourage individualism and promote anonymity, become models in the eyes of the novice; their attitudes and physical mannerisms are going to be imitated unless she is an uncommonly mature and strong-minded young woman. The novice-mistress is in a particularly influential position. From the day the novice comes in it is she to whom the girl has to go for advice, for help and for consolation at every turn. It is she who encourages each of her charges to share every thought with her because she herself has been taught that to be a real mother in God to them, which from the highest motives she wishes to be, nothing less than bearing every responsibility for them will serve. She stands in this relationship with every novice for anything up to three or four years. In that time, with the best will in the world, she can cripple their development as human beings by over-mothering alone.

Where that does not promote infantile behaviour the chances are high that authoritarianism will. It was Pius XII who had become sufficiently aware of this problem to say that 'What psychology teaches is doubtless true, that a woman in authority does not manage as easily as a man to strike the exact balance between severity and kindness.' The precise nature of authoritarian deficiencies in women superiors has since been remarked by a number of commentators from Cardinal Suenens downwards. It seems that these are more or less the same as those anyone can spot in the world at large. There are superiors, timid by nature, who let things slide until they blow up disproportionately over some trivial matter and their sisters become either aggressive or huffy. There are others with a natural taste for power, who believe like St Teresa in obedience for its own sake, who reduce some of their nuns to abject fear. There are some who think and even talk in terms of 'annihilating' the will of their subjects. A chaplain reports that 'During a conversation a superior let out the word annihilation. She checked herself and said she had been recommended not to use the word but to replace it with humiliation.' If such a superior has under her some nuns strong enough to withstand this philosophy she will have a house which is divided into a resistance movement and a group of humble servants; she will cultivate the latter to inform upon and to isolate the former, whose days will be marked by increasing bitterness.

Whatever kind of superior a convent may have, there is a built-in tendency to perpetuate either herself or like-minded sisters in positions of authority. The Central Council of a woman's congregation has made its own point on this :

It is noted that with few exceptions most female congregations have a Central Council composed of a majority and sometimes a totality of older members. Commonly enough elections for renewal of terms of office have their own particular psychology : a nun very easily feels that she must not be ungrateful to a retiring Superior even if there is an obviously competent candidate to take over her office, and so she votes for the present holder. Another point is that although freedom to vote as one wishes is theoretically guaranteed there is often a fear, founded or unfounded, that in the end the votes do not remain secret, and this obviously inhibits freedom. Finally, most of the time a serious renewal is almost impossible, owing to the fact that the Superior-General, once in office, nominates at her discretion all the general staff of local Superiors who are therefore devoted to her and who are ex officio members of the next General Chapter. Thus it follows that the tendency to maintain the status quo can easily prevail.

Manifestations of infantilism are about as diverse as you would expect to find in the average primary school. At a community level the processes which produce this pheno- menon can be responsible for a degree of uniformity in con- ventual demeanour and decorum that a middle-aged man's great-grandmother might recognize as contemporary. Some- one has said that the convent is the last stronghold of the studied middle-class manners of the nineteenth century; women who have lived fifty years together call each other 'Sister' and not by Christian name; a nun I once met said that no she certainly wouldn't dream of kissing a sister who had come home after a long time on a foreign mission 'be- cause we don't want to be effusive'. At an individual level all forms of childish behaviour have been remarked upon here and there. In the nun whose whole day focused on the moment when she would intercept the superior at the top of the stairs, take her apron from her and fold it for her. In the nun who became utterly distressed because Mother forgot to congratulate her on the anniversary of her profession. In the nun of forty-odd who burst into tears the first occasion she was given a job without precise directions for every stage of it; she had performed the task a hundred times before, but before there had always been someone to lead her through it from start to finish. An American priest has noted another kind of infantilism.

There are people who feel like ducking when they see a sister coming. They love the sisters but they say 'They will wring you dry. They will take your car for every and any occasion. They will use your gas and oil with no thought of the inconvenience to you. They are about as responsible in these matters as adolescent youngsters are. As the adolescent brings the car home with the tank nearly empty, so also do the sisters.

There has been such a concentration – mostly by men – upon infantilism and authoritarianism among women in the last year or two that outside observers of the religious life might well have concluded that such problems were exclusively feminine. They aren't, though they may be more prevalent in the convent than in the monastery. There are men as neurotic about physical contact with others as any nun; it was Father Raymond Raynes, Superior of the Anglican Community of the Resurrection until 1958, who 'had a way of becoming completely impersonal at moments of stress, or when he had to make physical contact. When a woman cried on his shoulder he put his arm round her and held her with the flat of his arm but kept his fist clenched so he should not grasp her. When you helped him out of a chair he would not take you by the hand, you had to hold him by the wrist.' It was a friar who once told me that as you grew old in his community hypochondria set in and nearly everyone worried about his health and was dabbling with special diets by middle age. It is a Jesuit who has said that members of the Society don't mature much psychologically during the first seven years of their training because they are given no serious responsibility in that time. There are male superiors who exact obedience as strictly as any Mother, whose doors are constantly being opened by a succession of brethren asking Father if they might do this, that and the other, for permission to do almost everything short of going to the lavatory. Even in Taizé, that launching pad of the avant-garde, a streak of authoritarianism, doubtless benevolent in its operation, is detectable. Although nearly a quarter of a century has passed since the community settled down, although its observances were codified in the early 50s, Roger Schutz has still not established a procedure for the substitution of anyone else in his own place as prior; and when a brother arrives late for the office he strides past both altar and cross without so much as a glance in their direction and makes straight for Prior Schutz's seat, where he kneels and receives a paternal hand upon the shoulder before he takes his own place in the choir.

Thomas Merton, the Trappist, describes what may await the monastic novice in terms which echo the writings of Suenens and Huyghe on women religious.

Too often they see men who have abdicated their human identity and reality (in good faith) and are leading lives without human authenticity, simply passive, evading responsibility, and humanly impoverished, often to a serious degree. For example, they see men who have been in the monastery for years and whose simplicity is not that of spiritual childhood but frankly that of neurotic infantilism. They see men who seem to be obeying and who, in fact, are simply the products of a life of over-control (the idea that every slightest move of the monk and even his inmost thoughts are not supernatural and monastic except when subject to complete control is disastrous for modern man. False supernaturalism). These people cannot be entrusted with the simplest job without expecting instructions and commands at every step. They lack sound judgement and even common sense. They are often eccentric and their spirituality tends to be both naïve and bizarre. Yet because they maintain a servile attitude they are praised and rewarded. In point of fact the emptiness and futility of their lives are a real scandal to the young monk. How often do we not hear novices and young monks say 'If I remain in the monastery will I become like Father so-and-so?' This is one of the main problems of the young monk today.

It is a problem which for men and women springs fundamentally from conceptions and applications of obedience and authority that are about as old as Christianity itself. In spite of all its colossal weight there have from time to time been a few brave enough or reckless enough to flout the unequalled authority and risk the unique sanctions which the Church imposes upon its religious. When the Council of Trent forbade any more convents of nuns to be opened (which, in fact, at that time meant that no more women's communities could be started because the convent was the only kind open to women) St Vincent de Paul still founded an institute to care for the sick by sidestepping the rules. 'It cannot be said', he remarked,

that the Sisters of Charity are nuns because if a woman is a nun she must be enclosed. Being a nun means being enclosed and the Sisters of Charity have to go everywhere. . . . For monasteries you have the houses of the poor, for cells your rented rooms, for chapels the parish churches, for cloisters the streets of the town, for the enclosure obedience, for grilles the fear of God, for veils holy modesty.

When the Vatican Council of Pope John XXIII began it was under an oath of secrecy not to allow anyone but partici-pants to know what had happened at each day's session. A religious who is now generally acknowledged to be the American Redemptorist Francis Xavier Murphy got round that one by publishing in four volumes a report on the daily proceedings of the Council, whose accuracy has never been challenged, under the pseudonym Xavier Rynne. But these are scarcely norms. And even when a religious order is prepared to tolerate the critical voice within its ranks it can be overruled by the Vatican itself. The most notorious example of this in recent times concerned the Eng-lish Dominican Herbert McCabe. At the beginning of 1967, as editor of *New Blackfriars*, he wrote a leading article which considered the defection of the theologian Charles Davis; in it he agreed with Davis that the Church was 'manifestly corrupt'. A little later he was removed from the editorship and for a short time he was suspended from his priestly functions, all on orders from the Master-General of the Dominican Order in Rome. Although the case has never been proved there is strong circumstantial evidence to sup-pose that neither of these sanctions would have been ap-plied if pressure had not been put upon the Master-General from some quarter inside the Curia, the papal court through which the Catholic Church in general is governed.

The norm, however, is less spectacular than that. It con-sists of men and women enduring a régime based upon authority and submission to it with varying degrees of diffi-culty and different measures of sacrifice; for some it is a mat-ter of easy acquiescence and for others it is nothing less than a painful slog from one day to another. It means moments of crisis which attack different people at different times; for some who have entered a novitiate at the earliest possible age there can be a crisis in high adolescence, which has something to do with a physio-psychological rebellion against chastity, but which is also a rejection of control over other than sexual powers which the individual begins to feel might be limitless if only they could be released; for women there is often a crisis in the mid thirties, by which time they normally should have borne children but here recognize subconsciously at last that they never will; for anyone there can be a crisis between ten and fifteen years after entering a community, when the first enthusiasm has dwindled and the religious life at last assumes its correct perspective as a monotonous routine which is not always going to provide the elevation of spirit necessary to bear the individual serenely through difficult patches which will surely recur, maybe growing longer each time, for the rest of his life. And all these crises in some way or another mean a clash with authority, either submission to it or defiance of it. Once acquired, religious obedience, which is rubbed in so deeply from the beginning of a vocation, is hard to shed. If it is true that there is no such creature as a lapsed Catholic who in his marrow does not have a lurking fear of hell to the day he dies, it may also be true that there is no defected religious who can ever shake off completely a disposition to be obedient.

After twenty-three years in a convent Monica Baldwin obtained her release and returned to the world outside. She wrote a best-selling book about her life inside and outside the nunnery and she called it *I Leap over the Wall*. Twenty-five years later she concluded, in a spirit of some repentance, that she had defected in 1942 after a long period of self-will in which she had never really understood the true nature of religious obedience. 'I deceived myself,' she said, 'I now realize. Obedience was my stumbling-block.'

Obedience is a stumbling-block to many who have remained inside their convents and their monasteries. Because it has been so often a stumbling-block, and an apparently senseless one at that, the reformers are abroad in the religious life today, who would modify the existing conceptions of authority, making them more humane where they seem to be tyrannical, more intelligent where they appear to be brainless. The reformers must, and they know it, go gently;

not only because the Church is conditionally and deeply averse to revolution and change but also from a charitable consideration of the ageing and the old in religion who have spent their springs and their summers and sometimes their autumns too in a pattern which has been fixed for generations; these cannot be expected as a matter of course to accept, much less to enjoy, radical changes now. This is not to say that the reformers are entirely youthful and the opponents of change are all approaching pensionable age; the most revolutionary and the most luminously spiritual religious I know will never see sixty again. A superior who has already changed much in her order in the past few years and knows very clearly what changes she would still like to see refuses to do more until half a dozen or so of her old ladies have died. 'They've put up with a lot since I took over, she says, 'and they've put up with it generously. But this place has been their home longer than it's been mine and I think they have a right to recognize something in it of the home they first came to as long as they're here.'

It is impossible to guess the proportions of religious who are hot for change, who are implacably opposed to it, or who would obediently acquiesce whichever party gained the upper hand. But just as an increasing number of religious have abandoned their vows in recent years and walked out rather than put up any longer with things as they have been, and just as an even greater army might defect if they did not think that a substantial adaptation of the religious life to the twentieth century were imminent, so there is an incalculable number of people who are fighting to preserve the status quo. One of them is Brother Gregory O'Donnell, of the Institute of The Brothers of the Christian Schools, a teaching body founded in 1680 by Jean-Baptiste de la Salle. Since the 39th General Chapter of the Institute ended its long deliberations in Rome in 1967 and decided to make alterations in the Rule, Brother Gregory has been frantically busy trying to stop this happening. Quite apart from the representations he has made within his institute he has showered his objections and supporting arguments in sheaves on no fewer than forty-one newspapers throughout the world, from the *Salford City Reporter* to the *New York Times,* from the *Cork Examiner* to the *Indian Express* of Bombay. He has also lobbied the B B C, two members of the British Government and his local Member of Parliament. His defence of the Rule is a very simple one. It was, he says, the code by which the institute's founder wished the Brothers to live. It was moreover, something which he, Brother Gregory, solemnly promised to keep for the rest of his life when he was fully professed in 1956. Not only did it carry the express wishes of de la Salle, but it was backed by the full authority of Benedict XIII, who was pope in de la Salle's day and who issued a Papal Bull of Approbation to ratify it.

In the Bull we hear the ageless voice of the Church's authority at its most dogmatic and its most florid :

We ordain, moreover, that these present letters shall be and continue, always and ever, in full force, and obtain their full and entire effect; that they be not compromised under the revocations, limitations or suspensions of any similiar or dissimilar favours whatever, and any other contrary dispositions whatsoever, but shall always be excepted therefrom; and that as often as such contrary arrangements shall appear, so often shall these presents be and continue to be restored, replaced and fully re-established in their original and most effective state; and that so and not otherwise it is to be decided and pronounced in all the premises by all judges whatever whether ordinary or delegated, even the Auditors of Causes in the Apostolic Palace and Cardinals of the Holy Roman Church, even Legates 'a Latere', Vice-legates and Nuncios of the Holy See. And if anything to the contrary should be attempted in or about these matters by anyone under whatever authority, whether knowingly or through ignorance, We declare the same to be null and void, any Apostolic Constitutions or Ordinances to the contrary notwithstanding.

Which seems a fairly conclusive point in Brother Gregory's favour. Which also illustrates the ass that authority can make of itself when it is as inflexible as religious authority so often is, with its talk of observing points X, Y and Z for ever and a day, without leaving itself a loophole for reappraisal later on. Brother Gregory, of course, will not win because his superiors are bent upon reform and they have authority over him. He doubtless realizes this. On 2 February 1968 he wrote to the pope.

Dear Holy Father, I am writing for permission to come to Vatican City to work there, if necessary for the rest of my life, at some useful task even in the garden. For four years I have been objecting to changes in the de la Salle Rule which I have promised to observe for the rest of my life as I had it in 1947. . . . Since in conscience I am unable to change my will I think I would be less of a burden on others doing something useful in Vatican City and trying to observe the Rule alone. I am, Holy Father, your most humble and obedient inferior and subject, And loyal subject of Her Gracious Majesty, the Queen – *Gregory O'Donnell.*

There are more than one and a quarter million religious in the world today. A lot of them will be as dismayed as Brother Gregory at the winds of change that are now starting to gust through their lives. Many will be in the same daily humiliated condition as the novice who was perpetually sat upon by her Mother Mistress. The religious life at present is on the change and it is not a comfortable time for anybody except the ones with unshakable calm and self-possession and hope, with certain faith and a capacity to endure all things. These are not the commonest ones. And among the rest the casualties are occurring all over the field of battle. The dichotomy of the religious life today, the tensions and strains which at the moment run from end to end in conflict with each other, were not so long ago illustrated grimly in an English Anglican convent. In 1967 it lost two of its nuns. One was an old lady who had lived most of her life under an unchanging system and who could bear the confusing new reforms no longer. The other was a young woman driven to despair by the humiliation of the novitiate. Within a few months of each other they committed suicide.

VOCATION

QUESTION When did you become a monk?

ANSWER When I was fifty. I was a soldier from 1912 until 1924 and then I worked in the leather trade.

Q Why did you become a monk?

A God lit up the way and I came here.

Q Were you married?

A No.

Q Are women a bad thing?

A Yes.

Q But look, I'm married; what should I do?

A You should tell your wife you're going to God and then you live together, like brother and sister, not in bed. The best thing would be to tell her to go into a convent and come yourself to be a monk.

Q What about children?

A Put them in an orphanage.

Q But nobody loves them there.

A Of course there must be love in an orphanage, like there is in a monastery.

Q What was your life like before you became a monk?

A In the army I smoked fifteen cigarettes a day, women, drink, went to the theatre – but those were bad things.

Q Why is the theatre bad?

A Because you see naked women and that's scandalizing.

Q But sometimes the actors wear clothes?

A Yes, but such light ones you can see what's underneath.

Q How do you see the Devil? (meaning what image do you have of the Devil?)

A I've never seen him – only great saints see him. How should I see him?

Q Yes, but what do you think of him?

A He makes us like the bad things, women, smoking . . .

Q Why must a monk not smoke?

A Because it makes him think of other bad things he could do.

Q What do you think of life here?

A If you have good will it is easier than life outside – you have a
roof, food, clothing, and you go to church often.

That is a conversation with a Greek Orthodox monk on
Mount Athos, the eighty-year-old porter of the monastery of
Dyonisiou; it is said to be fairly representative of Athonite
attitudes. No doubt more or less the same answers could be
elicited from cross-questioning a chosen section of the
monastic population in the western Church. At any rate, it
reveals a state of mind – unintelligent, illogical, bigoted,
prudish, narrow, and extreme – which a cynical world is
very ready to accept as a normal mark of the monk or the
nun; it suggests a form of escapism from Life with a capital
L which much of the secularized world understands to be
the sine qua non of the religious life.

The disbelieving, and certainly the cynical, can scarcely be
expected to make any other assumption when there is nothing which has been so wrapped in mystery and secrecy as
the reasons why human beings beome religious and so, by
taking vows of poverty, chastity and obedience, put themselves socially and morally at right-angles to the rest of the
race. To a large extent this follows from incompatible vocabu-
laries and concepts. The language religious employ more
often than not to explain the attractions of the life to them is
the language of mysticism and theology; they are forming
their explanations within a supernatural context which the
outsider generally has either rejected or simply cannot com-
prehend. There are other reasons. One is a perfectly understandable reticence on the part of a religious to share, unless
it is absolutely unavoidable, the most intimate details of his
or her life; it is not a habit that any but the neurotic acquire
in any section of society in normal circumstances. And reticence here tends to be heightened because the religious is
defensively aware that he has defied the norms of a society
which harbours a number of derogatory suspicions about his
motives.

There is also an element sometimes not so much of self-
deception as of inadequate self-awareness; a failure to ana-
lyse oneself either deeply or accurately enough. It all adds up

to a failure in communication which is no greater and probably no commoner than the failure of anyone to explain why and how he fell in love with someone. The chances are that unless the individual is extremely articulate and analytical he'll utter no more than a string of clichés about love; and unless he is uncommonly honest and aware of himself and his motives he will gloss over some significant detail either from ignorance or from a fear that it might be interpreted as unworthy of him.

The religious life abounds in its own clichés about discovering a vocation and the most common of them tend to be that 'I knew God wanted me', that 'I knew I had come home when I first visited the community', that 'I wanted to give myself completely to God.' Even with the best will in the world the explanations can sometimes sound heavily muffled. A thirty-two-year-old monk writes :

From the age of fifteen or sixteen I was quite certain that I was meant to be a priest, and also that the priesthood involved for me some form of poverty and celibacy. I knew virtually nothing about monastic life and had very little interest in it until I was persuaded to take part in a parish mission run by my community when I was an undergraduate. On this mission another member of the team (a woman) told me that I should offer myself, she thought, to the monastery. This came as a complete surprise to me, but nevertheless seemed exactly the right thing, and I knew at that moment that this was what I had to do.

A sixty-three-year-old nun writes : 'During the years in which I was seeking the will of God as to vocation, and following where he seemed to be leading, I was not brought face to face with marriage. Had I been so brought I could only have considered it in the light of vocation.'

Largely because the modern world has mostly viewed the monastic or the conventional existence with scepticism, the defensiveness of religious themselves has become as traditional as the habit of obedience. It is unlikely that a quarter of a century ago even a tartly qualified concession to the popular view would have been allowed. Yet in the 60s a French Oratorian is prepared to concede that

If the romantic vision of the monk who has become such out of disappointed love is an over-simplified caricature, it is quite true that certain people need as it were to have actually experienced the vanity of idols we fashion for ourselves if they are to realize the unique value of God alone. Of others, on the contrary, it might be said that it is the very purity of an affection denied by circumstances or destroyed by death which leads them to go beyond it, perhaps when threatened by despair.

It is certainly difficult to imagine that until very recently one of the most crucial issues to be settled by a vocation to religion would have been confronted as boldly as it has been by Bishop Huyghe. 'It is not sufficient to reject the world,' he has said.

. . . What would have been the candidate's attitude towards marriage if she had not had a religious vocation must be discovered. One who is incapable of genuine human love cannot consecrate herself fully to God. . . . Only one who would have been capable of the fullness of human love in marriage can engage herself in the religious life with the certainty of finding therein the full flowering of her chastity.

And then, in extension of this principle, he adds : 'One can enter religion to care for the sick or the aged, or to teach; one can even enter for less worthy motives. But unless these motives are eventually transformed one cannot persevere long in the religious life.' And it does indeed take all sorts to make a religious world.

There are some religious who can tick off precisely the moment they decided that it was for them, like this fifty-one-year-old who has been in her Anglican convent for more than twenty years. She had been brought up in a nominally Christian family, in childhood had a vague idea of becoming a missionary, in adolescence had a notion that she might take up religious education and go to work among natives in South Africa.

My first job on leaving college was as children and youth worker in a parish and it was when I had been there, very happily for three months, that this appalling idea of religious vocation simply settled itself in my mind with a ghastly sort of conviction after I had read something about it. For about a year nothing happened, no further thought of it came, and I hoped I had imagined the whole thing, though always with a sense of something hanging over me. Finally, on All Souls' Day 1940, about 7 p.m. on a wet evening in the middle of an air raid, I just 'knew' absolutely clearly and unmistakably that this was what I had to do, and that I was to get going on it at once. For about half an hour I walked up and down regardless of falling shrapnel, with a certain degree of exaltation, but after that it was sheer going against the grain. It cut across everything I had planned to do – all my ways of using my life, quite good ways, too, of serving God as I thought – and going to a convent just seemed the end (well, I mean, just think of the clothes; no suggestion of a reformed habit twenty-five years ago!). But short of deliberately refusing what God asked, and so cutting him out of my life, there was no alternative. I had to go forward along this way that was now so painfully clear.

There are others for whom there never was such a clear-cut moment of decision. This sixty-four-year-old nun, for whom the religious life was a recurring prospect over a long period, for example :

My parents were happily married for nine years but were childless. They believed my birth, when both were forty, was a direct 'Yes' to their prayer to God. Accordingly, having been born on my mother's birthday, I was given a Christian name meaning 'Gift of God' and when I was christened the occasion was for my mother the real dedication of her child to God for his service. I cannot remember a time when I did not know this, and in an infantile manner was aware of God, Jesus, heaven and angels as a real part of my whole life, and of myself as truly belonging primarily to my heavenly Father. So, when between $7\frac{1}{2}$ and $8\frac{3}{4}$ both parents died, my real life and comfort lay in that verse 'When my father and my mother forsake me, the Lord taketh me up' (Psalm 27).

Within a few years she had decided to become a teacher on some foreign mission; at sixteen she toyed with the idea of becoming a nun but 'life was opening up and I wanted to enjoy it, and I knew enough of one religious community to realize how hard they worked, what few relaxations or pleasures they enjoyed, how tied they were by obedience. But I saw, too, their deep joy, their kindness, patience, compassion, and I was much attracted by the liturgical side of the religious vocation.' She went to university, however, 'fell in and out of love' with boy friends who were mostly ex-servicemen older than herself, and

though I looked young and unsophisticated many of these grown-up boys came for advice. They got advice with no foundation of human experience. This was really, I believe, the religious vocation; the committal of one's whole, fully alive, fully natural and supernatural self to the love of God made known in Jesus, through his spirit's direct action. It was something which made communication with others, at a deep level, easier and not difficult and it brought in an element of detachment from any particular person which contributed to the foundation of a wide and varied circle of *real* friends. These friendships (one can count at least twelve, off-hand) have remained with *very* infrequent communication of any kind, especially during the twenty-four years of life in an enclosed community.

In her fourth year at university she fell in love with an ex-serviceman several years older than herself. 'Again, there came the challenge – "Whom do you most desire, him or me?" It was as definite as that on one particular evening. My real love for Our Lord drove me to leave the decision in His hands, so I antedated my offer for service abroad and was accepted by the missionary society to whose missionary union I belonged.' She was twenty-four and she had not been in the missionary training college a month before 'as I knelt in the chapel one evening, the realization of the religious vocation was suddenly clear, as it had been eight years earlier. This time I said "Yes".'

The history of the religious life is studded with examples of people who had some mystical or visionary experience while in a secular condition, which changed their whole course of action from that moment. It still happens, even though the individual has difficulty in conveying the exact nature of the vision, just what it was that he or she felt so vitally. A woman in her thirties who for several years had been teaching religion in her diocese, steeping herself in St

John of the Cross and other mystics, began to feel that for her an answer to the cosmic struggle between good and evil which she identified with the Second World War might be the religious life of prayer and contemplation. It was not a straightforward choice though.

In spite of the satisfying nature of my vocation in religious education there still persisted in me an interior sadness due to a desire for marriage. This was finally resolved for me in 1947 by a spiritual experience, the authenticity of which I have never once doubted. Our Lord (in what St Teresa would have called an intellectual vision; i.e. nothing seen with the human eye) asked me to give to him this thing which lay at the heart of my sadness. In the one moment I gave and he took, at the same time giving himself to me in a moment that was superlatively satisfying and at the same time radically painful. I have never since been troubled by the sorrow of unfulfilled human love.

A Benedictine monk sheds a little more light on the vision as he experienced it.

The call in part was started off as a live question for me in 1953. My first visit abroad – Portugal. The weather was superb, although it was January, and I was staying with friends on a farm behind the Estoril coast, overlooking the Atlantic. In a peaceful moment drinking in the scenery and my good fortune, the thought crossed my mind that if the world and its beauty could produce this foretaste of happiness, what would heaven be like. Surely the sacrifice of everything this world can offer would cost little? Personal economy, maybe; but it was a profound experience which stimulated a haunting question. Until that moment I had always considered marriage as my way of life, with lots of children, to the exclusion of a priestly or a monastic vocation which I did occasionally think about and reject from time to time. Now the vocation question became an open one. About a year later, during night prayers, I was reflecting on the day's happiness and I looked out of the window at the myriads of stars; aware of them, perhaps for the first time, as each being in the mind and care of God. Again the wonder of God surprised me, and his generosity. The thought then struck me that a return of generosity and service to God, be it a token compared with his, was possible. I immediately shrank from the implications of this thought; but, again, it would haunt me and I knew it raised a question which, if I failed to face and answer it, I might regret all my life. But slowly I accepted that the only way to see if God wanted me to devote my life to his service was to try out my vocation as a monk, which I regarded as a more difficult calling for me than being a secular priest. And this I did.

Whatever else may have propelled them towards the life there is, for some, the realization that it has offered a form of security that was important to them and might otherwise have been missing. An Anglican monk who was a solicitor and then a priest before taking vows as a religious six years ago, and who says that only a second dissolution of the monasteries would now drive him to any other life, can see several pressures which helped to put him where he is.

My age [he is sixty-five]; the fact of having sipped at so many flowers and found the experiences delicious but unrepeatable – two gorgeous goes at university, the enjoyable experience of a loose war-time discipline with the Royal Marines, clergy house life under a wise vicar, with regular offices etc. weaving into an unpredictable menu of cosmopolitan work and pleasure; contact with a number of religious communities and the knowledge that I am incapable of directing (efficiently or amicably) a staff of housekeeper, parish workers, secretary, assistant priest (and their husbands and wives); and the inability to know how either to spend or save money.

A monk who has been with his order for thirty years thinks that his vocation

was, in a sense, an escape from a world which seemed to me to present almost overwhelming difficulties in my case. I also think very strongly now, that in spite of periodic wobblings since profession, I feel very much more sure of the vocation than I did at the time of profession, at times almost overwhelmingly sure, but it's because of a kind of strengthened weakness. My life before I began to think about the community was one of revolt against a revolt in my family life from respectable Victorian belief and church-going. My father had broken with religion at an early age and become an agnostic and, furthermore, had separated from my mother. I felt incredibly the lacuna in life left by the absence of family ties and bonds. I do not think this made me *sure* that the life in community was my vocation, but it led me to suspect that I might find an anchorage here, and I think I have.

An unhappy home is a recurring factor in the development of a vocation, even though the individual sometimes seems to be barely aware of this. Here is a nun of sixty-seven, who entered her convent in her fifties.

I would say that the call was present in embryo in childhood, in that God was wholly real, first as a refuge from fear, then as a compelling voice of conscience. After confirmation he flamed into a new dimension – Creator, Source of all life, Lover of men, Light. He streamed into my little life and my whole being went out to him in a love so absorbing that I really ceased to want anyone or anything else. Through years of light it persisted, then through years of loss, darkness or intellectual doubt. It was some years before I recognized it as prayer, but it filled life. . . . I was immature but the desire, the search, the love, remained central, however faulty the attempts to live by it. Bad health, frustrating circumstances, family claims piled up in seemingly endless succession and wild ideas steadied down to two firm alternatives: contemplative life in an enclosed community or prayer in the middle of the mess, i.e. doing an ordinary job completely identified with my fellow workers. . . . I never thought of renouncing the world, but of helping to draw the world back to God through the deepest identification in prayer, in whatever outward setting God chose to put me. . . . God settled the choice through circumstances. For years it was the ordinary job in the middle of the mess. Then the circumstances changed, and with them the inward pressure. Family needs had been met, health had improved, and work which had hitherto been an instrument of service and growth turned into an obstacle to the new response demanded. Total commitment now pointed to obedience and silence in an enclosed community. What made me sure of the truth of this vocation? The persistence through all circumstances of the central purpose, and the recurrent, recognized pressure of God in many earlier decisions of life. My attitude to marriage was one of personal detachment from the age of about eighteen, because I knew that God had claimed me to give myself directly to him. There must have been unconscious influence at first from the fact of my own maturity and the disharmony of my parents' married life. But even after I discovered myself as a woman I continued to be much more conscious of relationships with people as human beings than as specifically men or women.

A forty-nine-year-old nun, professed in her convent for twelve years :

When I was confirmed I just knew that God wanted me to be a nun, but I did not. So I did nothing, but God did not leave me alone. I soon saw that I should have to try sooner or later and then I began to make excuses. I said I was too self-willed, too undisciplined, too unstable, too proud and that these things would have to be put right before I could possibly try a possible vocation. But of course they did not get right and I began to realize the reason – I just was not doing what God wanted, and therefore of course nothing went right. In the meantime I did nursing and midwifery and moral-welfare work and eventually at thirty-two found myself running a home for young girls who had venereal disease; while we treated them medically we tried to help them rehabilitate themselves. Here I found myself up against evil as I had never met it before. The best of the girls were often so in the power of evil that if and when they wanted to go straight they had a terrific struggle and spiritual battle. Then I began to see why God kept on saying 'be a nun'. The Lord provided two people to whom I could speak – a nun and the chaplain of the house – and so at the age of thirty-two I eventually found my way to my community, the Lord smoothing out one mountain after another.

I have had no experience of human love in terms of the man-woman relationship; in fact I grew up terrified of men and frightened of marriage, though I did think it would be rather nice to have a home and family of my own. This attitude was the result of strained relations between my parents; my father, having been a spoilt posthumous child, was inconsiderate and demanding; my mother thought the way to cure him was to deny him and so there were rows. Secondly my mother was a cold sort of person; she made little show of affection and so, being an affectionate person at heart, I became ashamed of it. Thirdly I was indecently assaulted by an uncle at thirteen years – hence the fear of men and the setting up of a great tension because (a) I had no one to tell about it and (b) the incident itself was pleasing and I was not able to reconcile this with the knowledge that it was wrong. However, when I started nursing I made some good friends among the nurses but none among the medical students, from whose advances I shied like a frightened cat. In particular I made friends with the family of one nurse and this home became a second home to me and showed me what affectionate family life was like, and community life has just continued that.

A fifty-four-year-old nun, professed in her convent for thirty-two years :

I had no ordinary home. I do not remember my first home. As a small child of about two I went to live with a woman who took in children for a living. There were about ten of us, all ages. She was cruel and unkind to all of us. We were sent to Sunday school to get us out of the way, but there was no religion in the home. At the age of six I was sent to a new home where there was a husband and wife and one son. At this time he was in good work and they had a nice house which was in great contrast to what I had been used to, but this did not last, as in 1919 times were difficult and he lost his job and they had to move to a new place. There was no practice of religion here either; his family were Wesleyans and there were relics of Nonconformist practices – no pleasures on Sundays etc. At the age of nine I went to a Church school but was not allowed to go to church. But I must have got some glimmerings of teaching in the day school as I asked if I could be baptized and was refused. At twelve I came to live with my 'aunt' who had paid for my keep and was no longer able or willing to do so. I had always disliked her and was very unhappy with her and disapproving of her way of life, although I did not fully understand the implications of it at that time. No religion here, but very anti-religious.

On leaving school at fourteen and having to produce a birth certificate before I could get work I discovered that the 'aunt' was really my mother and that I was illegitimate. This was a very great shock indeed and made me even more disapproving of her way of life. When I was fifteen I got knocked down by a taxi on my way to work and was taken to hospital. The people for whom I worked gave me letters for a convalescent home run by a community of Sisters. On arriving I astonished them by inquiring if I could be baptized. So I was duly instructed and baptized in their chapel. It was at my baptism that I first became conscious of the call to the religious life. I had an overwhelming sense of God and his claim upon me as I stood at the font, this call to serve him alone, but I did not speak to the Sisters about this as I thought that they would regard it as impertinent of anyone as ignorant and lowly as myself even to think of such a thing. The Sisters were anxious for me to remain at the convent but I thought that as a Christian it was my duty to go back and see if I could do anything to improve matters at home; we are terrible optimists when young and think all things will come right if only we make an effort to do something about it. So I went back and got a fresh job, but there was very little I could do. One night when my 'aunt' was lying on the floor hopelessly drunk and I was sitting up with her till she regained consciousness, as she was liable to do violent things like upsetting the oil lamp, this thing happened.

It was 12 p.m. and she was lying there muttering about rats and mice when I became aware again of that same compelling Presence which had claimed me at the font; and the voice said to me, 'This is the result of sin. This is what sin does to man. For this sin I died and you must give your life to me in prayer in union with my Offering.' And I could see the crucified Lord reaching out his hands and knew that in some way there is really something that a person can freely give and that it is of value to and accepted by God in and through his Son. This was a most tremendous experience; it seemed to embrace not only what was before my eyes as the spoiling of a human being but all the sin and sorrow of the world which lay upon his heart as he hung upon the cross. . . . It soon became clear to me that I could do no good living in that house and that if I wished to remain a virgin, I must not stay. So after a night when the lodger tried to come into my room and the next night when my 'aunt' in a drunken fit smashed my bedroom windows I ran away and went to the people who had brought me up. I very easily got work and began to go to church. Here I was again overwhelmed with this sense of vocation. I began to find out about the religious life in its various forms but was rather frightened of the enclosed kind, being a very energetic and active person. I thought that I would serve God just as well if I became a missionary. In those days I was not old enough to go to a really good hospital for training, this being the only possible way, as I had no money and would have to earn while learning, so I went to a convent of nursing Sisters for a period of preliminary training. Getting into the religious atmosphere of a convent just brought up this inescapable vocation again and I began to read books like *Holy Wisdom* etc. and spend all my free time in chapel.

Eventually she was put in contact with the Mother Superior of an enclosed convent.

The Mother was marvellous and most understanding when I told her the history of my call, and said the convent accepted people on their merits and not on their family history and I could become a postulant as soon as I was free. So I came on the day after my nineteenth birthday and found in the Rule all those things to which I had been drawn; this life of prayer in union with the Saviour, the offering of one's whole self to him to be used according to his pleasure. *How* this helps the world is a mystery but I do not think it matters that one cannot give an exact explanation. I have never doubted the reality of this call and the urgent need to answer it in this way and at this time. I have often doubted my ability to fulfil it, but somehow the Lord has held on to me through thick and thin. It is a bit like marriage if you have a vocation, you have to go on with it for better or for worse till death – but in this case death will not be the parting; only the parting from the old self that the new life may begin.

You will see that I had no desire to reject the world but to reach out and embrace it with the Divine Love – to become a channel for all men to receive this Divine Love. I think that modern inventions help us to understand this a bit – you need a wireless set before you can receive a message which is all the time going through the air – so the Divine message for men can be picked up and transmitted through those set apart and called to this work. It is not to be heard for oneself alone but for the world.

When I went to get my medical certificate before going to the convent the doctor said to me, 'But why go into a convent? You have got a perfect body for child-bearing – it really is your duty to marry and have children.' I should have loved to have had a large family of children and have always been glad that I had a perfect body in this respect; why should not God have the offering of a perfect thing? As I came so young I had no ordinary experience of the human love between men and women. I took special care to avoid it as, being red-headed, I know that I am attractive to men and I wanted to give my whole virginity to God, especially in view of my family history and the call to reparation. I have often wondered if this was a mistake, and if I should have become a fuller person with some such personal experience, but it seemed at the time to be most necessary. I have not found this lack of experience to prevent my sympathy and understanding of those who have.

A positive urge to give themselves without at first focusing on an object or a means of their giving is a fairly common denominator among women in religion, rather commoner than among men; though sometimes at an early age they have decided to direct their energies towards God. For one woman 'the call' came while a child 'in the form of a strong desire to follow God in the closest, costliest and most direct way I could. It seemed to me natural to turn to the traditional way of life under the vows of religion.' For another, 'When I grew up I had a great urge to give myself entirely to something – as a governess to a family, or as a teacher to a school, but both were disappointing.' So was something else. 'Human love did not seem to be satisfying. It had a way of breaking down. I wanted something total. The human relationship in religion is of quite a different quality. It tastes of eternity.' Sometimes the giving is evidently required by family circumstances. A seventy-year-old nun 'had a great longing to go to university but had no thought of anything like the religious life. When I left school it was my obvious duty to look after an old arthritic aunt who had been so very good to Mother and all of us.' When the aunt died she was twenty-six and finally got to Oxford, where she was happy but where she also made a retreat and decided to test her vocation. As for the possibility of marriage,

I do not know what might have happened if I had met anyone I could have cared for enough. I lived a quiet life and did not meet many people. I think most normal women have a sort of background longing for a husband and family. I was eighteen in 1914, so I grew to maturity with those awful casualty lists coming out every day, and said to myself, 'My aunt needs me and there are too many women to have husbands. It is reasonable I should be one of them.

She is not the only nun of her generation to have been affected by those casualty lists. For a woman of seventy-six 'the few "boy friends", as they are now called, to whom I was more intimately drawn, were killed in the First World War. But my attraction to the married life was really based more on love of children and mothering, the essence of which is love in sacrifice.'

There are many religious who seem to have by-passed any love relationship which might have ended in marriage or who, with varying degrees of consciousness, have avoided it. For one sister :

Before coming into the religious life my chief experience of human love was in my own family and home, to which I was very devoted. When I left home to earn my own living I found the world a somewhat hard and unloving place. I enjoyed the friendship and intimacy of a few kindred souls. I had no boy friends. I think I was always looking for the ideal man who never existed. When I took up nursing I found so much satisfaction in caring for the sick, for whom I discovered I had a special love.

For a nun,

Questioning about marriage hardly entered my life. I was one of a family of six and I think I hoped that I would marry. I was very fond of children. My life was full, I liked my work, I played games a great deal, so I came into contact with people quite a lot. I had good friends and friendship meant much to me (mostly with people of my own sex). When I went to the mission field I made no promises not to marry, but at the age of fifty, on coming to this convent, I just thanked God that I was single and so able to enter.

For another nun

the experience of human love has always been unsatisfactory, though there was a brief period when I thought that as a married woman it would be possible to live a Christian life almost parallel to that of a religious if one's partner were of the same persuasion. I now know that this would never have materialized in the given circumstances, and that God allowed me to have that experience even while he was preparing me for this life.

For a third

marriage seemed to be a very beautiful way of life, as witnessed by my own home, but I knew it was not the Will of God for myself. There was an urgency to love God in a more direct special way. I was aware also, of course, of the many sorrows experienced through unhappy marriages etc., having come into contact with such while visiting in parishes in earlier years. These sorrows, I feel, can best be alleviated and supported in intercessory prayer.

For a fourth there were

deep friendships with one or two schoolgirls when I was between seven and seventeen years old, but no friends among the other sex, partly due to the circumstances of my education, which was in all-girls' schools or colleges except for my years at prep schools; partly because I had no brothers and because as a family we did not mix much with other people; and partly because I knew very early on that my life should be a celibate one entirely given to God; this was an entirely satisfying thought to me. I did not, of course, realize at an early age the deep psychology of one's emotional and sexual make-up. This came later through sharing in my sister's experience of these things as we grew up together; for unlike me she went to a mixed school and fell in and out of love several times before she finally married. I realized ultimately, of course, that I was giving something up, but it seemed a small *personal* thing (for which I felt myself unsuited) in face of taking one's place in the Purposes of God which would be what one would be doing in taking one's place in the religious life. Moreover, having seen what hypertensional crises could be raised in a family by two highly emotional people such as my father (Anglo-American) and mother (Irish) getting married, and knowing myself to be the heir of both these temperaments, I did not consider myself a very suitable woman to marry any man, certainly not to pass on a hypertensional temperament to children. I also thought God had arranged my nature like that on purpose so that I should realize and see the way to following the religious life without having any confusing side issues about whether or not to marry.

There are others in religion who have tasted a kind of love and found it wanting. A monk decides in retrospect that

fear of commitment to any relationship was partly responsible for my lack of progress in two matrimonial possibilities, but neither was vested in enough romantic quality to have been seriously considered. I had considerable promiscuous relationships, particularly during the war and after, with people to whom I hope I shall remain always grateful. Promiscuity was brought to an end by a far deeper relationship for two or three years with someone with whom a complete involvement would have been thoroughly unsuitable on either part. Since then, ten years ago [he has been professed for five years], there has been no sexual involvement or tension.

'Since leaving school and being ordained', says an Anglican monk,

I had a series of girl friends with most of whom I engaged in passionate love-making. In each of them I was seeking one to whom I could commit myself body and soul, but in vain. It was much more a case of restless lusting than of genuine love, though on their part there was an obvious desire for marriage. The only time I fell in love was with a nun (already doubtful of her vocation before we met) shortly before my call to the religious life. We still write and meet when we can, now that all passion is spent, and we are so grateful for God's merciful dealing with us and for our continuing friendship. I may add that the understanding and achievement of true celibacy comes hardest of all the demands of the religious life. Since joining my community, knowing my susceptibilities, I take care (I trust!) not to allow any relationship to develop to that point where in other circumstances marriage might seem natural.

A nun, now thirty-four, recognizes that

On one level I was always surrounded by loving care; I loved my home, enjoyed school and university, and made many friends – boys, girls and older people. I also learned compassion for people through various vacation jobs. But there was another level. I was seduced at the age of eight and from then until I came to the convent I was sexually promiscuous. I had these affairs frequently and of course that led to other vices, but I managed to keep that side of my life very strictly hidden. I experienced fear and pain and frustration and loneliness, and sex became for me a sort of greed, unconnected by love or life. I was so amoral about this that at first I did not even mention it to the community. I did not come as an escape – the escape would have been not to come but to have gone on in unreality; or did I come as a penitent. I simply decided to give myself wholly to God. It is difficult to remember how one felt long ago, but I think I felt that it was the only real thing to do, to hand my life over to God, who was the only one to know the real me under the outward show. It did not occur to me to 'give myself' by doing good to others; that would have seemed a sort of presumption. It had to be all or nothing and God only; so I chose the strictest religious order I could and asked them to have me at once.

It is possible for someone to experience the shock of love for the opposite sex for the first time after becoming a religious. This is how it happened to a seventy-year-old priest in an Anglican community. He was one of seven children whose parents were devout Christians. 'In 1915, when I was nearly nineteen, I joined the army and soon dropped most of my religion. I was very ignorant of sexual matters but I was full of curiosity and longed for erotic experiences, and the upshot of that was that I learned to masturbate.' Some time after demobilization he had 'a conversion experience which ... was like falling in love. And, from then on, I have always known that my life was God's.' He became ordained, worked first in a parish and then overseas as a missionary, before deciding that 'I needed the mutual help and support of a regular community.' He became a monk in 1933 and since then has had no doubts that it was his true vocation. But

the one difficult sacrifice I have had to make as a religious has been not to have a wife and children. This has sometimes been hard, but I feel sure that in my own case the sacrifice has been right because it has been spiritually fruitful, and in accordance with Matthew 19.12. I tried to accept celibacy as a vocation from the time I was at my theological college. I had never been in love with any woman before that date. After profession I was twice very strongly attracted to two women, one at the age of forty-three and the other when I was nearly sixty. I fancy that either of them might have consented to marry me if I had embarked on a courtship, and on each occasion I felt nearly overwhelmed. On the first occasion I told a prayer group of my dilemma and asked for their prayers and on the second occasion I talked it out with one of my brethren and asked for his prayers; and on each occasion the temptation passed away from me.

It is possible for an uneasy love affair not perhaps to continue or to mature but to swing into a quietly satisfying friendship after one partner has taken religious vows. The case of the man who fell in love with a nun before himself becoming a monk was one example of this. Another is that of a nun who was forty-two before she tested her vocation in the convent which was finally to become her home. She had sensed her vocation while she was working as a medical missionary in Africa

and I found this incompatible with marriage to the man I would have wanted to marry. As I knew I could not marry him and thought it would be wrong to let a man propose if you did not mean to accept him (I think now it would have been better and kinder to let things come to a head) I held him off so that he cannot have known where he was with me at all. Consequently we had an uneasy friendship until I came to the convent. Then I had to explain what I meant by vocation and told him that I had previously had one to be a missionary. This made him realize how things stood and since then we have had a very satisfying relationship. My Superiors know about it and he comes to see me each year and I am allowed to write to him once or twice between visits. Apart from my letter to him about vocation and his answers we have never referred to our personal relationship; we just sit together when he comes and talk about this and that in an atmosphere of relaxation and peace. This sounds rather dull but isn't. Christ said that if anyone gave up wife or child or parents for him they would have a hundredfold. This is not just an exaggerated way of putting things for emphasis, the relationship *is* stepped up a hundredfold. Christ also said that in heaven there would be no marrying or giving in marriage but we should be as the angels of God. I used to think 'How dull!' But now I know that it would be worth anything to love one another with the burning love of the Cherubim, and although we haven't got there yet I can see it as a possibility in heaven.

It is also possible for the homosexual to find in a religious community the framework within which he or she can be more at ease than would have been likely in the world outside. A lay brother who had been in teaching and in show business before taking vows says :

I should never have got married even if I had not become a religious. I am completely homosexual. Before becoming a religious and before I was a schoolmaster I had been very promiscuous and found no satisfaction in it at all. The only human love that was in any way successful was with a coloured boy of my own age, who was a revue dancer, as I was at that time. We were in different shows. We lived together for several years completely platonically and were very happy – nearly all our interests being shared. Since joining the order I have had two very intimate and close friendships, both with men much younger than myself and both in the community. They run simultaneously and are completely satisfying.

In the case of an Anglican priest who is a monk :

My love for others has been for those of my own sex. There was one instance at university when marriage might have been a possibility, although from my point of view this was much less strong than the girl's. There was a good deal of affection on my part, but nothing like a love so strong that marriage could have been an outcome. This kind of thing happened again in a parish. But before becoming a religious the deepest human love I have experienced in either giving or receiving has been from those of my own sex. Since discovering my vocation and following it the pattern of human love in my life has not changed. It has, however, deepened. I think that I can best express it by saying that in the religious life I can be as God made me, and accept myself as God made me. There is a great sheet-anchor of love in a community which I find satisfying. By nature I am a very affectionate person and can fully give and receive the kind of brotherly affection which is necessary to me.

A woman who entered her community sixteen years ago at the age of forty-seven 'would probably have married had not circumstances seemed deliberately to circumvent it. I had two friendships with women, both circumvented in the same way. Since being here I have been allowed a friendship with another Sister, and have grown increasingly close to my large family and outside friends.'

Inside the community the experiences of warmth, friendship, love in any recognizable sense and form, are about as varied as they have been for the individuals concerned in the world before taking vows. Whether it is out of loyalty or not it is rare for anyone to concede that in these particular terms the life is as bleak as some have found it outside; there is, rather, just an occasional hint of disappointment borne bravely and then sternly overcome. A nun who had known several good friendships before her profession says that

> Perhaps at first I expected to find the same kind of friendship and was a little disappointed. But that was just foolish and didn't last long. Love and kindness was there, expressed perhaps in a different manner, but quite honestly human affection is not needed in the same way. Living and growing together, giving oneself to the whole in God, is wonderfully satisfying.

A Benedictine monk who as a youth never went round with girls except one, a Jewess, with whom he fell in love and was later to meet after his profession when she was married to an American businessman, seems to suggest that a vacuum can be created between the monastery gate and the cloister. When he met his old sweetheart during his annual holiday at home, 'She was well and happy and I was glad. I have no regrets. My experience of human love since then? It's difficult to describe. There are many friendships both within and outside the community. I still feel the thirst to give and receive human love and affections – perhaps more than ever.'

But a nun of sixty-seven, on becoming a religious, 'found a warmth and depth of human love quite beyond anything I had known before, an openness to each other and a true sharing in all our joys and sorrows, and in difficulties something on which you know you can always depend'. For another there has been 'much happiness in human relationships, with my family, friends, those I cared for in the course of service, and most especially my Sisters in religion and pre-eminently Superiors, of both sexes. I think a fearlessness in human loving has grown with the years in religion.' A third speaks of

> the amazing joy of having so many sisters. I rejoice in the loving naturalness of our life together at recreations – both formal when

conducted by Mother and informal when we wander together in the garden or sit and talk together in the common-room. We are encouraged to be natural and really human. I find great richness in the pooled experience of so many women of varying ages, backgrounds and interests.

It is almost commonplace to find in a religious community people who have been there for half a century and more. And there is maybe nothing more astonishing to a secular world, which is permanently and continuously in a state of vivid flux, which is forever packed with incident, where high contrast in every form shapes the pattern of days, than the fact that there are many people who have lived for so long a life of comparative monotony and immobility and who can say at the end of it that never for one moment have they doubted that this was indeed their vocation. But there are. More frequently they will say, like this monk of three decades, that they have not *always* felt absolutely sure of their vocation but that 'on the whole, by and large, I have grown more sure. I have, indeed, been through experiences of very considerable abandonment by God but this, I think, is very usual in the religious life.' A nun who has just celebrated her jubilee says that she has never seriously doubted the rightness of her option for the religious life : 'Occasionally I have wanted or tried to do so in moments, hardly even hours, of stress, but have never succeeded.'

Stress usually derives from some personal friction or else from some collision with the vow of obedience, in which case it can take the oddest forms. A septuagenarian nun recalls that

It was not until 1945, when I had been professed fifteen years, that I had a terrible shake over the question of obedience. We had been told that, although we were enclosed, the Bishop had given us permission to go out to vote for Sir Winston Churchill in the general election. Greatly as I admired Sir Winston as a war leader I could not vote for that Conservative programme. So I stated my difficulty and was of course allowed not to vote (the Labour candidate was divorced and in favour of easier divorce). No one was unkind to me, but it gave me a queer sort of shock. It was only a priest who said to me, 'Remember – "Ye have not chosen me, but I have chosen you" ' that brought me back to the certainty and wonder of vocation.

A wavering vocation is more likely to be felt by the young, rather than the old in religion. A thirty-one-year-old Benedictine monk says that 'Of course, one still has moments of doubt and dissatisfaction with oneself. But reflection and prayer usually seem to restore the balance. My doubts and misgivings are about my own inadequacy, not about the certainty of my vocation.' An Anglican monk of thirty-eight does not think that his vocation has ever seriously faltered 'though there was a time not long ago when I did have a depressing stretch. I am sure that this was owing to the kind of work and the place where I was. As the tensions were not just something that I felt myself, but were common to the other brethren in that particular house I did not take seriously any temptation to throw in the sponge.' A forty-five-year-old contemplative nun who has been professed with her order only two years can say :

that almost from the beginning of my life in the community I have had a deep, underlying conviction that this was God's call for me. But at all stages I have had times of rebellion and been tempted to give up and return to an easier life in the world, because I was unwilling to bear the cost of the necessary purgation of my inherent selfishness. Thus, as a postulant or novice and since profession, at times an inner voice has said, 'Why carry on what seems a stupid waste of my life when I could have a good job, be successful in the world, comfortably off financially? Why not return home to my mother and so prove my love for her? Why not use my medical training and experience in the world and have the satisfaction of knowing I was helping people?' And at times there has been the whisper, 'Is there a God at all?' I am sure that those times will go on, as faith will only grow and mature as it is tested; but knowing that the testing will never be beyond what God knows each one can endure.

A forty-two-year-old sister, professed with her community for ten years, says briskly : 'Since becoming a religious the conscious certainty of my vocation has been almost entirely

absent. This is neither unusual or important. It was a func-
tional thing which served its purpose in enabling me to
know God's will for my life – it was not intended to be a
permanent prop of reassurance.'

And the purpose of it all? There are some religious who
see it almost entirely in personal terms, like this monk.

There is no particular virtue in living the Christian life in
community as opposed to the world of the parish, the factory, the
commercial undertaking, the Services or the home. Neither is there
any particular virtue in living it in those worlds rather than in the
cloister. There is no more virtue in working in freedom from the
worry of making ends meet and coping with the income tax than
there is in trying unsuccessfully to cope with these things and
paralysing the rest of one's work. There is no more virtue in accommodating one's idiosyncrasies, talents, opinions and inabilities to
the mind and milieu of the community than to that of the office or
family. The commitment for life certainly plunges a brother into
the joys, distresses, responsibility and creative activity of a family;
into the work of a corporation or cooperative society; into a freedom in which he is relieved of many difficulties which he is by
nature incapable of solving; into a brotherhood in which he is supported by corporate prayer and intention. The immediate worship
and service of God (which is the first requisite of all Christian work)
is not the monopoly of the monastic, but is practised among all the
faithful, priests and laity. For me personally, the religious life has
made this practice possible again. I might also add that it has given
an untidy mind a framework in which to pray, think and live.

Others see their life as a signal to the rest of the world. A
monk says :

Although we reckon to have certain aims in the order I would
say that we are here to demonstrate the truth of learning obedience by the things we suffer. We appear to give up all sorts of
things, but if this is where we should be, then we are happy with
the things that are provided for us here, we are the praying heart
of the Church, and therefore the worship of God is first in our
lives. Everything that people see, and by which they mostly judge
our lives and our usefulness, is the outcome of this life of worship
and prayer. Our founder said that we were a lot of men trying to
be good. I think that this still holds – because it is what we are
that is more important than what we do.

A contemplative nun compares the convent to

an experimental laboratory into which some are called to work out in a particular way the problem of how man can give himself to God and to his neighbour, and if this is the basic spiritual need of human life, then it is worth doing. This experiment involves every part of one's being – physical, mental, emotional and spiritual. If any part is left outside the experiment goes wrong, the gift of oneself to God is incomplete, and we have nothing authentic to give to others. People come to us either in person or by letter, expecting to receive the results of our experiences in Christian living and community, that they may work out the principles in their own particular vocations. This is part of the overspill from our prayers which they have a right to expect from us.

Another nun appears, in the more conventional language of piety, to collect all these ideas and wrap them into one generalized diagnosis of the religious life. The object, she says, is

that all the members of the community should become mature persons, unified in themselves and in ever-deepening relationships with God and so with each other; and so be a family of love, and by doing so to fulfil the purpose for which they were created, and so to give glory to God. By their increasing growth in sanctification and union with God to be channels of this love to the world, participants in this thirst that all men and all creatures should be drawn to unity, to respond to his love for their healing. Thus called to share in God's reconciliation, to stand in the centre of the world's forces of evil in the victory of Love's triumph on the Cross.

So far, we have had religious talking piecemeal about a number of sides to their vocation; the quotations have been deliberately extracted from often lengthy answers to a questionnaire in order to form a coherent pattern of experience and belief in a highly complex subject. By contrast, here are three unedited statements of vocation and what it means to two men and a woman.

1 *The Jesuit's story*

(He is a Scholastic, aged twenty-five; which means that he is at that stage of Jesuit training in which he is grappling with philosophy and theology before eventual ordination as a priest. He took his vows four years ago.)

I joined the Jesuits on leaving school; before that I could have been described as a pious Roman Catholic schoolboy. I came from a large family with a very religious atmosphere. Weekly mass was taken for granted and occasional weekday mass was encouraged. Everyone took morning and night prayers seriously and the family normally said the rosary together in the evenings. Both parents were active members of our parish. My father was very active in the Legion of Mary and all the children joined the Sodality of Our Lady as they grew up. Out of the six children so far to have left school, two are Jesuits and one is a nun.

I was never very sure that the religious life and no other was my vocation. I realized that there was a shortage of priests and I regarded the priest's work as being extremely important. I also realized that I had the necessary academic ability to be a priest myself. With the encouragement of my elder sister (a nun) I reluctantly admitted to myself that there was no excuse for me. I thought of the Jesuits partly because I was at a Jesuit school and partly because I thought that they, more than any diocese or order I had come across, would be able to use my academic ability. I did not consider very seriously the difference between religious priests and the diocesan clergy. When I tried to discuss the matter with a priest at the college it soon became clear that he had already made up his mind that I had a vocation to the Jesuits. After that I went through the formalities required for entering the noviciate, never quite sure that I was doing the right thing. I might add that the fear of hell was a predominant driving force in my life at least until I joined the noviciate.

Before I joined the Jesuits I considered celibacy to be merely an unwelcome condition of becoming a priest. I was never very steady with one girl, but I enjoyed dancing and mixed social functions, and I had a few close friends who were girls and one in particular of whom I was very fond. On the other hand I was singularly short of friends among my contemporaries at school.

Since becoming a religious I have been able to make close acquaintance with a number of girls. One of them is a particularly close friend, and is also very fond of me; I am not sure of the exact meaning of the term 'in love' and whether it applies or ever did apply to my relations with this girl. I can say that at a time when I was reconsidering my commitment to religious life I discovered that thoughts about her were considerably influencing my judgements, and I found myself unable to accept the fact of my vow of perpetual celibacy: this state of affairs was, however, of short duration and I was able to correct it almost as soon as I realized that it had arisen. I do not regret the relationship, which has been a stimulus both to my work and to my religious observance. So my experience of human love has been limited, what I have experienced I consider to be very valuable in my life, but I do not believe that any person's desire of, and need for, love can be satisfied by any one person. I might also remark that one of the main considerations which have kept me in the order over the past couple of years is the help and stimulus I have found from friends within it, and my commitment to them.

On a number of occasions I have found it necessary to reconsider the value of and my attitude towards religious life as practised by those members of the order with whom I have come into contact. I now regard the concept of 'choice' to be more fundamental than the concept of 'vocation': the idea of some inner call I regard as irrelevant – what matters for me is that I have chosen and can continue to choose to live the religious life, and that the order chooses to have me. Every time I have reconsidered either the value of religious life as I have found it (taking into account the possibility of my own particular adaptations) or my own suitability for it, I have decided that I would do more good within than without – or more harm by leaving than by staying.

One doubt I have about religious life is that it gives me an authority and status in the Church which I have not really earned for myself. This can create a tension between my own convictions and those of the superiors who have given me the status. Each has in some way to take responsibility for the statements of the other and the question arises as to whether this is possible with the fairly radical differences of opinion that exist and whether honesty is being sacrificed. One objection I have to the living of the religious life in the order to which I belong is that the religious life seems to become in the minds of many an end in itself which has to be preserved as such. Certain practices and customs are held by many as binding on all irrespective of their usefulness to particular individuals or communities, and the situation in which they find themselves. Religious life becomes a particular style of life rather than a group of persons living for a common goal, so that 'common life' achieves a status out of proportion to its value. This is not to deny the need for some regularity, and I am reasonably content with the community in which I normally reside – but I am not content with the attitudes of many who are in positions of authority.

This over-emphasis on religious practice does seem to produce in people an odd scale of values. The concept of 'supernatural' is not supposed to be in any way contrary to reason, but in the minds of many it has become so distinct from reason that it does in fact result in attitudes and conclusions which to most people would seem to be unreasonable. Friends of mine have been put onto work simply in order to 'give them experience' or even 'to test their obedience'. Their suitability to the work, the 'natural' value of the work, or the responsibility towards those outside the society for whom the work is intended – these considerations were apparently deemed irrelevant. In one case this involved two years at the prime of his life. Other examples are the expensive and long training without consideration of the usefulness for the individuals concerned – the long academic training for priests even in the case of non-academic persons seems to me absurd, and to have people doing degrees at university which they do not use seems to me to be a scandalous waste of time and of benefactors' money. I am also out of sympathy with teachers of morals who have had little pastoral experience, with hours of rising and retiring unnecessarily out of conformity with the society in which we live, with injunctions on wearing a very distinctive dress and other difficulties imposed on social contact with non-religious, etc.

This slightly odd 'religious logic' becomes, to my mind, a more dangerous influence owing to our over-rigid rule about staying with non-religious, and difficulties imposed on eating outside one's house of residence (at least during the dozen years of formation). Religious tend to become isolated even while living in very populated areas, and over-concerned with the particular problems of religious life which are rarely examined in relation to other people's problems. In this way, for example, realistic attitudes towards the value of money can be completely lost, apart from more serious topics such as the possibility and limits of authoritative government, the nature of social problems, etc. Many have gone through the prescribed training and come out extremely human but many, to my mind, have not, and the danger to one's

own personal development – a danger which is not simply overcome by a critical frame of mind – does create a certain amount of
moral concern.

I understand the primary aim of the founder of the order to
have been to serve the Church in any way the Church requires,
and this is fundamental to my understanding of religious life,
though I would give less importance to the hierarchical Church
than he did and would emphasize that the Church goes beyond
explicit Christians. Thus I demand of myself a utilitarian justification of my life and my work. I regard the purpose of my religious life as being to make the best possible use of my talents,
taking into account the needs of the society in which I live: if at
any stage I decided that I could make better use of my talents outside the order I think I would leave. But this should be understood
in a very broad sense, taking into account the effect of my change
in status, and of the various interpretations that might be given to
my action, the betrayal of trust that many, both inside and outside
the order, may feel. A realistic assessment of what can be done
outside the order is required, and also a realization that human
happiness is more important than material welfare.

As for the function of the public vows I have taken, it seems
to me that primarily they are a witness and a challenge to the
world and their main purpose is to provoke a rethinking of attitudes and values; this applies as much to the religious himself as
those with whom he comes into contact. The vow of poverty is a
challenge to the rat race; how effective this can be when one is a
member of a large organization with substantial funds remains
questionable, but living slightly below the standards of one's associates can suggest that happiness can be obtained as much by having a little less as by having a little more. A recent interpretation
of poverty as being more concerned with working hard than with
the standard of living is also relevant. The vow of chastity is, I
think, an effective challenge to the place of sex in the modern
world. I would like it also to result in a greater availability –
which at the moment is true of major tasks, but unnecessarily
limited in daily life by rules of residence, and a tendency to require an over-particular exercise of the superior's sanctions – and
a witness to a distinction between sex and love, though we cannot
simply draw a line between them. The vow of obedience is a challenge to the value placed on independence: I would like it also
to suggest that we can go a long way by trusting men who make
mistakes like everyone while remaining realistic about the mis-

takes – a public acceptance of the fact that nothing can be perfect and that we must do our best with what we have. The religious life as a whole is my witness to my beliefs in the importance of religion (in some form) and the value of a commitment to serving rather than personal gain.

I might also point out that although my answer is stated in secular terms I am not entirely in favour of a 'secularized religion'. My own interest in philosophy results in a personal tendency towards a secular language, and I am very sceptical of anything that completely prohibits some sort of translation into secular categories.

2 *The nun's story*
(She is sixty-one and she has been professed for thirty-nine years, first in an active order of Anglicans, later in an Anglican contemplative convent.)

Born in a university city in an intellectual milieu, reaching the age of adolescence in the reactionary years of the First War period, at an early age I developed all the tendencies of revolt against traditions and conventionalities which was so typical of the age. Deeply involved with the moral and psychological distresses of one of my brothers and violently opposed to the idea that there was a God of Love because my eldest and much loved brother had been killed in the war, I made an absolute fetish of chucking over all religious observances, very largely to make a show of my independence and probably also as a form of shocking my parents, which was one of my chief aims of life.

This form of self-determinism carried me well into my own university years. I have no doubt at all that any psychologist would have summed me up as a good example of the will-to-power complex, as my undoubted gifts of leadership had ample scope on every level to be given expression to. It is all the more remarkable, therefore, that when the Lord caught up with me, it was through the overwhelming cosmic pressure of suffering and frustration by which the years of the middle 1920s were so characterized.

In the vacation I went down to the East End and saw something of what those years of unemployment meant, and the moral decline of the brother mentioned above so overwhelmed me that it became obvious that something more than a philosophy of self-determinism was needed to provide an answer to the problems of the age.

If religion was to be the answer it had to be all or nothing, and therefore, when I returned to the sacramental life of the Church and the practice of prayer there could be no half measures and the religious life presented as far as I could see the most complete self-committal to God in the service of others. At first I revolted against the idea and tried to escape from it; to no avail. I tried my vocation in an active teaching order the year after I got my degree and twelve years later was transferred from the active to the enclosed life of my present community.

This transference must again be seen in relation to the world conditions of the time in which I was living. By 1940 I was a Mission Sister and participated to the full in all the suffering and emergencies arising from the German bombing of the area I lived in. This was the culmination of a gradual process which had been there from the beginning – a realization that the Christian is called not only to try to ameliorate the *effects* of man's selfishness and depravities, but to go far deeper to be in God's process of reconciliation of that evil which is the source from which sin as we know it is derived. In terms of Christian commitment this means the witness to the power of prayer and the transforming grace of Christ's Passion being brought to bear on the world's deformities. This is the primary essence and function of the contemplative life and it was the challenge of World War Two that made me realize that for me personally the contemplative rather than the active life was the only way to fulfil my vocation.

Probably in the process of translation of Mgr Huyghe's book the unfortunate word '*reject* the world' has given a wrong impression. Religious vocation can never be negative, but for those so called the most positive way of serving the world. If there is an element of escapism then the religious life has no more virtue than any other form of negative way of life. I think it is quite wrong to put the question of human life in opposition to the call to the religious life; the two are not in opposition.

If a candidate for the religious life has had first-hand experience of sexual love in its fullness, it would be far truer to say that the call to the religious life is the completion of the human experience. In my own case I was engaged and can truly say that the experience was one of complete satisfaction at every level of one's being. We both realized there was a call from God not to abandon our love for each other, but to take it into the most complete form of dedication of which we were capable. This meant in effect that before we could think of marriage I had to try my vocation to the religious life.

My biggest query was not the rightness of what we were doing, nor even shrinking from the cost of it, but whether I was asking more in terms of sacrifice from the man who loved me and whom I loved. The whole thing was obviously only made possible by the fact that he as well as myself could sincerely and with a sense of complete fulfilment put the will of God first before any desires and wishes of our own. But the point I want to make is that we found each other by giving up each other, and certainly I can say now that this completely satisfied experience has gone on with me all my life, as I know it has with him, and has been the foundation of my fulfilment of human relationships within the religious life, and with all the manifold needs and problems that are brought to a contemplative community to pray for and to help resolve. In other words, having known human life at its best I was a fulfilled person, and so ready to be more completely sanctified by religious life if I let it. A religious community should be a place where human relationships can be fulfilled in depth, united as we are by a common aim and purpose, and with the consecration of the whole man and woman to God, life is balanced and all the faculties and emotions are redirected and thus gradually reach their full potential.

My years as a religious from 1929 to 1968 must be seen against the background of the changes in the world and in the religious life itself. There have been peak crisis points – e.g. from 1938 to 1941 and from 1948 to 1954, when I would have given anything under the sun to have got out of the religious life. This was *not* that I doubted my own personal call, but that I doubted profoundly whether the forms of religious life as we know it, either active or enclosed, could meet the challenge of the times or provide the setting where the real Gospel life of service of God and man could be fulfilled.

One was brought up against extreme forms of autocracy in government, outdated and outmoded social traditions which had been brought into being and absorbed by religious custom, the right initiative and freedom of the individual thwarted, and a general lack of Christian love and trust which seemed shattering and incompatible with the aims and ideals which religious life professes. Therefore as a younger nun I have been both frustrated and disillusioned, but somehow never doubted that the call for me

was a true one and that the religious life as a whole was a microcosm of the whole macrocosm of the Church, in its stuckness and
blindness. That is why for the last ten to fifteen years it has been
increasingly thrilling to be aware of the spirit of renewal and reform within the whole Church, and to realize that our community
has its part to play in this ecumenical age, in cutting right out
from the clogging conventionalities which have bogged down the
Church's and the religious life's witness, and to get down to the
fundamental principles which are both biblical and patristic in
origin.

The purpose of our community is that of all contemplative enclosed life (1) To bear witness to the primacy of God and to actu-
alize this Godcentredness right through the whole life, so that
nothing lies outside the ordinances of his will, as revealed through
the Christian premises and the Rule and Constitution of the community. This means in actual fact the sanctification of the whole
life so that the prayer and relationship – in fact the whole lot –
are seen as one whole, and one human activity is not put in opposition to any other. (2) Prayer is the life and work of the community. (3) The overspill of the prayer is the love and caring and
compassion of God's love for mankind, and an expansion farther through ecumenical channels (personal dialogue and encounter). Therefore (4) Love of the brethren, the giving of oneself
to serve the community and, through the community, the Church
and the world, with all that means of self loss, is the primary
purpose of the contemplative life.

Religious life and probably contemplative life in particular has
from the second century stood for the challenging and counter-
balancing of the conditions in the Church and world in any given
age. It is not higher than nor better than any other form of Christian witness, but it should provide for the individual the conditions
under which he or she can more completely give him or herself to
God and show forth to the world in terms of love and joy and self-
committal what it means to be a Christian. This community is
taking full part in the aggiornamento, which means an ever-
expanding form of apostolate as a proof of prayer, but the fundamental principles do not change in any age, and it is to these principles each successive generation must turn and see how far its
practice is answering the needs of the time.

I do not think I have stressed here sufficiently that religious life
should be seen in terms of *relationship*: man's relationship with
God, perfected in and through vocation; man's relationship with

man in God, perfected in and through vocation. This is only the Gospel – thou shalt love thy God, body, soul and spirit, and thy neighbour in God. Religious life is *Relationship* – not a code of moral life and behaviour; therefore it is organic and progressive.

3 *The monk's story*
(A Benedictine monk, aged thirty-two. He took simple vows eight years ago and solemn vows five years ago.)

About the age of thirteen I was conscious of a desire to do something large and generous with my life. I had no notion what this could be, and the desire itself was completely formless except that, having had from my Irish mother a 'good Catholic upbringing', I felt the Church to be the biggest thing around, in fact the only true thing. Therefore my life must in some way be involved in it. I didn't equate this with being a priest, but because my then Jesuit form-master at the local Catholic grammar school was the most loving and lovable person I had so far met I wondered whether his life was the thing for me. The 'religious' and priestly ideal meant nothing, or at least was completely remote; but this man somehow broke the conventional Jesuit behaviour pattern by showing an unconditional and disinterested concern for us, for our growth. I remember in particular that he took what I said with complete and unaffected seriousness in a way no one else quite did, which may explain why my one-year contact with him left a deep impression which still remains. Without moralizing he communicated a sense that life, our life, was intensely worthwhile, wholesome, and could be terrific fun. I don't think there was much, if any, romanticism or fantasy in my view of him; I wasn't shattered, though naturally puzzled and dismayed, to hear of his very severe mental breakdown soon after leaving us. He remained for me a vital person.

Through later school years and two years' National Service, I had no deep desire to do anything in particular with my life. My non-Christian father, remote in childhood owing to physical separation during the war years, was a solicitor and joining him seemed a sensible thing to do, especially as his business was self-made and the idea of a son inheriting it meant much to him. So it was with this fairly formed intention that I went from National Service to university, yet with a sense that this career, and indeed any career acceptable to most people I knew, was not quite real for me, somehow not adequate to my deepest desire and need. My father had very generously made it clear that any desire to be a priest would have his support, but this was not then appealing.

At university my only intimate friends were Old Boys of the school run by my present monastery. Through them and some of the younger monks also at university I came here first, largely out of curiosity to see the place which had produced my friends. The sophistication of their minds and the depth of their thinking about religion were a revelation after the prosaic and second-hand quality of religious instruction at the grammar school. Coming to the monastery for a few days was a deeply moving experience; a glimpse of a new, strange and curiously attractive world of which I wanted to be a part. I had no intellectual notion of what the monastic life was about – I wanted to be whatever these men were. Very simple so far.

At school I always moved happily in a like-minded group of friends, free of any emotional intensity. This pattern more or less repeated itself on National Service, except that the R C bit gave me a certain sense of apartness in this new irreligious atmosphere. My faith now demanded at least some degree of nonconformity to the group ethos, at least in terms of Sunday Mass and saying night prayers by my billet bed, scrutinized by at least one hostile witness. But I was on easy terms with almost everybody, and very dependent on a group of new but firm friends. It was at university (age twenty-one) that I first consciously and intensely loved anyone in particular. My narrowly formed R C conscience turned this experience into a morbid, guilt-ridden infatuation. This temporarily fixated relationship clogged the vocational issue because the person I loved (A) intended to join this monastery after university. This was at once a draw to the monastery and a repulsion from it; while desperately wanting to be always with A I felt guilty about this desire, which seemed a radical disqualification for the monastic life. Another friend, whom I now realize I loved more deeply (B), joined the monastery a year before I left university. I missed B very much in my last year and the thought of him in the monastery was a terrific pull, unclouded by the increasingly paralysing guilt associated with my immediate contemporary. My desire to be with my friends won out, although I seriously considered joining another monastery.

It seems clear to me now that it was quite simply human love which brought me here, although the attraction and inspiration of the place as a whole suggested a larger worth-whileness in living the life my friends proposed to lead. In letting my love lead me in this way I wondered very much whether I was really escaping, doing the nearest and most immediately appealing thing instead of something less congenial and more mundane, like my father's job. I couldn't exercise this doubt, and entered the monastery hoping rather desperately that all this would be resolved positively or negatively in the noviciate. It wasn't!

Things were further complicated by the noviciate-induced feeling that the search for and service of God were paramount, with love of other people as a kind of by-product of the God-and-prayer business. This made my emotional involvements a worry, a distracting irrelevance; yet I could never feel in my bones that they were no more than that. The fact that other people were absolutely important for me suggested that I was really in bad faith and should leave, or at least make the kind of psychological break with my friends which others seemed to find workable but which I felt to be beyond me. The recognized guides (books and older monks) had things to say about 'the problem of particular friendships', but they weren't adequate; they treated this as a *problem on its own*, never suggesting how such a relationship could be creative.

Sex was a closed book, so that the fact that my love included sexual attraction and desire made me think, at least with a part of myself, that it was outrageous, sinful, lustful, sacrilegious even. Words like 'sublimation', heard occasionally in the monastery, suggested there was an answer to be found, although the word itself was never enlightened in any practical way by the speaker. But I could never feel in my bones that loving another monk in this way was simply taboo, although often thinking that I ought to leave because of the intensity of the emotional-sexual pressure in the rather hothouse enclosed noviciate atmosphere. A further complication was the sense of not-quite-really about so much of the God-and-prayer business; this, I felt, was something I had to be able to take on and make my own, yet it never really connected with the rest of my life in any satisfactory way.

The first glimpse of anything I could honestly call 'certainty' about my vocation came in my fourth year here, when I began to be deeply influenced by an older monk. This was the year in which I had to try to reach a final decision about solemn vows, due that September. The terms in which superiors posed the problem – 'Do you really want to serve God in the monastic life?' – were artificial, presenting me with what I felt to be an unreal and therefore artificial question, although part of me felt this *ought* to be the real, decisive question. So it was a flash of light when this older monk (C), who had recently taken a more genuinely personal interest in me than any other older monk, suddenly said: 'The real vocational question is "Do you want to share the problem of this community?"' This struck home because it pin-pointed the sort of bond I already felt with the monastery in a way which seemed to unify all my hitherto fragmented concerns. The tension involved in my love for B was by no means resolved, but here at last was a conviction which made sense; a desire to help and serve this community in any way I could. In particular I thought of the commitment as helping the monks to resolve a spiritual crisis which their communal and personal history had clearly left radically unresolved at the time. I don't know what I thought I could do, but I wanted to be in on anything that happened. C communicated a strong sense that out of so much darkness and confusion some tremendous good would surely come. A deeply intuitive person, this conviction possessed him. Then, in the pre-solemn vows retreat, an old monk with the reputation of a highly intelligent eccentric, suddenly said, 'The eyes of the heart should be on all the brethren all the time.' I wondered why I had had to wait four years to hear this from a monastic preacher: I took solemn vows.

Subsequently I became ever more involved in C's struggle to articulate his new-found conviction about the Christian life and the monk's life ('You either marry or go it alone – if you take the second option it turns out to be going it with everybody.') His preaching was the service of the community as the key to what it meant to be a Christian and a monk. Deeply influenced by Teilhard de Chardin, he discerned a unity in the whole of creation and in personal experience, which was for me a liberation. I could never understand how I was such a help to him, since I seemed little more than a sounding-board for his ideas. He was so conscious of the mawkish sterility of even the most positive elements in the received teaching on particular friendship that he seemed to deny the relevance of emotional intensity between people, despite a message of love. So while giving me a firm conviction that we were working towards a re-birth of our own community in an unimaginable oneness of mind and heart, he couldn't fully resolve my personal uncertainty. I thought he would have been dismayed and outraged had I told him of my real feelings towards my contemporaries. There was very great emotional intensity in his talking and teaching, but a very deep inhibition prevented any clear articulation of this.

Recently we have been given a new insight into the equation of the communal and the personal which simplifies the whole business and leaves me with a new and deeper certainty that the love of one another is the only worthwhile thing, that it is this and only this which creates community, that only growth in this love will equip us for service in the wider world beyond the monastery to which we must increasingly look. This is no longer a largely notional conviction, still less a maudlin sentimentality, but an increasing intuitive awareness of the reality of others and of how we can in fact help to create each others' lives. The obverse of this is an increasing realism about the impossibility of really loving, the recognition that whatever real further change we can initiate in one another will be, like what has happened to us so far, a gift to us all.

This, then, is my present vocational certainty: a clear-headed involvement in the creation of a community to serve the world in a way which will hasten its end. I see this as the unification of my hitherto fragmented experience in the ability at last to begin to love others straightforwardly and wholeheartedly without fear or scruple. One consequence is that the options are now open in a new way: I am no longer worried as to whether or not I am a 'queer', but neither am I worried about what would happen if I were to fall in love with a woman. Ultimately I doubt whether full spiritual freedom can be reached without an intense man-woman relationship, but I don't see the sexual consummation as essential. Indeed, it seems that relationships which by-pass the immediate consummation have a special function in building up the whole human community and precipitating its final fulfilment in God – this is what I mean by the end of the world.

I should add that what has brought me to my present certainty is a sense of *being loved* unequivocally. The sense of being wholesomely and unconditionally loved has begun to release in me the power to love, so that more and more people are now clear to me as growing vessels of the Spirit, in whose growth is my salvation. This may sound a piece of abstract or pietistic wishful thinking, but I am writing out of an experience which has rapidly stripped me of many illusions and self-defences, out of a newly discovered sense of my own real self and others' real selves which is deeply unromantic and open-ended (but emphatically not *unfelt*). An older confrère not at present resident in the monastery has called this the recovery of sanity; if it reads like the belated discovery by a deeply neurotic person of a basic human truth familiar in childhood to more normal people then my language has failed me.

This is a love which *is* for ever; I am certain of my brethren, whatever they may do, say or think, now or in the future. This certainty works outwards into other relationships, producing for instance a new and exciting freedom in family relationships and leading to an increasingly direct and genuine contact with a wider range of people.

As hinted above, I think the purpose of our life together is to bring the world to an end by the practice of an all-embracing, open-ended love. Few monks would accept this without cavil – many would find it incomprehensible or shocking. And this conviction would be an absurd, delusive fantasy if it didn't illuminate Christian and monastic tradition. But all the classical monastic doctrines now take on a new fullness of meaning: the search for God, loving obedience, communal prayer (effective sign of our love's present achievement and future fulfilment), so-called private or personal prayer (to facilitate some depth of reflective awareness of reality, of all that is and how it moves), the flight from the world (i.e., the darkness, whatever requires exorcism in Harvey Cox's sense, of *The Secular City*). The world is intensely present in the monastery; this stripped-down way of living together heightens consciousness of what is truly dark and unresolved in all our lives.

The monk least of all can avoid the burden of consciousness of the whole human spectrum and the insistent challenge to new ways of spiritual action which that consciousness provokes. Perhaps we can define the monastery's function as exorcism. True, that is the Church's function – but the monks are explicitly and consciously committed to this task. If a monastic community can be exorcised, what task is beyond it? I have known sufficient exorcism to believe total exorcism possible.

THE TURNING-POINT

'Suddenly, the fact of being a human being seems wildly liberating.' – SISTER MARYELLEN MUCKEN-HIRN CSC, *American Catholic Exodus*, p. 119

'Monks are found to view the question of reform in different ways. The seasoned religious will tend to see it as the rusty turnstile through which we all at one time or another must want to pass. But he will be quite happy at having himself turned back in time. To him it represents an artificial device which does not so much introduce to the promised land as separate from it. He has so often seen monks getting stuck in that turnstile for good. He thinks of sound men wasted on a superficial cause, going round and round, with self leaning nearer to the centre of it.' – DOM HUBERT VAN ZELLER OSB, *The Benedictine Idea*, p. 81

THERE have been many great turning-points in the history of the religious life. Benedict was responsible for the first of them, when he brought order out of chaos, when he introduced the idea of a close community life, when he composed the theme which has been developed and re-arranged but which has never been substantially challenged as the basis of monasticism from his day until this. Francis and Dominic led another change of direction by taking their disciples and their faith out into the world, to convert it by exhortation instead of praying for it and for themselves within the security of the monastic walls. Ignatius founded a society to defend the faith against all comers and by all means when it seemed likely to be demolished by the Reformation; it was the first time the Church found itself with its back to the wall, attacked by an enemy from within its own ranks on its own terms; and that was a turning-point, too. Yet none of these shifts and changes are of greater significance than the ones taking place today. History may eventually see the middle of the twentieth century as the moment when the religious life lurchingly rounded a bend much more acute than Benedict navigated fourteen hundred years ago. It is so sharp a turn, and the vehicle traversing it is so top-heavy with tradition, so uncertain in its steering mechanism, that some gloomy souls at present wonder whether it will, in fact, make it safely; they can foresee the awful possibility of flying off at a tangent half-way round and ending up catastrophically in some utterly irreligious ditch by the side of the road. This is, of course, no more than the predicament of the Church at large, writ small in the microcosmic world of the cloister and the wimple and the threefold vow.

Like the Church as a whole the religious have seen the need for changes in the structure of their lives, some of them fundamental. Reappraisal has nowhere been more agonizing than in the matter of religious poverty.

Religious poverty as it is generally interpreted today entails the inability of the religious, the monk or the friar, the nun or sister, to possess anything. Whatever they need is provided by the community, in many instances frugally enough, in others on a more lavish scale. The individual's poverty consists in not owning anything in the sense that he (or she) has no dominion over what is provided for his (or her) use. Communities, as such, may be considerable property owners, powerful corporations with large resources. Now poverty as it is experienced (as distinct from practised) outside the monastic enclosure is somewhat different in scope; it embraces a whole family, not just individual members of it, and although it consists in a lack of property (in this it is the same for the private individual as for the monk or nun) it includes also the consequences of such a lack, among which is to be numbered insecurity and dependence on others – and also dependence on a weekly wage packet or, in unemployment, on the allowance made by the state insurance system, if any. It is probably in this last respect that the contrast with religious poverty, as it is interpreted by canon law, is particularly obvious. A solemn vow of poverty, provided the religious is not guilty of some heinous offence, nowadays amounts in practice to security for life. All this is not to say that canonical poverty is meaningless or has outgrown its usefulness, but the contrast between it and actual poverty has been shown in this way in order the clearer to show the ideal of poverty practised by the Petits Frères. They *share* the poverty of those among whom they live – lower-paid labourers, peasants in under-developed countries, casual agricultural workers and the like. This 'witness to the poverty of Christ' (in de Foucauld's words) is the clearer because it is easily understood by those whose lives they share.

That, as it happens, is the comment of a layman. But much the same attitude is today being struck by priests and by religious themselves. The Bishop of Arras has pointed out one traditional offence against real poverty which has been perpetrated under the guise of fortifying chastity. He has cited the example of the nun travelling from a community in Paris to another community in Lyons, who has been obliged to take two sisters with her – one as her chaperone, the other as chaperone to the chaperone on the return journey; which has made the cost of her journey four times what it need have been. An English Benedictine monk, recalling the vast baroque palaces like Melk inhabited at great expense these days by brethren of his order, has observed that there seems to be something wrong with an economy which requires an income of about £1,000 per head to keep a monk in holy poverty. An American Benedictine has pointed out a local flaw in the system.

Trips away from the monastery or convent are a problem. Custom varies. In some congregations a time away each year is regularized, ten days or more either in a mountain retreat owned by the community or with the family or friends. For those who are allowed to 'go into the world' for a period in the summer a real problem exists. . . . In our sophisticated society eager friends want to give the returned solitary a good time, meaning an entertaining time. Friends are so generous; trips to Florida or Cape Cod or Europe may not cost the monastery a cent. Of course, it would be against poverty to be spending all that money on a first-class fare to the south of Spain, but if the friends pick up the bill . . . the Superior may be nonplussed or a little hesitant, especially when friends have been good to the house – perhaps built the library and set up a fund for further education of the young religious; it would be ungrateful to refuse. After that a precedent has been set. Next

year there are other tempting offers, which can hardly be refused
when the first has been accepted. People tell us that these trips are
very economical. But economy is not the same thing as poverty.

An English Carmelite prioress has detected another jarring
note.

What convents and institutions should be interested in today is
the tableware used by the average unpretentious family: deal
tables instead of oak benches; stainless steel rather than hand-
carved or turned wooden spoons; not pottery platters and earthen-
ware ewers that look charming and medieval, but Woolworth's
china, glassware, or even that ultimate abomination of our century,
plastic.

And René Voillaume, Prior of the Petits Frères, has suggested a more subtle danger to the life of poverty as it is
known in real rather than religious terms. He has written
that:

We need a clearer idea of the relationship between the priestly
calling of a Petit Frère and the general mission of the priest in the
Church. This calling of a Petit Frère to be a priest involves its
own difficulties. The reason which made Brother Charles of Jesus
hesitate when he was thinking about ordination to the priesthood is
today as valid as ever; it is the difficulty of reconciling the status
of a cleric, and the signs of a dignified position which the Church
attaches to it, with the social status of poverty and toil essential to
the calling of a Petit Frère.

Alongside poverty the religious concept of obedience is
being re-examined. Nothing has struck more firmly at one
tradition than Cardinal Suenens's insistence that the chief
consideration 'is not the abdication of one's own will nor
the submission to a person, it is loyalty to the common good
as an expression of God's will. ... The superior has the
final decision, the last word – but not the second-last word.
... To think that one obeys in the first instance in order to
renounce one's own will, is to start on a path that leads nowhere ...' And, taking him at his word, religious have
started to make their own caustic observations on the
application of obedience. An Anglican deaconess has written

that 'For a religious to have to telegraph to England from Africa before accepting an invitation out to a meal even in connection with the work suggests a caricature not only of obedience but of religious poverty.' The criticisms have begun to produce results. Some of the greater deferences to superiors have now been abandoned. In the Belgian Congregation of Benedictines the abbot is now addressed as 'père abbé' instead of 'révérendissime père abbé'; at the Belgian Abbey of Maredsous the abbot's ring is no longer normally kissed by his brethren when they have audience of him. Various antique mortifications practised under obedience are on their way out; since 1967 the Poor Clare nuns have been allowed to sleep lying down instead of sitting up in special beds, as they used to.

The very heart of the religious life, the liturgy, is being overhauled perhaps more thoroughly than any other part of it. An Anglican superior has pointed out the difficulty for an active religious of reconciling his work with the need to say the seven-fold office each day; it has very often meant cramming a number of the offices together either before or after work so as to fulfil the quota ordained by tradition, 'which is as if a man should kiss his wife good morning and good-night at the same time, in order to get it over and save him having to do so later on when the time comes'. His own order, the Community of the Resurrection, has experimentally dropped the lesser offices since the beginning of 1967 and now makes do with matins at 6.45 a.m., mass at 7.15 a.m., a 'midday office' at 1 p.m., evensong at 7.0 p.m. and compline at 9.45 p.m. The English Congregation of Benedictine monks, which tends to include a lot of schoolmasters, not only rises and retires now at the more academic hours of 7 a.m. and 11 p.m., but has altered its liturgy so that 150 psalms are chanted in a fortnight instead of a week. The Dutch Augustinian friars have not only trimmed their offices; they have also re-bound their breviaries as loose-leaved books because they expect to be amending their forms and patterns of worship for some time to come. At the Benedictine monastery of Mount Saviour, in New York, they have taken a leaf from Taizé's book by redistributing the psalms so that 150 can still be chanted in a week while short periods of reflective silence are introduced into the office. At the Benedictine abbey of Bec, in France, they are conducting the most radical liturgical experiment of all. On Sundays women oblates, who live a modified Benedictine Rule in the world, sing part of the office and mass in the choir with the monks.

While experiments with the structure of the religious life have been carried out there have been moves to redirect it, where possible, to more effective employment in the world. In the United States three Franciscan Missionary Sisters have taken a downtown apartment in Portland, Oregon, where they teach remedial reading to backward children and counsel slum dwellers; forty Glenmary Sisters have detached themselves from their mother house in Cincinnati and started a new community in Appalachia to teach and nurse among the poor. In Britain the Anglican Community of the Resurrection closed its priory in a middle-class London suburb in 1968 and moved across the city to premises in a slum area; with the monks went a group of deaconesses to share in social and pastoral work there. Even ten years ago the idea of men and women religious joining forces in work, let alone sharing the same buildings to eat and sleep in, would have stunned anyone in the religious life, from a Carthusian nun to a Presbyterian minister doing his shift with the Iona community. It is, in fact, no more than a restoration of the dual community which existed in the early Middle Ages at Whitby and elsewhere. Yet nothing shows the extent to which some religious would re-adapt the life more than the pressure which Dutch Dominican novices successfully applied to their superiors in 1967 to let them study agriculture rather than theology, so that they might go after profession to work rather than to preach in underdeveloped countries.

Many of the changes now afoot are doubtless the result of much cross-fertilization that has been quietly taking place during the past few years. As in the Church at large, denominational boundaries are counting for less and less – which is not, by any means, to say that they count for nothing yet – and are being crossed more and more frequently and with a greater sense of security. This is not just a matter of occasional visiting; it has, in some cases, meant residence over a long period. There have been Catholic and Orthodox priests at Protestant Taizé for two or three years now. Swedish monks of the Protestant Brotherhood of the Holy Cross have been living with the Benedictines of Ehrlach in Austria. At the abbey of Boquen, in northern France, American Episcopalians and Methodists have been sharing the common life and worship of the resident Trappist monks. And in the process of these visitations different ideas and outlooks have been channelled back and forth between the various sects of the Church involved. At the same time guests and hosts have discovered that not much of importance divides them in their understanding of what the religious life is and should be about. One of the Franciscans who has been attached to Taizé has written that 'If we did not have the separate Eucharist – the great sign of unity which still reminds us of our separation – there would be almost no difference between us.'

Other influences have been at work besides those exerted by itinerant individuals. Few things have shaped the present course of the religious life more than the philosophies of Taizé and of the Petits Frères, as they have been expounded in the writings of Roger Schutz, Charles de Foucauld and René Voillaume. They run so closely parallel as to make one almost suspect collusion, though neither Voillaume nor Schutz has ever acknowledged the existence of the other in print, so far as I am aware. Yet together they have damned the traditional concept of religious poverty for the sham thing it so often has been. Together they have rejected the idea of converting, in any accepted sense, the agnostic or half-believing world. Together they have insisted on the prime importance of contemplative prayer in the midst of worldly activity and have tried to exemplify this in their communities. Together they have argued that the Christian duty in the world is unselfconsciously to take the next man as you find him and to offer him everything in the way of care and affection that he wants; nothing more, or less. In tandem these philosophies, the one Protestant, the other Catholic, are gradually being absorbed across the religious world.

They are not, perhaps, as codes of conduct, very distinguishable from some that have been spawned by pure agnosticism; and agnosticism too can be seen pressing the religious world into a different shape. There never was a time when more mass movements driven by high humanitarian ideals were shifting without a thought for God across the face of the earth. Many American religious superiors have seen the unrest in their communities, the defections of people in vows and the comparatively sudden lack of vocations, as a direct result of what they call the Peace Corps mentality. In the Peace Corps and in its equivalents in other countries (Voluntary Service Overseas in Britain, for example) the religious and potential religious of this generation can see a philosophy in action which is far closer to the precepts of the Christian gospel than most of the social patterns established by the Church; and if the Church cannot learn to follow this example then they will, heedless of official Christian sanctions. Thomas Merton has suggested another reason why, at this particular point of time, the religious world should have begun to move from its fixed positions again. He thinks that those who came to monasticism before the Second World War were comparatively little influenced by thinkers such as Marx and Darwin, Kierkegaard and Nietzsche, Freud and Jung, Adler and Sartre, Heidegger and Teilhard; most of this thought was not only banned from the monastery by the enclosure; it was forbidden the average Catholic at any stage in his education. The end of the war not only prised open the enclosure a little but it also brought a crop of vocations in men already acquainted with writers who had all 'in one way or another concerned themselves very deeply with the predicament of modern man; with his special needs, his peculiar hopes, his chances of attaining those hopes . . .'

The cross-fertilization process is probably going to be taken many stages farther than most Catholics and Protestants can imagine at the moment – or, in many cases, would care to think of. For an attempt has been made to integrate the Christian and the Hindu religious life and it is at present quietly flourishing in the Kurisumala Ashram. This is a monastery in Kerala, in south-west India, founded jointly in 1958 by a Cistercian and a Benedictine who had gone separately to the country in the hope of establishing some kind of contemplative life there. The Cistercian, the Belgian Dom Francis Mahieu, had already been involved in an experiment at Trichinopoly, in Madras, where two French priests, Father Monchanin and Father le Saux, had started an ashram (the Hindu term for a group of disciples living in community under a spiritual guide) on completely Hindu lines. The two priests had taken Hindu names, becoming Swami Paramarubananda and Swami Abhishiktananda. They had worn the saffron habit of the Hindu monk, had gone barefoot, and lived on a vegetarian diet in small thatched huts. They had worshipped in a chapel designed like a Hindu temple and their Christian liturgy had been in a mixture of Sanskrit, Tamil and Latin. It was far too bold an identification with its local religious culture for Indian Catholics and so it foundered for lack of vocations. But out of it came Kurisumala.

Kerala is a stronghold of that eastern branch of Catholicism, the Syrian Church, and this has added another ingredient to the intriguing mixture that has been made there. When Kurisumala was started :

The Rule of St Benedict was adopted as the basis and it was interpreted according to the strict Cistercian observance. The centre of the monastery's life became the Syrian liturgy with its emphasis on biblical theology. A quiet period of silent prayer varying from five minutes to a quarter of an hour is practised after each liturgical exercise. This is done in Indian fashion by sitting cross-legged on the floor. Other measures have been introduced to conform in general to the pattern of Indian life. The monks go barefoot, eat with their hands while sitting in the cross-legged position, sleep on mats on low wooden beds, and wear the kavi or saffron-coloured dress of the Indian sannyasin. For deeper spiritual contact with Indian tradition, they are studying Indian philosophy and religious systems, and practise some yoga exercises. They are cultivating their lands and developing a dairy farm and a medical dispensary.

There has been a small but steady trickle of vocations. A cynic might well suppose that the adoption of certain local habits of dress, diet and posture is merely a bait in order to proselytize more successfully. The only trouble with this theory is that it discounts the effect of the local environment and culture upon the proselyte's own system, when these are embraced as closely as they have been by the Christian monks of Kurisumala. Already the weightier monastic journals of Christendom have thoughtfully noted comparisons between classical Hindu literature, such as The Upanishads and the Bhagavad-Gita, and their Christian equivalents. And one of the Kurisumala monks, Dom Bede Griffiths, has reported back his own conclusions for the future:

It seems to me that it is the task of the Church in India to bring the light of Christ, of Christian revelation, to bear on this original intuition (of the classical Hindu philosophers), to complete the Vedanta, as it were, by introducing a new point of view. In this way we should not be simply introducing a new doctrine but continuing the work of Sankara, Ramanuja, Madhva and the other doctors of the Vedanta. But this means that we have first to enter into the intuition of the Upanishads, to understand Hindu doctrine as it were from within, and this is surely the work of a contemplative. No amount of conceptual skill will suffice, no attempt to graft St Thomas on to the Vedanta. There must be the discovery within ourselves, in the depths of our own souls, of the Self, the Atman; and what can this be but the discovery of Christ? Thus the study of Hinduism, if it is to bear any fruit, must lead us to a renewal in depth of our own religion, a rediscovery of that mystical presence of Christ in us which lies behind all our theology. But this discovery will be along lines which are indicated by the Hindu tradition.

And though talk of bearing fruit may still have an ominous sound to the cynic, no one ever entered someone else's intuition and came away unmarked.

The purely western religious life has enough problems of its own to sort out before it begins to take any strain which will be imposed if at some time in the future it tries to graft onto itself elements of other religious philosophies. The most formidable one, at present, is the condition of the individual. No one can be sure precisely what has motivated the increasing number of people who have abandoned their vows and walked out of the religious life in the past few years; it is likely that many are not sure themselves. Certainly some will have gone because they do not believe that the world (or God) is adequately served by the religious life in its present state. But many have opted out simply because they themselves can no longer endure the life; and the thing that ought, where it doesn't already, make religious authority ponder very deeply the elements of the life is the fact that so often the defections remove men and women of considerable experience, who have been monks, nuns or friars for several years. They have not gone back to the world after a small flirtation with religion, but after a thorough trial which may have lasted a decade or more. It is possible that this has always been the case and that until comparatively recently we never heard about it; it is rather more likely that until recently the sanctions of the Church seemed so terrible that they deterred anyone from breaking religious vows but the men or women who were past caring about the ultimate fate of their souls. The breach in the enclosure which admitted Freud and Nietzsche, Sartre and Teilhard and the rest also admitted doubts about the terrors promised defectors by the Church. It is the richest irony confronting the Church, both in the microcosmic world of religion and in the world at large, that to have invoked non-Christian thought in a genuine attempt to understand more clearly the Christian vocation on earth has meant enormous disillusionment with Christian practice and sometimes with the faith itself; has meant, in the Church as a whole, a colossal loss of even nominal membership. It may seem inevitable to the non-Christian, but that doesn't relieve the confusion among the Christians.

The individual pressures which have caused people to leave the religious life in order to save themselves from what they have taken, consciously or not, to be a kind of personal destruction have been against a system which has traditionally been designed quite deliberately to suppress the distinctive quality of the individual. They have been pressures against a concept of obedience which has meant the total renunciation of will. They have been pressures against a concept of chastity which has meant that a demonstration of warmth and affection in any terms the world would recognize has been vilified as something not far short of promiscuity and which has seen to it that behaviour a long, long way short of that has been hallmarked as the norm. They have meant, at last, that religious have seen themselves too often being moulded in the image not of Christ but of Tennyson's Maud – 'faultily faultless, icily regular, splendidly null'.

So the traditional view of the 'particular friendship' has been increasingly under attack this past two or three years. A pointer to the way ahead has been provided, yet again, by the Petits Frères. Standing pat not on twentieth-century psychology but on the habits of Christ himself, René Voillaume has indicated the impossibility of genuinely loving people in general without burnishing the capacity for love in a deep relationship with one or two in particular.

It is true that the love of friendship which unites us to our Lord also demands that we should love all our brethren in like manner. But this seems obviously impossible, unless indeed we are talking about something other than genuine friendship. The restrictions imposed by human life on earth make it impossible for us to acquire and exhibit feelings of friendship towards any considerable number of our brethren and, *a fortiori*, towards all those who cross our path. How, then, can it be possible for the love of friendship in our Lord's name and expressed towards all men to become the perfect fulfilment of the commandment to love? In fact, however,

Jesus does not ask us to acquire a conscious feeling of friendship towards everybody, but to have a heart sufficiently open and humble and alert to others, and above all to be spontaneous enough to be capable of friendship should it become possible here and now. We must understand the commandment to love and try to obey it in terms of what is possible in our human situation as it actually is, a situation so confined that in reality we are able to have a few friends only. Why should this surprise us? Was not our Lord so restricted by his circumstances on earth that he was unable to have more than a very few men and women as his intimate friends?

A Dominican has pushed the point even further and nearer the knuckle of the religious life. 'In the last resort', he suggests,

it is better to run the risk of an occasional scandal than to have a monastery – a choir, a refectory, a recreation room – full of dead men. Our Lord did not say 'I am come that ye may have more safety and have it abundantly.' Some of us would indeed give anything to feel safe, about our life in this world as in the next, but we cannot have it both ways: safety or life, we must choose.

While the choice is being made the pressures continue to build up, the defectors continue to return to the world outside, and some of those remaining turn to psychiatry for salvation. In one case, at Cuernavaca in Mexico, a whole monastery put itself under the psychiatrist, an adventure that ended in its dissolution. It was an attempt by the prior, Dom Gregoire LeMercier, to resolve the tensions and the individual problems of the monastic vocation and it deserved better than its ultimate end. LeMercier is a Belgian who had been professed as a Benedictine at the abbey of Mont-César before the war. After serving as an army chaplain he went, on demobilization, to Mexico and in 1951 established the monastery of Santa Maria de la Resurreccion near Cuernavaca, in accordance with the primitive Benedictine observance as practised at La Pierre Qui Vire and elsewhere. He was the only European in a community of Mexican Indians.

In 1960 he had an ecstatic vision, 'a host of brilliant, multi-

coloured flashes of light, of extreme beauty, followed by a
screen over which passed a succession of faces, stopping at
one beautiful face radiating goodness. LeMercier began to
weep, feeling his own inadequacy before God's love, a
curious mixture of defeat, of God controlling him, and of
great joy, which lasted several hours.' He called in a
Freudian analyst, a Dr Quevedo, whom he knew to be interested in religious questions. After several months of treatment by Quevedo LeMercier felt able to say that 'The long
ascesis of psychoanalysis has led me to a spiritual life which
I had been unable to reach after thirty years of monastic life,
filling me with a joy and confidence which nothing can de-
stroy.' At about the same time it was discovered that he had
contracted an operable cancer in his left eye; and medical
opinion was that the cancer had begun at about the
same time as LeMercier's vision.

LeMercier was so impressed with his general improvement at the hands of Quevedo that he decided to begin
group therapy for his monks. It became a part of the novitiate and it was managed not only by Quevedo but also by a
woman, Dr Frida Zmud. This was a deliberate choice by
LeMercier. He argued that sexuality was too often ignored
or suppressed by those offering themselves to the religious
life and that confrontation with Dr Zmud on the threshold
of their intended vocation would bring them face to face
with the issue most crucial to their survival as human beings
in the religious life. They would be forced to recognize their
degree of sexuality and they would have to decide before they
got anywhere near life vows whether this allowed them to
cope with existence in a 'homosexual' society. The result of
the early confrontations was that a number of professed
monks left and returned to the world, sometimes to get
married; many novices failed to complete their training.
But by 1965, when the psychiatrists had been attending
Cuernavaca for four years, thirty monks were in residence
and LeMercier claimed that the life of the monastery had
become more effective and more harmonious. Departures
had diminished. In 1962 fifteen men had left, in 1963 six-

teen, in 1964 five, in 1965 two. Vocations were increasing.

The astonishing thing is that the Vatican allowed the experiment to go so far before prohibiting it. The Archbishop of Mexico City had, after all, been calling LeMercier a demon and the Abbot Primate of the Benedictines at the time had said he was a shame upon the order. In fact, in 1961, when the psychiatric treatment had been going for only a few months, the Congregation for Religious had sent two observers to Cuernavaca to find out just what was happening there; it is said that they reported to Rome in Le-Mercier's favour. It was not until October 1965 that Le-Mercier received the imperial summons to present himself to Cardinal Ottaviani, at the head of the Curia. He was told that the experiment must end and that he must return to Belgium. He refused and asked that the matter should be put into the hands of the pope. The pope appointed three cardinals to examine the situation. In 1967 they delivered their verdict. LeMercier was to return to Cuernavaca but he was forbidden to dabble in psychiatry again; he was also to carry out spiritual exercises in the abbey of St Jerome as punishment for his obduracy. He did return, but not in the prescribed manner. In June 1967 he announced that he and his monks had renounced their monastic vows, had severed their connection with the Benedictine order, and would in future work in conjunction with the Emaus Psychoanalysis Centre.

The Vatican's verdict against LeMercier suggests not only alarm at the upheaval that might be caused if psychiatry were let loose across the face of the religious world. It seems to be yet another refusal to look the facts of life straight in the eye. It is one more example of the Catholic Church's disinclination to acknowledge the existence of sex *qua* sex in the lives of its professional man- and woman-power. In the case of religious this is not confined to Roman Catholicism. There is no reason to suppose that, in degree at any rate, the sexual composition of a religious community is much different from that of any other sort; it will contain some who are highly sexed and some whose sexual drive is low; it will include both heterosexuals and homosexuals of different potencies. The fact that most of these at the beginning of their vocation are either unaware of their sexuality or are attempting to ignore it, with the whole weight of religious tradition actively encouraging them to do so, is the one thing that distinguishes them sharply from most other groups of people. Sexuality is not a thing that can be ignored or that can leave the individual unaware indefinitely. It can obviously be repressed, but at some cost. It can doubtless be channelled into something short of full physical expression, but again at some cost, if it is not to cause – in the terms of the religious life – some scandal. The cost of repression in the circumstances is sometimes scandal when sexuality asserts itself beyond control; more often it is an emotional and physical crisis which either causes the individual to abandon vows and walk out or which damages his personality for the rest of his life, turning him at best into something like Tennyson's Maud. A monk I know had to leave his order, with the connivance of his superiors and brethren, after medical and psychiatric treatment, because after many years under vows he had reached this critical point; for much of that time he had suffered a permanent headache; for the twelve months preceding his release he had endured a nightmare every single night and its pattern had always been the same – he or someone else had been killing him. If from the outset of his religious vocation he had been taught to channel his sexual energy in some way short of scandal he might have been able to continue as a monk – as he wanted to do, even when he recognized that he must and could not – with nothing more than a sense of loss; and perhaps the sense of lost sexual outlet is for the religious the imitation of Christ on earth, the small crucifixion which is to be borne without despair.

But all this needs to be recognized and if there is one thoroughly frightening thing about the religious life it is the general failure to recognize sexuality for what it is, for what it can be, and for the part it plays in personality. The most fundamental questions about sex are left unanswered, not only in literature written by religious for religious but in the verbal training of novitiates. What, for example, is the monk to do if he wakes up in the middle of the night bursting with sexual desire? Is he to masturbate? Is he to fling himself on the stone cold floor (as the handiest alternative to St Benedict's nettlebed) in the hope that this will cool his ardour? Or is he merely to seize his breviary and trust that prayer will drive the demon out? A superior, far less inhibited than most, says that every one of these methods has been tried though very few people in religion are prepared to admit the existence of the first – or even of a situation which may require it. Novices in that particular community are advised to try working themselves to exhaustion, or the cold floor, or prayer if need be. They are told that if none of these methods succeeds they will have to masturbate to relieve their tensions. They are also told that if by the end of the novitiate masturbation is still the only way of coping with their sex they had better pack up and return to the world. One cannot be sure, but one gets the impression that very few novices elsewhere have ever been given such straightforward advice. And from no one else have I ever heard it suggested that life vows will one day have to be scrapped altogether in favour of renewable vows over much shorter periods, purely because of the sexual problem.

An unflinching look at sex is the chief need of the religious life if the problems of the individual's condition are to be resolved. At the same time the whole ethos requires re-examination if monasticism and other forms of religious practice are not to founder slowly through lack of vocations from people who do not believe that these can any longer serve a valuable Christian purpose in their present shape. Again this is the problem of the Church as a whole in miniature. The Church has not yet shaken off the double standard applied to the world by St Augustine of Hippo, and the religious life has been pickled in it even more deeply than the secular. Augustine was not the first Christian to insist on it; Clement of Alexandria advanced the theory at the start of the third century, two hundred years before him; but Augustine was its supreme exponent, particularly in his book *City of God*, which was written under the influence of Christian Rome's capitulation to the barbaric Alaric in AD 410. Its opening words set the tone for what is to come. 'That most glorious society and celestial city of God's faithful is partly seated in the course of these declining times, wherein he that liveth by faith is a pilgrim amongst the wicked.' From there Augustine takes some time to get to the heart of his philosophy. But in the twenty-eighth chapter of his fourteenth volume he writes:

Two loves therefore have given origin to these two cities – self-love in contempt of God unto the earthly; love of God in contempt of one's self to the heavenly. The first seeketh the glory of men and the latter desires God only, as the testimony of the conscience, the greatest glory. That glories in itself and this in God. That exalteth itself in its own glory; this saith to God 'My glory and the lifter-up of my head'. That boasteth of the ambitious conquerors led by the lust of sovereignty; in this everyone serveth other in charity. . . . [In the earthly city] the wise men follow either the goods of the body, or mind, or both, living according to the flesh, and such as might know God honoured him not as God, but became vain in their own imaginations, and their foolish heart was darkened: . . . but in the other, this heavenly city, there is no wisdom of men but only the piety that serveth the true God and expecteth a reward in the society of the holy angels and men, that God may be all in all.

If any five sentences have fixed the Christian Church, and especially its religious life, in an attitude of superiority over the rest of mankind for the last fifteen hundred years then those are they. For the Church needed no pressure to identify itself with the heavenly city and inside the Church the progression was continued; the religious state was held to be more estimable than the secular, the contemplative higher than the active, the celibate worthier than the married. A number of biblical texts have been adduced to support some of these theories – St Paul's apparent penchant for celibacy and the Martha–Mary passage in Luke among them – by Christian philosophers ever since. But the arguments have always been made within the framework built by St Augustine, who in some of his other writings enlarged upon specific points. 'The mother', he wrote elsewhere, 'will have a lower place in heaven than the daughter, because she is married, while her daughter is a virgin. ... Both will be in heaven, but the one as a bright star, the other as a dim one.' This is a philosophy which has been challenged from time to time; St Thomas Aquinas insisted that the monastic life was no more than one of many ways of striving for perfection, not perfection itself or the only way to perfection; every word of Charles de Foucauld, René Voillaume, Roger Schutz and many other religious writing today makes the same point. Yet the philosophy has remained as the basis of the religious life, has been accepted as its justification. When, in 1950, representatives of all forms of Catholic religious life met in Rome for their first general congress they called themselves the General Congress on the States of Perfection. When, in 1967, the BBC made a television film of the Trappist monastery at Nunraw in Scotland, an old monk told his interviewer that he wouldn't stay in the cloister three days if he didn't think he was thereby going to heaven. A booklet which the Benedictines of Buckfast Abbey offer the tourists refers to 'the more perfect life of the monastery'. A French religious writes of 'the white-hot Christianity of monastic life'.

St Augustine is no longer good enough in a world which is no longer prepared to accept self-assertion as the only evaluation of either man or institution; which prefers to make its own judgements, and to make them on performance alone. Over the past decade the Church's realization of this has quickened; it will be one overpowering reason why it has attended of late to the Bultmanns, the Bonhoeffers and the Teilhards, who much earlier than the official body of the Church sought to reorientate Christianity in a twentieth-century context; why it has thrown up more recently the writings of men like Kung and Robinson, working with the same end in view; why, within the sphere of Roman Catholic influence, many of its leaders were seen to be

clamouring for adjustment to the age they live in at the
Vatican Council. Faithful Christians call all this the
movement of the Holy Spirit, while the agnostic host sees it
as an accommodation to a world which the Church can no
longer hope to influence unless its ways are mended. Which-
ever it is, movement and accommodation are unmistakably
there. They are also present within the religious life. It is
being seen increasingly both by secular and religious Christians that the doctrines of Augustine must be replaced, that
the Church's claims must henceforth rest upon a different
theology, based less upon a notion of perfection than upon
one of vision, less upon an attitude of superiority than upon
one of service. Gradually the theology is being hammered
out; but it has not yet been formulated into a code which
the Church as a whole can assimilate. The question for
religious, no less than for the Church of which they are a
part, is whether it can be done fast enough before the whole
structure crumbles irreparably. An American has already
dared to suggest that his order, the Dominican, will have
disappeared inside twenty years. The temptation, for the religious as well as for the Church, is merely to make adjustments to the existing order of things, either as a concession
to popular demand or to provide a breathing space before a
thorough overhaul. Yet the writing on the wall is too
emphatic to allow either any longer. Its tale for the Church
in general is one of increasing disobedience to the most rigid
rules (in, for example, the growing number of Roman
Catholics who practise non-Catholic methods of birth
control) and of mounting unconcern for the more lenient
requirements (in the dwindling congregations of Protestantism). Its tale for the religious life is one of scanty vocations
and of vows being abandoned at a rate unheard of before.
A few turns of the spanner in the religious works are not
going to correct that. There must be, as Bishop Huyghe
has pointed out, a complete re-reading of the Gospels rather
than a return to the ideals expressed by the founders of
religious orders.

There is a resistance to the notion of radical change in

the religious life; there was bound to be. There is no reason
to suppose that the reformers, who may be among the most
articulate of religious, are anything but a small minority.
There are cries for change from half a dozen countries of
Europe and from the United States, but they have not been
heard so far from Spain, Italy or Ireland. A few years ago
the Abbot of Montserrat was deposed on orders from
Rome, for speaking out once too often against General
Franco; which may be a straw in the wind of general
change, or which may mean nothing more than the fact
that the abbot was a Catalan and therefore a dabbler in
purely local politics. And even where the religious radicals
are reaching for their battering rams and their sapping
equipment there are brothers in Christ preparing to withstand the siege. 'I know of enclosed nuns more than a thousand kilometres away from Paris', writes a horrified French-
man, 'who are so well informed about what goes on in the
world that they find flats in the capital for their friends,
who cannot succeed in doing so by their own efforts. The
altruism which they display in this form is assuredly not the
end for which they were enclosed.' That man would
not only exorcise property advertisements from the convent but newspapers in general and intellectual preoccupa-
tions in particular, for 'the monastery is not a "thinking
shop". To make of one's solitude the means, not of a truly
spiritual life, but of an intellectual life, is one of the subtlest
ways of adulterating it.' The opponents to change rarely
express themselves as bluntly or as crudely as that. More
frequently they appeal vaguely to history and to the sense of
continuity which embellishes so much that is beautiful and
awe-inspiring in the religious life. An Anglican contemplative monk says that 'Conservatism, then, as a looking back
to past tradition, is a necessary element of monasticism;
otherwise it could not remain true to itself.' An English
Benedictine writes that 'any work which rules out manual
labour and also takes monks habitually away from the enclosure and the choir can hardly be called Benedictine'. This
is demonstrably true but it dodges the main question at

issue, which is whether Benedictinism – among other forms
of religious life – has anything more to contribute to the
evolution of Christianity; whether it ought to be modified
even more than it has already been, to a point at which it
can no longer be called Benedictine. An Anglican has suggested that a particular difficulty facing reformers of the
religious life within the Church of England is that in most
of its communities there are still one or two people who can
remember the founders and who see any change at all as a
positive betrayal of someone they knew, admired and followed obediently. Judging by the regularity with which St
Benedict's name is invoked without any supporting argument it sometimes seems as if many monks of his order can
claim, across fourteen centuries, a similar acquaintance.

There is resistance to reform which speaks out point-
blank against it. There is also acquiescence to the idea of
reform which seems to speak of nothing more daring or
dangerous than adjustments. No one has made more for-
ward-sounding noises in print than the American Trappist
monk Thomas Merton. His view of what ought to happen
next to monasticism was set out in a paper which has circulated widely in religious circles in the United States and
elsewhere since it was written in 1964.

The adaptation required by our time will not be effected by
simple tightening up of the organizational structure and increased
centralization of control. On the contrary, more than anywhere
else, a relative decentralization would seem to be needed in the
monastic order. Yet at the same time the idea of the Ordo Monas-
ticus would seem to call for closer and more active interrelation-
ship between the various monastic communities of all the families
now existing: Benedictine, Cistercian, Camaldolese etc. (It might
be well for a change in legislation that would permit a change of
stability allowing transfer from one of these families to another
with no more complication than is now required to transfer from
one monastery to another within the same order.) Within the Order
it should be recognized that different monasteries in diverse situations will have needs that greatly vary. Instead of detailed legislation in the matter of usages imposed on everyone, there should be
greater respect for local differences, and the local abbot should be

able to regulate details of horarium and observance for his own community. .... Everything should be done to favour and encourage those who seek to maintain and to increase the silence and solitude of the monastic life, and its primitive simplicity. ... Monastic silence should be maintained, along with enclosure, separation from the world etc., but in a somewhat different spirit; more flexible, less rigid, less forced. To this end, individual monks should have greater freedom in going apart from the others to read and meditate in their lectio time, the problem of machines in and near the monastery must be frankly confronted, and recreation should never become a formal observance. There is on the part of many monks an earnest and reasonable desire for experiments in a simpler, more primitive and more solitary form of domestic life. Furthermore, the insistence on absolute unification and perfect conformity of all in one form of observance should not be carried to the point where it may in fact interfere with the development of an individual monk who may have special needs; e.g., for greater solitude. Our cenobitic life should normally open up to a life of deeper solitude. For the sake of 'détente' and in rightful concern for human needs of modern man, which constitute a general problem, the following should be considered in general as *not acceptable solutions* – habitual use of TV in a monastic common-room; habitual smoking; recreation in the sense of conversation and play together; habitual use of cinema and radio in a common-room. But the following might be considered acceptable in accordance with the situation of individual houses – swimming; reading of works of literature (including novels of genuine value, under proper guidance); long walks (alone) in forest or countryside; skiing, horseback riding, boating, fishing. These of course would not normally be allowed to interfere with the obligations of the monastic life (including manual labour) but time could be made for them on certain feasts. General use of such recreation would not be encouraged but only special cases. Also the local abbot should allow his library to be suitably furnished with reviews which will enable the monk to keep up not only with current developments in theology and philosophy but also to get a general view of world trends. But habitual reading of newspapers and topical magazines should not be allowed. Examples of such magazines as would be permissible: *Etudes, Blackfriars, The Commonweal.*

There are many in the religious life today who will regard that as too radical for words, as a pollution of the pure, the authentic stream of monasticism; St Benedict, after all, would have had no truck with keeping abreast of current affairs in the world. There are many who will regard it as a very proper step forward, thoroughly in keeping with the times we live in without losing sight of the foundation on which the monastic life stands; a greater respect for local differences and a recognition that individuals have special needs do, after all, have a fine mid-twentieth-century ring. But there are some who will see it as no more than a half-hearted concession to popular noises off, in which tradition is not really undermined, in which nothing is really changed; and when there is to be no 'conversation and play' between brothers in recreation, when literature may only be read 'under proper guidance', one of the fundamental defects of the religious life for the individual will quite clearly remain unaltered.

It is difficult for an outsider, unburdened by the tradition, unconditioned by the life, not to accept the last diagnosis. Within the relatively narrow confines of monasticism, which is only a small part of the religious life, something much more drastic seems to be called for. This may mean a change in which some of its most distinctive marks – permanent or semi-permanent enclosure, a life of regularity, a strictly codified régime – will disappear forever. For it seems fairly certain that the present shortage of manpower will become more acute if things stay even as Thomas Merton would have them. Even his modified monasticism is so completely and unattractively at odds with the world, in terms of idealism and civilization as well as hedonism, that it is very difficult to see where the next generation of recruits is to come from; they will have been reared on a variety of Christian doctrine which takes much greater account of the world as it is than the present one. And it is precisely because they have been thrown up by the twentieth century, and not by the nineteenth or the sixth, because they have genuinely tried to assess human needs in the twentieth century and to supply them, within the framework of Christ's teaching, that the Petits Frères, the Taizé Communauté, the secular institutes and the worker-priests seem to point most clearly the way ahead for the religious life as a whole.

It will engage more closely with the underprivileged world than it already does. Instead of sending a wealth of its manpower to non-Christian countries in order to convert these to the faith it will spend its people more freely in meeting obvious social needs at home; and where it does go on foreign mission it will regard conversion as a happy by-product of its primary task, which will be to help others to achieve health, education and dignity. It will close any gaps that remain in its social services; like the one in the Church of England, where no religious community cares for old, sick and lonely men, though several have been founded to look after women. It will make much greater use than now of an enormous asset in the potential mobility of its members, who are without the ties and obligations of family and who can drop everything on the instant and take up any job; some religious may not savour the comparison but they can be flung into some long-term emergency situation as effectively as the Salvation Army is apt to respond to brief disasters.

This may seem to be a prescription for active communities alone, leaving the contemplatives locked in some timeless solitude of their own. But if Voillaume and Schutz and the other radicals of the past few years have made two things very clear indeed, and one of these is the need for greater rather than less engagement in the world as it is, the other is the futility of separating the contemplative and the active life. Even the outsider who cannot understand the processes of prayer must recognize its significance in a Christian context; at the very least it is the channel of communication with the source of inspiration. It may also be, as contemplatives maintain, in itself an effective instrument upon the world; or a duty, with a quota per shift to be fulfilled by divine requirement. On the first count alone, the inspirational, the most intense form of prayer life in pure contemplation without the immediate distractions of work to be done and people to be seen is of obvious benefit. On the second count, the instrumental, it is difficult to see how it can be fully effective if contemplation is conducted in the vacuum conditions traditional to this vocation; a man can only pray intelligently for a world he is well aware of and he cannot be well aware of it insulated behind permanently closed doors. And if there is indeed a divine requirement for prayer then somehow it will have to be sustained by the community. The insistence by the most worldly actives, the Petits Frères, of attaching a hermitage to each community, to which individuals can go for contemplation in solitude at regular intervals, surely suggests a pattern for the future for the whole religious life. This is a pattern in which no exclusively contemplative communities will remain, or exclusively active ones either. Instead all religious communities will be intensively engaged in the world's work; they will also have at their core the hermitage in which a proportion of their manpower will always reside, for the inspiration of intense prayer, for the application of prayer, for the duty of prayer; and while for a few individuals temperament may mean permanent or semi-permanent residence in the hermitage, for the majority it will be a place of periodic visitation.

Within the past decade a Benedictine has written that 'Monasticism has two things to offer to civilization of the future : sanity and hope. By stressing the right order of values, monasticism in a world of unbalance stands for sanity. By keeping alive, in a world of mutual mistrust, an awareness of man's dignity and of his relationship in charity to the rest of the human race, monasticism brings with it hope.' More recently still the Belgian Cardinal Suenens has said of all forms of religious life that

At a time when Communism is trying to impose by force a new social order which destroys the spiritual personality of man, it is more than ever important that the Church should be able to offer the world the picture of living communities, where a voluntary communism reigns, based on divine worship and brotherly love, as a foretaste of what in many aspects a society open to social Christianity and faithful to the Gospel would be.

At the moment both aspirations are within the realm of the possible rather than the probable. For monasticism badly needs to revise its human values if it is to stand for sanity; the way to sanity is not to be found by treating adults as if they were children, by prohibiting literature except under ominously proper guidance and by forbidding a free flow of conversation in the common-room. An awareness of man's dignity is not to be achieved by keeping mankind in general at even half-arm's length. It might be demonstrated more effectively than it is now not only by going out into the world more frequently but by bringing the world into the religious life more indiscriminately. If a community is to be a foretaste of a society open to social Christianity then it might well consider the possibility of including in its membership some regarded as outrageous misfits in the world outside; it will first have to be sure that it is itself, in human terms, balanced and sane and mature enough if it is to ease the misfit rather than be disturbed by him. And if a community is to exemplify voluntary communism then it will have to live voluntarily from start to finish; it will not have to maintain its membership under threat of penalty or even under the psychological pressure imposed by a permanent vow. It may well be that the East will be summoned to redress an imbalance in the West at just this point, by way of Kurisumala and other places where Christian religious are absorbing something of Hindu and Buddhist philosophy. The Buddhist monastery is not just a place to which holy men are attached for life; it is also a school to which the faithful resort for various periods at a particular stage of their religious and human development.

Traditionalists will doubtless boggle at this prospect. They may comfort themselves with the thought that hardly any of it is utterly new. There is a precedent in the history of the religious life for almost all these changes. The Franciscans, after all, attempted for a time and up to a point to live at the lowest level of the people they were preaching to. The teaching and nursing canonesses of the eighth century lived in chastity and obedience while in community,

but very often left to get married. The active community
with a contemplative core and most of its population shifting from one to the other at intervals would be no more
than a repetition of what Robert of Arbrissel attempted with
his Order of Fontevrault at the end of the eleventh century.
The traditionalists, however, will have to accept the fact
that if reform takes this tack it will not be because anyone is
modelling himself on the Franciscans, the canonesses or
Fontrevault. It will be because the reformers intuitively believe this to be the most Christian course from their reading
of the Gospels. And this is what distinguishes the present
religious reformers from most of those who have preceded
them.

The survival of the Christian religious life seems to
depend on changes of this magnitude. But then so does the
survival of Christianity itself. This may be an exciting time
for some religious to be living in, for the ones who have
fretted for too long under the impositions and pallid un-
worldliness of the old traditions and who can see the mono-
lith beginning to move in the right direction at last. It is a
time of some despair for others who are too old or ill
equipped by temperament and training to accommodate
themselves to more than small changes. It is not a comfortable time for any of them. The strains of the whole religious
world at the moment are crystallized in a recent sentence
written by an American. 'One older Jesuit in California reported to me tearfully that, as he sits down for meals in
common with his fellow Jesuits, an abyss separates him
from them, that the soldierly unity in the common cause of
the defence of the Faith that has always knit into one the
Companions of Jesus, has simply ceased to exist.' It is impossible for the outsider not to be saddened when he thinks
what will have gone from the religious life by the time that
abyss has been sealed and those ranks have been closed
again, and are turned in another direction. Does it really
mean that one day, before very long, there will be no more
haunting beauty of Trappist monks pacing, in the dress of
fourteen centuries ago, silently along a Gothic cloister? Does

it perhaps mean that a little later the spellbinding liturgy of Taizé will be heard only on a plastic disc or a magnetized tape and not be seen and felt for the mysterious drama that it is? Can it be that monks and nuns and other religious will be indistinguishable from other human beings eventually, except in their community life and in their quiet profession of poverty, obedience and chastity for a part of their days and occasionally for a lifetime?

For although the form, the understanding and the duration of the threefold profession will change and the shape of community will alter, these alone, in their essentials, are the sure survivors of this turning-point in history. The worker-priests and some members of secular institutes have shown that some people can fulfil the ideals of the new social Christianity in isolation from their fellows. But not everybody can manage without the support of a closely integrated community; as Kierkegaard said, there will always be individuals with that need. The threefold profession in community is almost the definition of the religious life. It is also the reason why the world in general will always regard the life as supremely irrational, if not derisory. It represents, as a cold-blooded choice, the greatest sacrifice that a fulfilled human being can make. But people with an ideal of service driving them on can often give everything they have, in defiance of ridicule and contempt. And a man finding his way to salvation must sometimes fly in the face of reason.

Bibliography

I SHOULD think that several hundred books – at least several hundred – with some bearing on the religious life have been written by now. The ones below are merely those I have read from cover to cover. The list includes all books referred to by title only in the chapter source notes.

American Catholic Exodus edited by John O'Connor, London, Chapman, 1968.

The Benedictine Idea by Dom Hubert van Zeller OSB, London, Burns Oates, 1959.

Brothers of Men by René Voillaume, London, Darton, Longman & Todd, 1966.

The Call of the Cloister by Peter F. Anson, London, SPCK, 1964.

The Call of the Desert by Peter F. Anson, London, SPCK, 1964.

The Collected Works of St John of the Cross edited by Kieran Kavanaugh OCD, and Otilio Rodriguez OCD, London, Nelson, 1967.

The Complete Monk by Dom Demys Rutledge, OSB, London, Routledge & Kegan Paul, 1966.

Conjectures of a Guilty Bystander by Thomas Merton, London, Burns Oates, 1968.

Contemplative Nuns Speak edited by Bernard Bro OP, London, Chapman, 1963.

The Desert My Dwelling Place by Elizabeth Hamilton, London, Hodder & Stoughton, 1968.

Dynamique du provisoire by Roger Schutz, Les Presses de Taizé, 1965.

God's Highways; the Religious Life and the Secular Institutes by J. Perinelle OP, Blackfriars, 1958.

I Choose the Cloister by Rosemary Howard-Bennett, London, Hodder & Stoughton, 1966 edition.

I Leap over the Wall by Monica Baldwin, London, Hamilton, 1949.

Introduction to Spirituality by Louis Bouyer, New York, Desclee Co., 1963.

The Life of a Nun by Françoise Vandermeersch, London, Chapman, 1967.

The Life of Raymond Raynes by Nicholas Mosley, London, Hodder & Stoughton, 1963 edition.

Living Today for God by Roger Schutz, Baltimore, Helicon, 1963.

Love or Constraint; Psychological Aspects of Religious Education by Marc Oraison, London, Burns Oates, 1959.

Maturity in the Religious Life by John J. Evoy s j and Van F. Christoph s j, New York, Sheed & Ward, 1965.

The Meaning of the Monastic Life by Louis Bouyer, Cong Orat., London, Burns Oates, 1955.

The Monastic Order in England by David Knowles, London, Cambridge University Press, 1941 edition.

Monastic Renewal by Dom Columba Cary-Elwes, New York, Herder, 1966.

Monks and Civilisation by Jean Decarreaux, London, Allen & Unwin, 1964.

The New Nuns edited by Sister Charles Borromeo c s c, London, Sheed & Ward, 1968.

The Nun in the World by Cardinal Suenens, London, Burns Oates, revised edition, 1966.

Obedience edited by Père Plé, London, Blackfriars, 1953.

The Park Village Sisterhood by Thomas Jay Williams and Allan Walter Campbell, London, s p c k, 1965.

Prayer by Hans Urs von Balthasar, London, Chapman, 1961.

Priest and Worker by Henri Perrin, London, Macmillan, 1965.

The Religious Life by Sister Edna Mary Dss. c s a, London, Penguin Books, 1968.

The Religious Orders in England, 3 volumes by David Knowles, London, Cambridge University Press, 1955, 1955 and 1959 editions.

Religious Orders in the Modern World, a symposium edited by Mgr Gerard Huyghe, London, Chapman, 1965.

The Religious Orders of Men by Jean Canu, London, Burns Oates, 1960.

The Religious Vocation by R. M. Benson, Oxford, Mowbray, 1939.

Renouveau communautaire et unité chrétienne by Annie Perchenet, Paris, Mame, 1967.

The Rise of Protestant Monasticism by Francois Biot o p, Baltimore, Helicon, 1963.

The Rule of St Benedict translated and edited by Dom Justin McCann o s b, London, Burns Oates, 1963 edition.

The Rule of Taizé, Les Presses de Taizé.

Saint Benedict by St Gregory the Great, being a new translation of the second book of the *Dialogues* by Dom Justin McCann, published by Princethorpe Priory, Rugby, 1941.

Secular Institutes by Gabriel Reidy OFM, London, Burns Oates, 1962.

Seeds of the Desert by René Voillaume, London, Burns Oates, 1964.

The Seven Storey Mountain by Thomas Merton, New York, New American Library, 1948.

The Silent Life by Thomas Merton, Dublin, Clonmore & Reynolds, 1957.

The Silent Rebellion by Donald M. Allchin, London, S.C.M. Press, 1958.

The Spiritual Exercises by Ignatius Loyola, translated by Fr T. Corbishley SJ, London, Burns Oates, 1963.

Teilhard de Chardin a biography by Robert Speaight, London, Collins, 1967.

Tensions and Change by Mgr Gerard Huyghe, London, Chapman, 1965.

A Time to Keep Silence by Patrick Leigh Fermor, London, Murray, 1957.

La Trappe in England by a Religious of Holy Cross Abbey, London, Burns Oates, 1946.

Unanimité dans le pluralisme by Roger Schutz, Les Presses de Taizé, 1966.

A Valiant Victorian by anonymous authors among the Sisters of the Church, Oxford, Mowbray, 1964.

The Vision of God by K. E. Kirk, New York, Harper Torchbooks, 1966 edition.

The Waters of Silence by Thomas Merton, London, Hollis & Carter, 1950.

Witness and Consecration by Sr Jeanne D'Arc CP, London, Chapman 1967.

The most valuable reference work I have consulted is:

The New Catholic Encyclopedia, New York, McGraw-Hill.
Other useful ones are:
Annuario pontifico, Vatican annually.
Directory of Religious Orders, Congregations and Societies of Great Britain and Ireland, London; Burns Oates, annually.

Guide to the Religious Communities of the Anglican Communion,
 Oxford, Mowbray, 1962.
A Guide to the Religious Life, London, Chapman, 1965.

Many religious communities publish their own periodicals. The
ones I have kept a regular eye on include:
C.R. (Community of the Resurrection), *F.L.G. Letter* (Community
of the Love of God), *Sitio* (Benedictine nuns of Burnham Abbey),
Nashdom Abbey Record; all of which are produced by Anglicans.
Among Catholics there are *Pax* (Prinknash Abbey), *Ampleforth
Journal, Downside Review, New Blackfriars* (English Dominicans),
The Month (English Jesuits), *The Aylesford Review* (English Car-
melites). There are several national or international religious re-
views: *Monastic Studies, Review for Religious, The American
Benedictine Review, La Vie spirituelle, Collecteana Cisterciensia,
Notes.*
There are two or three other reviews which regularly contain in-
formation about the religious world – *Herder Correspondence,
New Christian* and (quite the most prolific and most reliable source
of statistical information) *Pro mundi vita.*

Some fiction has been written around the religious life. Two pieces
which are better than most are:
The Two Nuns by Ann Huré, London, Macdonald, 1964.
Found Wanting by Joseph Martindale, London, New Authors,
 1967.

Finally, there is now a fair amount of Gregorian chant and other
liturgical music from religious communities available on gramo-
phone records. Three discs I would not wish to lose are:
Gregorian Chant – Missa VIII (de Angelis) cum Credo III sung
 by the German Benedictine monks of the Abbey of St Martin,
 Beuron, Archive EPA 37112.
Psaumes-Chorals sung by the Taizé Communauté, Edition Studio
 SM – SM 4509.
Missa Luba, a Congolese Mass sung by an African choir trained by
 a Belgian missionary priest, which catches the mood (Latin
 words, *very* African music) of local free expression referred to on
 p. 161 in chapter 5, Philips RL 7592.

Appendix 1

The Religious Population among Roman Catholics

	1967	1966	1962
Jesuits	36,038	36,038	35,086
Franciscans (Friars Minor)	26,940	27,009	26,876
Salesians	22,626	22,042	21,048
Christian Schools Bros	17,787	17,926	17,560
Franciscans (Capuchins)	15,710	15,838	15,708
Benedictines	12,070	12,500	11,500
Marist Brothers	10,221	10,356	8,974
Dominicans	10,003	10,191	9,841
Redemptorists	9,052	9,450	9,030
Oblates of Mary Immaculate	7,890	7,609	7,505
Vincentians	6,230	5,992	5,966
Society of the Divine Word	5,744	5,773	5,436
Holy Spirit, Congregation	5,147	5,200	5,200
Franciscans (Conventuals)	4,605	4,650	4,550
Augustinians (Hermits)	4,504	4,531	4,200
Passionists	4,340	4,135	3,935
Claretians	4,128	3,770	3,554
Discalced Carmelites	4,018	4,022	4,236
Christian Brothers of Ireland	3,900	3,814	3,500
White Fathers	3,749	4,013	4,055
Trappists	3,770	4,211	4,339
Marianists	3,434	3,490	3,250
Priests of the Sacred Heart	3,425	3,400	3,175
Missionaries of the Sacred Heart of Jesus	3,315	3,455	3,107
Brothers of the Sacred Heart	3,116	3,148	3,043
Holy Cross Fathers	3,110	3,352	3,127
Carmelites (Ancient Observance)	2,852	3,075	2,904
Piarists	2,501	2,540	2,455
Marists	2,446	2,343	2,277

	1967	1966	1962
Hospitallers of St John of God	2,318	2,504	2,527
Pallotines	2,281	2,400	2,250
Brothers of Christian Instruction of Ploermel	2,228	2,215	2,200
Picpus Fathers	2,135	2,052	1,962
Scheut Fathers	2,008	2,008	1,930
Premonstratensians	1,991	1,991	1,750
Montfort Fathers	1,985	2,000	1,722
Assumptionists	1,967	1,963	1,960
Brothers of Christian Instruction of St Gabriel	1,900	1,961	2,200
Society of African Missions	1,861	1,820	1,855
Viatorians	1,800	1,815	1,850
Servants of Mary	1,749	1,750	1,670
African Missionaries of Verona	1,703	1,710	1,570
Cistercians (Common Observance)	1,665	1,665	1,665
Franciscans (Third Order Regular)	1,650	1,592	1,420
Blessed Sacrament Fathers	1,641	1,645	1,580
Augustinians (Recollects)	1,571	1,615	1,490
Pious Society of St Paul	1,600	1,500	1,150
Brothers of Charity	1,566	1,559	1,567
Salvatorians	1,527	1,538	1,350
Oblates of St Francis de Sales	1,391	1,250	1,210
Maryknollers	1,381	1,356	1,442
Ministers of the Sick	1,309	1,380	1,297
Missionaries of the Holy Family	1,269	1,293	1,200
Mill Hill Fathers	1,207	1,204	1,152
Theatines	1,205	1,205	1,205
Little Workers of Divine Providence	1,202	1,090	1,055
Canons Regular of St Augustine	1,190	1,190	1,083
La Sallette Missionaries	1,175	1,179	1,069
Consolata Fathers	1,160	1,092	–
Mercedarians	1,061	1,230	1,163
Columbans	1,055	1,055	1,005
Carmelites of the Blessed Virgin Mary	1,028	1,028	–
Brothers of the Blessed Virgin Mary	1,000	1,000	1,041
Membership of Communities with fewer than 1,000 members	36,557	35,230	34,172
Total	332,997	332,993	319,006

WOMEN

	1967	1966	1962
North America	256,350	261,316	247,693
South America	107,358	82,945	73,885
Europe	576,814	591,360	591,577
Africa	30,702	45,616	25,408
Asia	101,710	79,443	74,010
World Total	1,072,934	1,060,680	1,012,573

The figures are those issued annually by the Vatican. In the case of the men they do not include those of communities with fewer than 1,000 members; there is no breakdown of women's communities. The list should be treated with some caution. In some cases figures have not been reported to the Vatican from the communities themselves in some years; and there is reason to suppose that the Vatican figures are sometimes at variance with those issued by various orders in their own handbooks – see, for example, a reference to the Benedictines on page 83.

Appendix 2

Declaration by the General Chapter of the Cistercian Monks of the Strict Observance (The Trappists) in March 1969

WE Cistercian monks feel a deep desire to interpret for our own times the traditions which our Fathers have handed down to us. Yet we must admit that we are faced with a variety of different trends in our Order which reflect its present situation. We may feel at times that certain of these trends could well obstruct the renewal and healthy evolution of the Order.

And yet, when these difficulties came to light at the opening of this Chapter for renewal, we all felt a profound sense of communion in the lived experience of our common spiritual values. We are convinced that the work of this Chapter will become constructive to the degree that we foster this communion and the mutual confidence which it inspires.

We shall do this by recognizing all that really unites us in the Holy Spirit rather than by trying to impose unity through a legislation that would determine observances down to the last detail. Individual communities can in fact look after such details according to local needs and in conformity with the directives of the General Chapter, so long as our wholly contemplative orientation is maintained. We are convinced that the best laws are those which follow and interpret life and it is in the concrete experience of our Cistercian vocation that we would first of all recognize this life.

Our wish is to clarify the content of this experience which we all share and by so doing to further as best we can the values which inspire it. That is why we feel moved to make the following declaration on our own particular way of life.

Following the first Fathers of our Order, we find in the Holy Rule of St Benedict the practical interpretation of the Gospel for us. A sense of the Divine Transcendence and of the Lordship of Christ not only pervades the whole of this Rule, but also permeates our life, totally orientated towards an experience of the Living God.

God calls and we respond by truly seeking Him as we follow Christ in humility and obedience. With hearts cleansed by the Word of God, by Vigils, by fasting and by an unceasing conversion of life, we aim to become ever more disposed to receive from the Holy Spirit the gift of pure and continual prayer.

This search for God is the soul of our monastic day, a day composed of the Opus Dei, Lectio Divina and manual work. Our Cistercian life is basically simple and austere. It is truly poor and penitential 'in the joy of the Holy Spirit'. Through the warmth of their welcome and hospitality, our Communities share the fruit of their contemplation and work with others.

We carry out this search for God under a Rule and an Abbot in a community of love where all are responsible. It is through stability that we commit ourselves to this community. We live in an atmosphere of silence and separation from the world which fosters and expresses openness to God in contemplation . . . treasuring, as Mary did, all these things and pondering them in our hearts.

The Church has entrusted a mission to us which we wish to fulfil by the response of our whole life . . . 'to give clear witness to that heavenly home for which every man longs and to keep alive in the heart of the human family the desire for this home . . . as we bear witness to the majesty and love of God and to the brotherhood of all men in Christ'. (cf. GS No. 38, AG No. 40, Letter of Pope Paul VI to the Order – 8/12/68).

This present General Chapter is convinced that the unity rooted in charity which has been the strength and beauty of the Cistercian Order ever since its origins (Letter of Paul VI to the Order) will best be served today by a deep sense of communion in the lived experience of our common spiritual values. That is why the present General Chapter, in its *Declaration on the Cistercian Life*, has already insisted on the contemplative orientation and the fundamental observances of our Order.

In the present Statute those observances which demand special attention in our times are presented in a more concrete fashion. Thus the fundamental values of our life are guaranteed without imposing a detailed uniformity where in fact a legitimate diversity should exist. Conditions are laid down so that each community in union with the other monasteries of the Order and following these guidelines may deepen its own living experience of the Cistercian life.

Guidelines

1. Faithful to the thought of their Founders, Cistercian monks live under a Rule and an Abbot. They live, united in the love of Christ, in a community which is stable and effectively separated from the world.

2. The Abbot as spiritual father of his community should try to discover the will of God. One important way of doing this is by listening to his brethren in the spirit of Chapter 3 of the Rule.

3. In our daily horarium we keep the balance between the Opus Dei, Lectio Divina and Manual Work as required by the Rule of St Benedict.

4. The hour of rising is to be so regulated that Vigils, which follows it, should keep its traditional character of nocturnal prayer – as we watch for the coming of the Lord.

5. The monk, who is tending to a life of continual prayer, needs a fixed amount of prayer each day. The Abbot will see to this for the community as a whole or for each individual in particular.

6. This search for a life of prayer should be lived in an atmosphere of recollection and silence for which all are responsible. In particular, the great silence at night and the silence in the regular places will be maintained.

7. Separation from the world demands that journeys out of the monastery should be infrequent and only for serious reasons. The use of radio and television will be exceptional. Discretion is needed in the use of other media of communication.

8. Our monasteries should practise generous hospitality, but this should not be allowed to interfere with the contemplative nature of our way of life.

9. Our diet should be simple and frugal. The monastic practice of fasting and abstinence should be retained.

10. The habit is to be retained as the distinctive sign of the Order; its use can differ from house to house.

11. The life of the community, as of each monk, should be marked by simplicity and poverty. Fraternal correction in the spirit of the Gospel is a help in this direction.

Conditions

12. Within the limits of the above guidelines, the monasteries of our Order are free to arrange the details of their observance.

An effective consultation of the community should accompany these experiments – though the manner of it may vary.

13. Anything in the second or third parts of the Constitutions, or in the Usages, which does not fall under common law, retains only a directive force.

14. The results of these experiments will be reviewed by the Visitor who will make a statement on them in his report to the General Chapter.

15. The experiments should be discussed at the Regional Conferences, so that communities may be helped in their work of renewal.

Appendix 3

The Rule of the Community of the
Sisters of the Love of God*

THE MONASTIC STATE

All Christians, whether monastic or secular, are called to sanctification. The Christian life may be manifested in many forms
but it is one in its acknowledgment of a total commitment of its
members to the service of God. For the monastic this commitment
must be a witness to the necessity of separation in order to fulfil the
vocation of a following of the way of Christ bound by the Vows
of Poverty, Chastity and Obedience.

There is one Christian way, there is one monastic life of total
commitment in which the Monastic Vows are an underlining
of the Christian baptismal life. Here lies its unity and its witness
both to the Church and to the world. In function, nevertheless,
there are differences of application as the life is directed either to
an active ministry made fruitful through prayer or, as in the contemplative life, to one separated not *from* but *for* the world to a
way of living that is disciplined for the work of prayer. Therefore
the Vows of Poverty, Chastity and Obedience shall always be
regarded by the Sisters as the foundation of their life and of their
witness to the Church and world. The requirements of the Vows
shall always be exactly fulfilled in spirit as in letter.

Profession under the Holy Vows provides unity. It is the re-
direction to God of the natural life of man in its ownership of
things, in the exercise of all creative powers and in the complete
control of all self-interest.

THE AIM OF THE COMMUNITY

The Community of the Sisters of the Love of God shall have for
its aim the glory of God. The Community is called to witness both
to Christ's repairing of man's disobedience and to the Divine
Will for unity by the sanctification of the individual lives of its
members through their union with the mysteries of the life of the
Incarnate Son of God.

*Anglican contemplative nuns.

Contemplative life and prayer is to be the realization in time of man's union with the purposes and will of God. Therefore the Sisters shall have the visible unity of Christ's Church as a Central theme of their prayer and offering.

The Sisters, while cherishing all that is distinctive in their own life and calling, shall offer special intention and intercession for the increase and perfection of the Priesthood and for the Monastic Life in all its forms.

They shall strive by their discipline and prayer and constant self-oblation to fill up what is behind the afflictions of Christ for His Body's sake, and to use their privileges of enclosure and of silence as a means to lead them to a growing union with God through Christ in the power of the Holy Spirit.

RECONCILIATION

There is in true contemplation an urgency to love God for himself and also a desire that all men should be drawn to respond to his mercy, to acknowledge and accept the reconciliation accomplished by, with and in Christ.

Asceticism is not an end in itself but a disciplined training for the renewal of the life in Christ to witness Christ in and for the world. The ascetic way both for the individual and for the community is a preparation whereby through grace all may participate in the re-creating ministry of Christ.

To be in Christ's reconciliation means to open the whole being in the common life to God through the stripping of self, and to gather and hold to his love the concerns of the temporal and the many requests for intercession which are brought to the Community. It is through Christ in the fellowship of the Spirit that the wholeness of spiritual power proceeds for the healing of the ills of mankind and of the world's disorders.

It will be by continually remembering that God has called each member of the Community into this common life, that the order and discipline of the individual life will bear the fruits of Christ's victory over sin and death. (St John xv)

ENCLOSURE AND SEPARATION FROM THE WORLD

The Sisters of the Love of God are constituted as a Monastic Community which observes enclosure.

Enclosure in answer to the Divine call is a withdrawal from

the secular estate to witness a more complete offering of the whole self, body, soul and spirit, to do God's will and to be the means of extending his love into the world.

The function of the withdrawal of the enclosed life is for the preserving and deepening of prayer in the Church. It is within this withdrawal that the needs of the world can be most completely seen in the light of God.

The practical application of this principle of enclosure both in regard to those who are permitted within the enclosure, and the occasions on which the Sisters may go out of the enclosure, shall be stated in the Customary. The Bishop, or at least the Warden, shall have knowledge of and give permission for these exceptions. In emergency the Prioresses of the Convents may act in accordance with the principles laid down in the Rule.

THE MOTHER GENERAL

In the hierarchy of obedience the leadership of the Mother General shall be the unifying source and directive for the common purpose and life of the Community.

The Mother General must remember that more than anyone else she is responsible for the maintenance and exposition of the distinctive spirit of the Community.

THE MOTHER GENERAL AND
THE MOTHER PRIORESSES

The principal duty of the Mother General and the Mother Prioresses is to lead those under their care with justice and charity, and to maintain a strict and faithful observance of the Rule and Statutes of the Community.

They shall always be careful to set a good example of such observance, regarding themselves as being bound, within the limits compatible with their office, by the ordinances of the Community.

They shall be careful to keep a strict impartiality in their administration both of those spiritual and temporal goods of the Community of which they are stewards during their tenure of office.

ENTRY INTO THE COMMUNITY

Those who seek admission to the Community shall always be received with courtesy and sisterly kindness as sharers in a common hope.

No consideration of wealth or poverty shall be allowed to influence the acceptance or rejection of any candidate provided that the Community has reasonable hope of being able to maintain her; nor shall any such contribution be regarded as entitling her to any favour or privilege.

Candidates who are accepted for probation shall be admitted as Postulants immediately upon their arrival, that they may have full privilege of entry into the enclosure.

They shall during the time of their postulancy be instructed by the Novice Mistress in the duties and obligations of the Novitiate.

NOVICES

Those who are admitted to the Novitiate shall bear in mind its twofold purpose of probation and training, and shall accordingly be entirely open with the Novice Mistress in all that concerns their daily life, while they give a cheerful obedience to all that she may enjoin. The demands of the life shall be accepted readily and joyfully as a means towards the purification of life which may entitle the Novice to hope for the privilege of Profession in due time.

The Novices shall be instructed by the Novice Mistress in the various exercises of the Monastic Life and in the Rule and Statutes of the Community, and in such other matters as she shall consider appropriate to their calling.

The simplicity and thoroughness of a good Noviciate is the foundation of the Professed Life.

PROFESSION

Throughout the time of Noviceship, the Sisters shall accustom themselves to look forward to their Profession as being the pledge of the acceptance of their offering to God by, with and in Jesus Christ in the unity of the Holy Spirit. Profession shall, therefore, be always regarded as a signal token of the love of God, and the utmost diligence shall be given to preparation for it. The offering must be thoroughly purified if it is to be brought for Divine acceptance.

No one shall be permitted to take the first Temporary Vows unless it be her intention to proceed to Final Vows if the privilege is granted in due time. Thereafter the offering continues until it is consummated in death.

The Professed shall be careful to maintain the spirit of sacrifice in its integrity, looking forward to, and preparing for its consummation with the same zeal with which she formerly sought its acceptance. All shall endeavour continually to be united with our Lord's offering in order that all their actions, words and thoughts may be permeated with the spirit of sacrificial love in the fellowship of the Spirit.

The daily dying to self is the necessary condition of that risen life in which the Professed is called to dwell with Christ.

POVERTY

Poverty as a call means far more than a simplification of life in a community of common ownership. It means possessing *nothing* for self, an entire dependency on Christ in whom all things are gathered up and in whom all things are possessed.

The positive application of Poverty is the cultivation of the virtue of holy indifference – to claim the possession of nothing but to use all things and opportunities to deepen that dependence on God wherein is true liberty.

In accordance with the spirit of their consecration to the mysteries of the life of the Incarnate Word, the Sisters shall always have in regard the Vow of Poverty. Its requirements shall be recognized throughout the daily life both in the appointments of the Convents and in the conduct of the Sisters.

No one who enters the Community shall claim anything for her private use, but everything shall be received from the common stock and shall be regarded as belonging to the Community. The careful and reverent use of all Community goods shall be recognized as an essential part of true poverty.

As far as possible the Sisters must avoid asking for dispensations. They shall shun all deviations from their common usages that are not absolutely necessary; all singularity shall be carefully avoided.

In daily life such small hardships and deprivations as may occur through the faithful maintenance of this standard of Holy Poverty shall be welcomed by the Sisters as offering fresh opportunities for realizing the conditions of their consecration.

CHASTITY

The distinctive dedication of the Community to the mystery of the Love of God must always be regarded by the Sister as emphasizing the dignity and power of holy Chastity.

Chastity is the submission of every creative faculty to their re-creation in Christ that the Sisters may take their part in our Lord's reconciliation.

It is by the faithful observance of this Vow, and the cultivation of the virtue, that the soul of the contemplative must seek to be trained for the vision of God promised to the pure in heart. All the faculties of mind and spirit must be purified by penitence and trained to familiarity with the things of God. There must be a continual exercise of love and desire reaching out towards God.

Chastity is the answer to man's selfish and destructive use of his natural powers both over nature and in his relationship with other men. The application of Chastity for the monastic includes voluntary perpetual celibacy.

In Chastity, which is the whole being set on God, we have the hidden joy that is beyond all natural attainment. It is there that all relationships are made perfect both in this world and in the whole unseen world. Herein is the wonder of the monastic life and of the whole family in God.

OBEDIENCE

Obedience is the means whereby the human will is re-established in its true purpose to be one with the will of God. Obedience must always be recognized as a free response of love.

Through all the authorized channels of leadership and in her relationship of mutual obedience and co-inherence with her Sisters throughout the Community, each Sister shall make her obedience as complete and generous as possible. The virtue of obedience can only be acquired by its detailed practice in small things as well as in great.

If any conscientious difficulty is felt about obedience it shall be stated.

No position of seniority in the Community shall excuse a Sister from fulfilling her obligation of obedience.

The Sisters shall seek by the faithful observance of Holy Obedience to keep themselves free from all self-pleasing and self-will that the spirit of sacrifice may be the more perfectly attained.

SILENCE

Silence, which is always to be regarded as one of the chief privileges of the Community, shall be observed with all possible strictness and its spirit must be faithfully cultivated, for it prepares the way for the union of the soul with the will of God and is an offering of perpetual reverence to his Majesty.

It should be remembered that silence must cover all the levels of the conscious life, for there must be an outward silence of speech and movement, a silence of the mind for the overcoming of vain imaginations and distractions, and a silence of the soul in the surrender of the will to be still and know that God is God, leading to a silence of the spirit which is the preparation for the fullness of contemplation.

Failure in silence is a real failure in chastity, just as failure in humility is a failure in poverty.

Silence can be broken not only by speech and gesture but also by idle curiosity, for it is in stillness that the spirit should be trained to deepen recollection. Remembrance of the morning's Eucharist, intercession, thanksgiving and adoration should fill the silent hours, while the mind brings its own contribution of thought stimulated by spiritual and other reading and instruction.

In order to maintain the spirit of silence throughout the day, the necessary speaking shall be brief and quiet. Silence must be guarded by each for others so that none shall invade another's silence thoughtlessly and without real necessity.

Silence should never be made an excuse for lethargy, whether mental or spiritual, but the life of the contemplative should be trained to exercise itself after the likeness of the Seraphim and Cherubim that worship round the Throne of God.

THE CELL

The Sisters of the Love of God shall endeavour to remember that the poverty and simplicity of their cell are meant to remind them of the poverty of Bethlehem and of the sacred solitude of the holy sepulchre and completed Sacrifice.

They shall, therefore, learn to regard their cell as a place where the Holy Spirit will reveal to them the mysteries of God and manifest to them the compassion and love of the Saviour.

The cell shall always be kept clean and tidy, and no one shall enter the cell of another without leave nor stay there longer than is necessary for the purpose for which she has been sent.

Immediately upon rising every Sister shall make the following act of self-oblation:

'All glory be to thee, my God, for that thou art, three Persons, one all holy God, very love.

'My God, I desire to love thee with all my heart, with all my mind, with all my soul and with all my strength. I here renew the consecration of my life to thee in union with the supreme oblation of Jesus Christ my Lord.'

THE SACRAMENT OF PENANCE

Confession has for its object the more complete purification of the soul for the glory of God and it should always be accompanied by great watchfulness and care with regard to all matters which generally make the subject matter for confession.

The Sisters shall therefore be very careful to avoid all known occasions of temptation, and must be prompt to resist it at once, and with all the resources at their command. They shall ever bear in mind our Lord's will for their perfection, and upon every occasion seek to unite themselves with him in his temptation, that they may with confidence dispel anxiety, fearfulness and scruples.

After any fault a Sister shall, if possible, make an avowal of it and instantly turn to God with an act of contrition, and that done she shall dismiss all fear and discouragement, nor should the remembrance of the fault be allowed to create an atmosphere of despondency and gloom. She shall rather seek to make amends for her failure by resuming her work and prayer with renewed vigour and watchfulness.

THE EUCHARIST

In the Eucharist the People of God thank God for what he has done and revealed to us through Christ who is both Word and Sacrifice, with whom we participate, priest and people alike, in the one Sacrifice of the one Body and Blood. Therefore to participate in this central activity of the Church's offering is the first duty of the Sisters, whereby they unite themselves with the oblation and satisfaction of our Blessed Lord, our great High Priest. All prayer and offering is in him, and in the eucharistic action all are drawn by the Holy Spirit to be offered by, with and in Christ in his offering to the Father for the sin and need of the world.

THE DIVINE OFFICE

The recitation of the Divine Office shall always be regarded not only as a fundamental duty in the Community but also as a privilege. Because of man's incorporation in Christ's risen life, the Divine Office is an extension of the holy Incarnation both in worship and mediation. Therefore the greatest care must be given to render it with a dignity which unites each individual in the corporate offering.

The recitation of the Divine Office shall be binding upon all those who are admitted to Profession whether under Temporary or Final Vows; and the Sisters shall recite their Office when absent from Choir.

In cases of necessity dispensation may be granted by the Warden or, in emergency, by the Mother General.

Novices, though bound to the recitation of the whole of the Day Hours, may be excused from the recitation of the Night Office by the Novice Mistress with the approval of the Mother General.

Strict silence must always be observed from the time of the ringing of the first bell, and all work should immediately cease; and no one shall enter the Choir after the second bell has rung without asking and obtaining leave.

The Psalter shall be recited or sung rhythmically and without haste, all the words being carefully uttered. All shall endeavour to take their part in such a way as to preserve a corporate uniformity.

LECTIO DIVINA

The study of scripture to form the basis of their prayer should be the first charge upon the Sisters' attention outside the Divine Office. Nothing can take the place of this.

The reading of commentaries, exegeses, and the writings of spiritual masters should be undertaken in such time as may be available for reading and study. Attention should also be paid to doctrine and to books which may help to the more intelligent use of the Liturgy and Divine Office in order that the Sisters may learn to pray with the understanding. Any tendency to pass lightly from one subject to another should be resisted.

The Sisters shall take care that spiritual reading does not degenerate into a matter of merely intellectual interest or of formal duty. The exercise of reading shall be begun with prayer and carried through in a prayerful spirit.

Sisters should from time to time consult the Mother General about their reading.

PRAYER

Prayer is the growth of a personal relationship between man and God. It must be directed so that every faculty of man is brought into the obedience of fulfilling the will of God. This requires both time and discipline and it is through the growth of the prayer that the true potential of each individual life may be realized.

Ideally the whole life is to be made prayer, but there must be times set apart for its solitary exercise. The prayer which the Sisters carry out in Chapel or cell, apart from their participation in the corporate Liturgy and Divine Office, is not regarded as a contrast to but as a continuing expression of this corporate offering.

An hour shall be appointed each morning for prayer with a further hour of recollection in the afternoon. A distinction should be drawn between the two hours. In the morning the prayer should be orison, whether the actual form be simple petition, pondering meditation or affective or contemplative prayer. A greater liberty is allowed in the use of the hour in the afternoon as long as the attention is set wholly on God. Sisters should consult the Mother General as to their use of this time.

In all their prayer the Sisters shall remember that the primary purpose is the worship of God rather than their own consolation or enlightenment, and that they are equally called to sacrifice themselves in their prayer, as in their lives, for the sanctification of their neighbour.

INTERCESSION

Contemplation gives both strength and purpose to intercession. As contemplative prayer is waiting upon God to be taught of God, both of the wonder of himself and of his will for the world, so intercession is the uniting of man's will to be one energy with the will of God.

The intercessor both perceives and realizes the knowledge of God's love and, with compassion, is concerned with the suffering and lack of purpose in the world. The intercessor sees the world in the light of God to hold it to the love of God for its healing and restoration.

It shall be remembered that the intercessory activity extends to the whole conduct of life in the Community, and forms an integral and important part of it. After the example and in the power of the Incarnate Lord every member of the Community should regard her life as called and set apart for this work of mediation, and should find in it further inspiration for faithfulness in obedience and generosity in self-sacrifice.

The power of the prayer will depend not on any intimate knowledge or carefully detailed exposition of the subject matter, but rather upon a comprehensive and penetrating sense of the majesty and mercy of him to whom the prayer is made and of the merits and compassion of him through whom the Sister pleads.

The Sisters are committed to pray for the dead and dying, remembering the countless numbers of those who have passed from this life spiritually uncared for and who specially need our prayers.

RETREATS

In order to maintain in its integrity the corporate sense of their vocation, the Sisters shall observe annually two separate weeks of corporate retreat, of which one shall be unconducted. They shall also keep a corporate day of retreat monthly. A Sister before her Profession anniversary shall in addition have a day of retreat.

Upon these days at least three hours shall be given to solitary prayer, and it is desirable that the opportunity should be taken for special examination upon the observance of the Rule.

The Superior may at her discretion grant leave for a Sister to have a period of retreat in the local 'desert' of each Convent.

FASTING AND MORTIFICATION

It is the common life that provides the primary means of self-loss, and the Sisters shall therefore accept with simplicity and fortitude any physical discomforts that may come to them through its poverty and strictness.

While the true spirit of mortification is in the affections and will, external and physical penances have value in so far as they contribute to that which is more perfect. Fasting and mortifications are traditional accompaniments to growth in the life of prayer and penitence to which the Sisters are committed.

RECREATION

All recreation should be regarded as part of the repairing of man's selfish and irresponsible attitude towards pleasure. Everyone shall enter fully into the spirit of recreation, contributing to the refreshment and enjoyment of all, and should realize the danger of any forms of withdrawal as detracting from the expression of love in the fellowship of the common life.

At formal recreation no Sister shall absent herself without permission. At these times conversation shall be general and private conversation shall be avoided.

MANUAL WORK

In the tradition of monastic custom manual work has its place in the sanctification of the natural world and is a sharing in the common lot of man. It completes man's offering to God in body and mind.

Every Sister shall accept with generosity and simplicity whatever work is given her in the Convent. Quietness of movement, recollection of mind and a consecrated energy should be accounted as part of the offering enjoined.

SICKNESS

The discipline of ill-health, pain and weariness must be accepted by the Sisters as offering opportunities for deepening their participation in Christ's re-creation through the Sacred Passion and Resurrection. These experiences should be definitely offered as part of the intercessory activity of the Community.

The sick shall make it part of their offering to avoid giving unnecessary trouble, and they shall accept with loving gratitude the care and kindness bestowed upon them.

A Sister should report anything that seems really prejudicial to her health that, if advisable, some alteration may be made, but she shall in any case accept at once the decision made on her behalf.

Only those who have permission or are appointed for it, shall visit the sick whether they be in their cell or in the infirmary: in any case the sick-room shall not be made a place of undue relaxation of silence or other rule but suitable means of recreation shall be provided as needed.

Those who tend the sick shall remember, as St Benedict says, 'care must be taken of the sick so that they may be served in very deed as Christ himself'.

CHAPTER OF FAULTS

The Chapter of Faults, an ancient monastic custom, gives the Community an opportunity for the deepening of mutual responsibility in the observance of the corporate vocation. It is an instrument for the increase of fraternal charity and for the mutual respect and knowledge of each other.

THE TIMETABLE

The timetable as arranged shall be of obligation and shall be acknowledged by all as the expression of the Community corporate offering.

THE RULE

Every Sister and Novice shall have a copy of the Rule for her own use and it shall be the subject matter for prayerful consideration and study.

The Rule when finally accepted may not be altered except by the authority of the governing body of the Community, according to the provisions set forth in the Statutes.

THE SPIRIT OF LOVE

As the heavenly City is builded of innumerable stones, each possessing its own intrinsic beauty and its own due place, so the living Church of Christ on earth is ever being builded by the perfecting of individual souls and their due relationship to one another in the oneness of charity.

This is especially true in the Religious family, where all depend for their growth in holiness upon the perfection of their relationship to one another in mutual obedience and holy love.

From their first entry into the life of the Community, therefore, the Sisters shall study to develop themselves in the spirit of love, setting the wellbeing of their Sisters and the perfection of the Community as a whole above any personal aims and desires of their own.

It will be within the safe protection of the life thus lived, that each will look to find her own spiritual life deepened and enlarged according to the spirit of Jesus Christ her Lord.

The Sisters shall pray for each other daily.

They shall always be watchful to use opportunities of unselfishness as far as the conditions of the life of Rule admit, bearing one another's burdens and avoiding laying burdens on others to relieve themselves.

No unkind, derogatory or critical words shall ever be used by one Sister of another, nor shall blame be imputed to another by any unless it be part of a Sister's duty herself to give correction or to report some grave irregularity; such correction shall always be administered with courtesy and the firmness of true Charity.

When anything is needed or when any complaint has to be made, the Superior or Sister appealed to shall always attend to the request with courtesy and consideration.

While the spirit of silence serves to separate each individual life unto God, the spirit of love must ever be binding all together in God, that in the unity of the Spirit all may seek their perfection by holy charity.

Source Notes

Details of books not cited in full here are given in the bibliography. The author and publishers are grateful to all copyright-holders for their permission to reproduce material from other works.

CHAPTER 1
Page

5, line 23 *Unanimité dans le pluralisme*, pp. 22–3
9, line 10 *Rule of Taizé*, p. 63
10, line 7 ibid., p. 71
10, line 13 *Taizé; communauté et unité* (Les Presses de Taizé), p. 10
11, line 7 *The Rise of Protestant Monasticism*, p. 86
11, line 35 *Rule of Taizé*, p. 52
17, line 3 *Unanimité dans le pluralisme*, p. 20
17, line 31 ibid., p. 56
18, line 25 ibid., p. 16
18, line 34 ibid., p. 49

CHAPTER 2

21, line 16 *The Call of the Desert*, p. 12
22, line 13 St Matthew xix, 21
22, line 16 ibid., xix, 12
24, line 15 *The Call of the Desert*, p. 29
25, line 33 *Saint Benedict*, prologue
26, line 4 ibid., p. 14
26, line 10 ibid., p. 14
26, line 36 *The Rule of St Benedict*, chapter 1
27, line 3 ibid.
27, line 6 ibid.
27, line 15 ibid., chapter 2
27, line 17 ibid., chapter 33
28, line 8 ibid., chapter 2
29, line 17 *The Religious Orders in England*, vol. 1, p. 292
29, line 25 *The Monastic Order in England*, p. 305
36, line 8 St Matthew x, 7–10
37, line 17 *A History of Europe* by H. A. L. Fisher, London, Collins, Fontana, 1960
40, line 5 *The Rise of Protestant Monasticism*, p. 63
44, line 11 *The Religious Orders of Men*, p. 97

Page

46, line 23 ibid., p. 112

49, line 10 *English Eccentrics* by Edith Sitwell, London, Arrow Books, 1960, p. 34 (By permission of Denis Dobson)

49, line 20 ibid., p. 35

50, line 10 *The Park Village Sisterhood*, p. 3

50, line 36 ibid., p. 22

51, line 4 ibid., p. 25

53, line 3 *The Call of the Cloister*, p. 64

CHAPTER 3

58, line 29 *The Life of Raymond Raynes*, p. 38

59, line 14 *Rule of the Community of the Resurrection*, p. 5

60, line 36 *Report of the Royal Commission on Ritual* (1867), Appendix B, p. 123

64, line 13 *The Church of England* by Paul Ferris, London, Gollancz, 1962, p. 197

64, line 36 *The Call of the Cloister*, p. 189

68, line 6 *Kierkegaard's Journals*, London, Collins, Fontana, 1958, p. 130

68, line 30 *The Rise of Protestant Monasticism*, p. 97

71, line 36 *What is the Iona Community?* by T. R. Morton, published by the Iona Community, p. 3

73, line 11 Figures from *Pro mundi vita*, No. 19, 1967

75, line 23 *Brothers of Men*, p. 13 (The biblical quotation is Luke xiv, 12–14)

78, line 10 ibid., p. 143

80, line 20 *Secular Institutes*, p. 82

82, line 25 *The Nun in the World*, p. 30

82, line 33 *Notes*, December 1966, p. 50

83, line 1 *New Catholic Encyclopaedia*, vol. 13, p. 674

83–4 Apart from the figures quoted from *Annuario pontificio* and the *Benedictine Catalogue*, all statistics on these pages are from *Pro mundi vita*, No. 18, 1967; *Pro mundi vita*, No. 10, 1966; or *The Nun in the World*, pp. 30–31

85, line 22 *Tensions and Change*, p. 45

85, line 31 *New Blackfriars*, April 1967, p. 375

85, line 34 The decline among Anglican women and the rise in men was noted in a article by Mark Gibbard s s j e, *New Christian*, 7 April 1966

86, line 1 Survey by Fr Vincent Strudwick s s m. Results privately circulated.

86, line 20 *The Nun in the World*, p. 117

87, line 7 *Religious Orders in the Modern World*, pp. 123–4

87, line 31 *Tensions and Change*, p. xii

Page

88, line 10 *Herder Correspondence*, vol. 2, No. 18, August 1965
88, line 28 *Tensions and Change*, p. 41
89, line 28 *De accommodata renovatione vitae religiosae*, London, Catholic Truth Society, 1965, p. 7
91, line 2 Figures from *Newsweek*, 25 December 1967, and *Time*, 9 February 1968
91, line 12 *Monastic Renewal*, p. 32
91, line 35 *De accommodata*, p. 18

CHAPTER 4

98, line 34 Figures from *New Blackfriars*, April 1967, pp. 370–80
100, line 24 Figures from *Benedictine Yearbook*, Ampleforth Abbey, 1967
109, line 26 *Priest and Worker*, p. 192
110, line 13 Figure from *New Christian*, 15 June 1967
110, line 35 *Rule of St Benedict*, chapter 49
113, line 3 *Monastic Renewal*, p. 189
113, line 26 Inquiry reported in *God's Highways*, p. 290
114, line 2 *Sitio*, July 1959
115, line 1 Constitutions of the Community of the Glorious Ascension, pp. 19–20
116, line 24 *La Vie spirituelle*, July 1967
117, line 2 Quoted in a monastic journal which has asked to remain anonymous
124, line 7 *Community of St Laurence Newsletter*, No. 16, Easter 1967
127, line 2 *Nashdom Abbey Record*, No. 36, Winter 1967
128, line 6 *The Religious Vocation*, p. 310

CHAPTER 5

131, line 6 *New Blackfriars*, April 1967
131, line 34 *Brothers of Men*, p. 79
132, line 20 *The Meaning of the Monastic Life*, p. 130
132, line 34 *Inside the Cloister*, Buckfast Abbey Publications, p. 9
133, line 28 *F.L.G. Letter*, February 1966, p. 6
134, line 16 *Contemplative Nuns Speak*, p. 220
134, line 23 *Historical Sketches* by J. H. Newman, London, Pickering, vol. 2, p. 452
134, line 27 *The Benedictine Idea*, p. 31
134, line 34 *F.L.G. Letter*, March 1966, p. 3
135, line 2 ibid., January 1966, p. 2
136, line 24 *Introduction to Spirituality*, p. 93
137, line 34 *Spiritual Exercises*, par. 47

Page

138, line 1 ibid., par. 48

139, line 7 *Introduction to Spirituality*, p. 68

139, line 16 ibid., p. 69

140, line 1 *Collected Works of St John of the Cross*, pp. 68–9

141, line 9 ibid., p. 113

141, line 23 ibid., p. 373

142, line 12 *Introduction to Spirituality*, p. 43

143, line 15 *Contemplative Nuns Speak*, p. 240

144, line 23 ibid., p. 28

144, line 31 ibid., p. 31

145, line 6 ibid., p. 59

145, line 9 ibid., p. 59

145, line 13 ibid., p. 68

147, line 33 A journal of a community of Anglican nuns. When permission was sought to reproduce the extract the Mother Superior
said this could be granted 'only on condition that it is entirely
anonymous, because since that was written the Community has
changed its custom and does not often use a grille now. This
does not in any way invalidate what we said on the purpose of
the grille where it is still retained.'

149, line 20 *The Waters of Silence*, p. 273

151, line 35 *The Rule of St Benedict*, chapters 16 and 18 (His biblical
authority comes from Psalm cxix, 62 and 164)

156, line 29 St Luke, x, 38–42

157, line 16 *Cistercian Nuns of Today*, Tenbury Wells, Worcs.,
Fowler Wright Books, p. viii

158, line 1 'Openness and Cloister', paper by Thomas Merton, privately circulated, p. 2

159, line 12 'Monasticism in our Age', by a monk C S W G, privately
circulated, p. 6

160, line 19 *Tensions and Change*, p. 34

160, line 32 ibid., p. 95

161, line 25 M. L. Algini in *La Rocca*, 23, 1964; quoted by Dom
Jean Leclerq O S B in *Monastic Studies*, No. 4, 1966, p. 150

CHAPTER 6

All quotations from Canon Law in this chapter have been taken from
the translation in *The Sacred Canons*, a commentary by John A. Abb
and Jerome D. Hanna, St Louis, Herder, 1960.

170, line 19 *The Downside Customary*, pp. 86–7

173, line 17 *Pax*, No. 315, Winter 1965

175, line 3 *Summa theologica*, IIa IIae q186 art. 8

175, line 16 *Obedience*, p. 81

Page

175, line 27 ibid., p. 85

175, line 38 ibid., p. 86

178, line 30 *Herder Correspondence*, vol. 2, No. II, November 1965, p. 323

179, line 34 *Rule of St Benedict*, chapter 58

180, line 14 'The Religious Life – A Call to the Love of God', paper by Fr Hugh Bishop, to the Oxford Conference on the Religious Life, 1965

180, line 21 *Monastic Studies*, No. 4, 1966, article by Dom Emmanuel Schuurmans, Abbot of Zundert, Holland

180, line 35 *Manual for Novices*, Loughrea, Eire, M. S. Kelly

182, line 31 *The Meaning of the Monastic Life*, p. 151

182, line 37 ibid., p. 149

183, line 22 *Hoja del Lunes*, 13 February 1967

184, line 3 *Obedience*, p. 106

184, line 22 ibid., p. 214

184, line 36 ibid., pp. 191–2

185, line 15 ibid., p. 210

185, line 29 *The Benedictine Idea*, p. 41

186, line 6 *Obedience*, p. 212

186, line 10 American nuns referred to in *Maturity in the Religious Life*, p. 151

186, line 28 *Tensions and Change*, p. 180

186, line 33 *Obedience*, pp. 55–6

187, line 6 *Monastic Studies*, No. 4, 1966, p. 100

187, line 9 *Religious Orders in the Modern World*, p. 155

187, line 12 *Maturity in the Religious Life*, p. 275

187, line 16 *Religious Orders in the Modern World*, p. 155

187, line 20 *Teilhard de Chardin*, p. 29

187, line 25 *Tensions and Change*, p. 234

187, line 27 *Maturity in the Religious Life*, p. 191

188, line 25 *Review for Religious*, vol. 25, No. 3, May 1966, article by Joseph B. Simms on 'The Particular Friendship'

189, line 1 *God's Highways*, p. 142

189, line 23 *Review for Religious*, vol. 25, No. 3, May 1966, article by James Griffiths s J on 'Religious Censorship of Private Communications'

189, line 30 *Maturity in the Religious Life*, p. 143

189, line 38 *The Religious Vocation*, pp. 306–7

190, line 8 *Witness and Consecration*, p. 64

190, line 14 *Tensions and Change*, p. 30

190, line 27 *Witness and Consecration*, p. 219 n.

191, line 9 *The Nun in the World*, p. 47

191, line 14 For St Paul's views on women see, for example, I Corinthians xiv, 34

Page

191, line 17 *Obedience*, p. 115

192, line 37 Pius XII on 15 September 1952, quoted in *The Nun in the World*, p. 143

193, line 13 *Obedience*, p. 199

193, line 26 *The Nun in the World*, p. 160

194, line 19 *Obedience*, p. 157

194, line 28 *Maturity in the Religious Life*, p. 289

195, line 3 *The Life of Raymond Raynes*, p. 202

195, line 16 *Maturity in the Religious Life*, p. 243

196, line 1 'Monastic Vocation and the Background of Modern Secular Thought' by Thomas Merton, privately circulated, pp. 13–14

196, line 33 *Religious Orders in the Modern World*, p. 8

197, line 13 *The McCabe Affair* by Monica Lawlor and Simon Clements, London, Sheed & Ward, 1967

198, line 29 *The Times*, 5 January 1968

CHAPTER 7

Except for the sources noted below, all the material in this chapter has come from the answers to a questionnaire I composed and circulated among a number of religious communities – both men and women's, Catholic and Anglican – in Great Britain. The questions were as follows :

(A) You were called by God to your vocation as a religious. But what form did the call take? What was the pattern in your life beforehand that made you attend to this call; that made you sure this, and no other, was to be your vocation?

(B) In *Tensions and Change* Mgr Huyghe writes (p. 78) of the aspirant to the religious life : 'It is not sufficient to reject the world. ... What would have been the candidate's attitude towards marriage if she had not had a religious vocation must be discovered.' What was your experience of human love before becoming a religious; to what extent was this satisfying? And what has been your experience of human love since then?

(C) Since becoming a religious has the certainty of your vocation been a constant in your life?

(D) What is the purpose of the religious life as practised by your community, bearing in mind that your own interpretation of this may not coincide precisely with that expressed by the founder(s) of your community?

202, line 1 *Anatomy of a Church: Greek Orthodoxy Today* by Mario Rinvolucri, London, Burns Oates, 1966, p. 61

205, line 1 *An Introduction to Spirituality*, p. 197

205, line 12 *Tensions and Change*, p. 78

Page

205, line 21 ibid., p. 79
219, line 24 The passage in St Matthew's Gospel reads 'For there
     are some eunuchs which were born from their mother's
     womb . . .'
232, line 28 *Tensions and Change*, p. 78

CHAPTER 8

242, line 17 *Brothers of Men*, p. 22 (Lancelot Sheppard's introduc-
     tion)
243, line 12 *Religious Orders in the Modern World*, p. 155
243, line 18 *The Complete Monk*, p. 213
243, line 25 *Monastic Renewal*, p. 192
244, line 6 Letter to *The Tablet*, 14 August 1965
244, line 17 *Brothers of Men*, p. 46
244, line 29 *The Nun in the World*, p. 142
245, line 1 *The Religious Life*, p. 315
245, line 21 'The Religious Life – A Call to the Love of God',
     paper by Fr Hugh Bishop to Oxford Conference on the Religious
     Life, 1965
247, line 19 *Ampleforth Journal*, Spring 1967, p. 19
248, line 37 'Monastic Vocation and the Background of Modern
     Secular Thought', by Thomas Merton, privately circulated, p. 3
249, line 32 *Monastic Studies*, No. 3, 1965, p. 200
250, line 22 *Monastic Studies*, No. 4, 1966, p. 131
252, line 29 *Brothers of Men*, pp. 52–3
253, line 13 *To Heaven with Diana* by Gerald Vann O P, London,
     Collins, 1960, p. 50
253, line 38 *New Blackfriars*, September 1967, article by Louis
     Allen
254, line 9 ibid.
258, line 6 *De civitate dei*, Healy translation, London, Dent
258, line 12 ibid.
259, line 3 Sermo 354 ad continentes 9; PL 39 1568
259, line 8 *Summa theologica*, a5 ad2
259, line 23 *Inside the Cloister*, Buckfast Abbey Publications, p. 2
259, line 24 *The Meaning of the Monastic Life*, p. 201
260, line 18 *American Catholic Exodus*, p. 187
260, line 34 *Religious Orders in the Modern World*, p. 107
261, line 15 *The Meaning of the Monastic Life*, p. 135
261, line 24 ibid., p. 136
261, line 32 *Monasticism in our Age*, p. 8
261, line 35 *The Benedictine Idea*, p. 46
262, line 5 'The Religious Life – A Call to Service', paper by Fr
     Michael S S F to Oxford Conference, 1966

Page

262, line 24 'Adaptation of the Monastic Life', paper by Thomas
  Merton, privately circulated, 1964
266, line 23 *The Benedictine Idea*, p. 229
266, line 32 *The Nun in the World*, p. 59
268, line 26 *American Catholic Exodus*, p. 187

Index

Aachen, conference of abbots at (817), 30, 172

Abbeys, *see* Monasteries and Convents

Abbots, Aelred, 32; Baldwin, royal physician, 29; Biscop, Benedict, 28; Clowns, William, 38; de la Mare, Thomas, 38; Hor, 24; Hugh of Cluny, 30; Odilo, 30; Wilfrid of Lindisfarne, 28; responsibility of, 28; live separately from monks, 29; congregational meeting of, 168; power of, 168–9

Abelard, Peter, 35

Active Orders (*see also* Benedictines, Dominicans, Franciscans, Jesuits, etc.), distinguished from contemplative, 98, 156–7; difficulties of prayer in, 245

Africa, Dominicans in, 37; the dance as prayer in, 161–2

Albigensians, 36

Alexandria, early religious sects in, 21 *et seq*

Alms, canon law on collection of, 165

America, arrival of Benedictines in, 55; Anglican Benedictines in, 64; postwar growth in, 82; 2,000 nuns abandon vows in, 91; Camaldolese hermit-monks in California, 96; Trappists in Kentucky and Utah, 97, 98; wealth of communities in, 112–13; false poverty in, 243; liturgical reforms in,

245; redeployment of religious in, 246; unrest in, 248; Jesuits in, 268

Anglicans, *see* Church of England

Annuario pontificio, 57

Aquinas, *see* St Thomas Aquinas

Arrupe, Fr Pedro s J, Superior General of Jesuits, 166

Art, at Taizé, 12; medieval monastic, 29; treasury at Kremsmünster, 97–8

Ascent of Mount Carmel, 139–42

Athos, Mount, 203

Augustinians (Austin Friars), 39, 40, 105; founding of, 35, 37; liturgical reforms, 245

Austin Friars, *see* Augustinians

Austria, 99; Benedictines in, 97, 247; monastic granges in, 116

Austrian Empire, contemplatives suppressed in, 47; Jesuit influence in, 44

Authority, *see* Obedience

Bacon, Roger, 37

Baldwin, Monica, 198

Ballot box, use in chapter, 169

Barnabites, 43, 172

Basilea, Mutter (Dr Klara Schlink), 69–70

Bea, Cardinal Augustin s J, 169

Bede, the Venerable, 29

Belgium, 19th-century growth in, 55; present shortage of vocations in, 84; deferences to superiors abandoned in, 245

Benedict of Aniane, 30, 172
Benedictines (see also St
   Benedict), 79, 97, 98, 104, 105,
   110–11, 112–13, 125, 126–7,
   135, 152, 176, 208, 224,
   243–4, 245, 249, 259, 261–2;
   Rule of, 25 et seq; early
   discipline, 27; early economy
   of, 27–8; spread from Italy,
   28; 17th-century reform of,
   46; return to England, 48; in
   Church of England, 52,
   60–64; in 19th-century
   Europe, 54; arrival in
   America, 55; numbers today,
   57, 83; in congregations,
   167–8; postwar growth in
   America, 82; as teachers,
   99–100; prayer life of, 130–31;
   power structure of, 167–70;
   vows of, 171; control of pride
   among, 185–6; Benedictine's
   account of vocation, 235–40;
   work with Protestants, 247;
   psychoanalysis of a monastery,
   253–5
Benson, R. M., 53, 128, 189–90
Bhagavad-Gita, 250
Bishops, visiting the enclosure,
   165; from religious orders,
   169; disbarred from religious
   life, 176
Blessed John Roberts, 47
Bonshommes, 35
Breviarum monasticum, 62
Brigittines, 128
Britain, Benedictines come to,
   28; reformation in, 40–41;
   revival of religious life in, 47;
   Benedictines return to, 48;
   French Trappists in, 48;
   early Cistercians in, 32; recent
   decline of religious in, 91;
   vocations exhibition in, 101–3
Brotherhood of the Holy Cross,
   247

Brothers of Christian Instruction,
   55
Brothers of the Christian
   Schools, 172
Brothers of the Holy Family, 55
Brothers of the Immaculate
   Conception, 55
Brothers of Our Lady Mother
   of Mercy, 55
Brothers of the Sacred Heart,
   55
Brothers of St John of God, 173
Brothers of St Francis Xavier,
   55
Browne, Cardinal Michael OP,
   169
Bruce, Miss Mary, 50, 51
Buddha, 21
Buddhism, 267
Buildings at Taizé, 7, 13; of
   Petits Frères in Leeds, 76–7;
   of Camaldolese hermit-monks,
   95; of English Jesuits,
   Benedictines, Trappists, 97–8
Butte, Mlle Antoinette, 68

Caldey Island, 53, 61–3, 118,
   169
Camillians, 43
Canon Law, on evangelical
   counsels, 163; on novitiates,
   176; limits to recruitment,
   176
Canonesses of St Augustine,
   fourth vow of, 171
Canons regular, in the early
   church, 33; precedence over
   monks, 172
Capuchins, 128; start Parisian
   fire brigades, 43; property of,
   164
Cardinals, from religious orders,
   169
Carlyle, Aelred (Benjamin
   Fearnley), 61–3
Carmelites, 37, 48, 125, 176,

Carmelites–*contd*
180, 244; founding of, 35;
reform of, 43; French inquiry
into income of, 113; novices'
manual of, 180–82

Carmelites, Discalced, 43;
numbers today, 57

Carthusians, 96, 122, 146, 151,
177; origins of, 33; numbers
today, 57; settle in America, 82

Celibacy, 59

Cenobites, 26

Censorship, among Camaldolese
hermit monks, 96; of mail
and phone calls, 189

Cerne Abbas, 65

Chant, *see* Liturgy

Chaperones, 187, 243

Chapter, general, 59; operation
of Benedictine, 168–9; lay
brothers excluded from, 173

Chapter of Faults, 153

Charterhouse (*see also*
Carthusians *and* La Grande
Chartreuse), John Evelyn and,
42

Chastity, Jewish sects and, 21;
basis of, 22; in canon law,
163; Carmelite training in,
182; precautions for, 187;
rebellion against tradition of,
197–8, 252

Christian Social Union, 59

Church of England, origins of
religious life in, 48 *et seq*;
Benedictines in, 52, 60–64;
Advisory Council on Religious
Communities, foundation of,
57–8; composition of, 166;
numbers in communities
today, 57; communities
accepted in principle by
bishops, 57; romantic
nostalgia in, 58; agitation
against communities, 58;
numbers of communities,

66–7; age of entry to
communities, 176; difficulty of
reform in, 262

Church of England communities:
Community of the Glorious
Ascension, 114–15;
Community of the
Resurrection (Mirfield
Fathers), 54, 58–9, 105, 195;
lay associates of, 79–80;
monk's life in, 106–8;
experimental offices in, 245;
redeployment of, 246;
Community of the Sacred
Passion, 104; Community of
St Laurence, 124; Community
of St Mary the Virgin, 104;
Order of St Augustine, 60;
Park Village Sisterhood, 50
et seq.; Sisters of the Church,
110; Sisters of the Love of
God, 86, 125, on prayer,
134–5; Society of the Divine
Compassion, 65; Society of
the Most Holy Trinity, 52;
Society of the Sacred Mission
(Kelham Fathers), 54, 58;
Society of St Francis, 65, 106;
Society of St John the
Evangelist (Cowley Fathers),
53, 58, 128, 189–90

Cistercians (*see also* Cîteaux and
Trappists), 31–2, 46, 99, 111,
172, 186, 249; and the
Reformation, 40; numbers
today, 57; postwar success in
America, 82; as farmers today,
116–18; timetable of, 152–5;
instruction of novices, 154;
burial of, 155; vows of, 171

Cîteaux, 5–6, 17, 31

City of God, 258

Clement of Alexandria, 257–8

Cluny, 5–6, 30–32

Codex iuris canonici, 163–6

Codex regularum, 30

Columbus, Christopher, 55
Community of the Resurrection, *see* Church of England Communities
Communities, general, beginnings of, 23 *et seq.*; mixed, 34; at Little Gidding, 42; first Anglican, 50; numbers in women's, 57; Protestant, 67–72, 247; decline among Anglican women's, 85–6; secular institutes, 80–81; criticized for rigidity, 87–9; purpose of 199 British communities, 101–3
Concordia regularum, 30
Congregation of the Sisters of Jesus Crucified, for sick and invalid women, 104
Congregations, Benedictine: Maurist reform, 46; English congregation established, 48; ordered to confederate, 54; reform of prayer life, 161; distinctions between, 167–8; numbers of, 168; Belgian reforms, 245; English liturgical reforms, 245; Solesmes, 99
Congregations general, federations of, 89; canonical definition of, 164; tendency to maintain status quo, 193–4
Constantine, emperor, 24
Constitutions, canonical definitions of, 164
Consuetudines, *see* Customary
Contemplation (*see also* Prayer), early Jewish sects and, 21
Contemplatives, suppressed, 47; distinguished from actives, 98, 156–7; purpose of life, 135; numbers of, 146; rigours of life as, 149–50; view of world outside, 158; contemplative

nun's account of vocation, 231–5; future of, 265–6
Convents: Burnham Abbey, 114; Holy Cross Abbey, Stapehill, 123, 126, 183, 186; Stanbrook Abbey, 48; West Malling Abbey, 61; dowries in, 164; lay sisters in, 172–3; limited to virgins, 177
Council of Chalcedon (451), 29
Council of Lyons (1274), 37
Council of Trent (1545–63), 42–3, 44, 196
Cowley Fathers, *see* Church of England communities, Society of St John the Evangelist
Cromwell, Thomas, 41, 168
Crutched Friars, 35
Cuernavaca, psychiatric experiment at, 253–5
Curia, religious in, 169; pressure on Dominicans from, 197; and Cuernavaca experiment, 255
Customary (Usages and Consuetudines), function of, 170

D'Andolo, Diana, 147
Dark Night of the Soul, 139–41
Darmstadt Sisters (Oekumenische Marienschwestern), 69–71
Daughters of the Heart of Mary, 128–9
Davidson, Randall, Archbishop of Canterbury, 62
Davis, Charles, 197
De accomodata renovatione vitae religiosae, 89, 91
de Ahumada, Teresa, *see* St Teresa of Avila
de Foucauld, Charles, 73–5, 142, 243, 247
de la Salle, Jean-Baptiste, 46, 199, 200
de Rancé, Jean, 46

de Recalde, Inigo Lopes, *see* St
    Ignatius Loyola
De votis monasticis judicium,
    39
de Yepes, John, *see* St John of
    the Cross
Deaconesses, 67–8; working with
    monks, 246
Decian persecutions, 21
Dialogues of St Gregory the
    Great, 25–7
Diocletian, emperor, 22
Discipline, 166; early
    Benedictine, 27
Discipline, the, *see* mortification
Dissolution of the monasteries,
    40–41
Dodsworth, Rev. W., 51
Dominicans (Order of
    Preachers), 98, 104, 125, 169,
    171, 172, 176, 197, 253, 260;
    founding of, 36–7; as English
    bishops, 38; fight Jesuits in
    New World, 44; numbers
    today, 57; question members
    about change, 90; as worker
    priests, 110; drop theology,
    246
Double standard of St Augustine,
    257–8
Downes, Douglas s s f, 65
Dowry, 114; canon law on, 164
Dress, 8, 9, 28, 31, 43, 59, 66,
    86, 128–9, 177
Duns Scotus, 37

Eastern monasticism, 24
Echallens, 67
Economy, of Taizé, 11–12; early
    Benedictine, 27–8; early
    Cistercian, 32; taxation of
    communities, 113; place of
    gifts in, 113–14; place of
    dowry in, 114; place of farm
    in, 116–18; a monastic balance
    sheet, 120–22

Ecumenism, 114, 246–7; at
    Taizé, 16
Edict of Milan (313), 24
Egypt, early communities in,
    21 *et seq.*
Ellacombe, Miss Jane, 50
Enclosure, medieval, 39; rules
    modified, 86; degrees of,
    145–8; canon law on, 164–5;
    solemn vows in, 171
Eremetical life, *see* Hermits
Essenes, 21
Eudes, Jean, 46
Evelyn, John, 42
Exemptions, from episcopal
    control, 29; Leo X prohibits,
    42; 17th-century orders and,
    46

Fasting, 151; and obedience,
    175
Father Ignatius, *see* Lyne, Joseph
    Leycester
Ferrar, Nicholas, 42
Fitzralph, Archbishop of
    Armagh, 38
Fliedner, Pastor Theodore, 67
Food, at Taizé, 11; of hermits,
    23; early Benedictine, 27–8;
    of Trappists, 112; monastic
    gluttony, 112; of
    contemplatives, 151
France, attacks on religious in,
    45, 72; Protestant communities
    in, 67–8; present shortage of
    vocations in, 84; Carmelite
    income in, 113; Carthusians
    in, 146; ecumenism in, 247;
    19th-century growth in, 55;
    worker-priests in, 108–10
Franciscans, 43, 98, 104, 172,
    267; friars at Taizé, 16;
    founding of, 35–6, 37;
    numbers today, 57; in Church
    of England, 64–6, 106, 111;
    tertiaries, 79; property of, 164;

Franciscan missionaries
of the Divine Motherhood,
177; Franciscan Missionary
Sisters, redeployment of, 246;
view of Taizé, 247
French Revolution, 47, 48
Friars (*see also* Franciscans,
Dominicans, Augustinians),
attacked by monks and secular
clergy, 37–8; as foreign
missionaries, 37
Friars Minor, *see* Franciscans
Friars of the Sack, 35

General Congress on the States
of Perfection, 259
Geneviève, Mère, 69
George III, visits French
Trappists, 48
Germany, 99; effects of reform
in, 40; Protestant communities
in, 67, 69–70; present shortage
of vocation in, 84
Germond, Pastor Louis, 67
Giles, Brother, s s f, 65
Glenmary Sisters, 246
God, religious impressions of,
144–5
Gore, Charles, 54, 59–60
Gospel, St Luke's, 156; St
Matthew's, 23, 36, 219
Grandchamp, 69
Griffiths, Dom Bede o s b, 250
Grille, 146, 153; as protection
from temptation, 135;
introduced by St Dominic,
147; still being installed, 147;
justification of, 147–8
Gut, Cardinal Benno o s b,
169
Gyrovagues, 27

Hairshirt, *see* Mortifications
Halifax, Lord, 61, 63
Hamilton, Hon. Charles, 49

Hardie, Keir, 59
Harding, Stephen, 31
Henry VIII, 41, 168
Hermits, 21 *et seq.*; decorative,
in England, 49; hermit monks
of Calmaldoli, 95–6; future
of, 266
Herrnhut, 67
Hinduism, 21, 267; influence on
religious life, 249–50
Holland, 19th-century growth
in, 55; present shortage of
vocations in, 83–4;
Dominicans drop theology in,
246
Holy See, property of, 164
Homosexuality, 188; and
vocation, 220–21
Hoyer, Conrad, 40
Huddleston, Trevor, c r, Bishop
of Stepney, 60
Hughes, Miss Marian Rebecca,
first Anglican religious, 51
Humiliation, practice of, 184–5;
'annihilation' of will, 193
Huvelin, Abbé, 74
Huyghe, Gerard, Bishop of
Arras, 85, 87, 88, 160, 186,
205, 243, 260

I Leap Over the Wall, 198
Infantilism, among nuns, 191–4;
among men, 194–6
Institute of the Brothers of the
Christian Schools, 46, 199–200
Institutes, canonical definition
of, 163–4; direction of, 166
Iona, 28
Iona Community, 71
Ireland, monastic colonies
arrive in, 25; as channel of
monastic influences to
England, 28; present shortage
of vocations in, 84
Iron Curtain, religious life
behind, 73

Italy, 99; departure from Benedictine rule in, 28; spread of Franciscans in, 36; new 17th-century institutes in, 47; Carthusians in, 146; 19th-century growth in, 55

Jarrow, 28
Jesuits (*see also* St Ignatius Loyola), 97, 98, 105, 169, 171, 172, 180, 187, 189, 268; foundation of, 44; fourth vow of, 44, 171; ups and downs of, 44–5, 47, 54; numbers today, 57; in North America today, 82; as worker priests, 109–10; prayer life of, 135; use of *Spiritual Exercises*, 136–9; direction of, 166–7; training of, 178; control of pride among, 185–6; Jesuit's account of vocation, 227–31
Jews, early eremitical sects of, 21; as monastic creditors, 29

Kaiserswerth, 67
Keble, John, 49
Kelly, Herbert, 54
Kierkegaard, Soren, 68, 269
Knights of the Sword, 35
Kurisumala Ashram, 249–50

La Grande Chartreuse, 31, 33; Roger Schütz and, 5
La Trappe, 46
Langston, Miss Emma ('Mother Emma'), 51
Latin, usage today, 64, 126–7, 151–3
Lay brothers, in St Benedict's plan, 28; as monastic servants, 30, 32; Camaldolese, 96; position today, 172–4
Lectio divina, see Spiritual reading

LeMercier, Dom Gregoire, O S B, 253–5
Little Brothers and Sisters of Jesus (Petits Frères and Petites Sœurs), 104, 108, 110, 244, 247–8, 264–5, 266; origins, 73–6; in Britain, 76–7; work of, 77–8; daily prayer of, 131–2; on love and friendship, 252–3
Little Gidding, 42
Liturgy (*see also* Offices), at Taizé, 13–15; expansion of in early monasteries, 30; Gregorian chant, 99, 168; psalms in, 151–2; reforms in, 245; Hindu influence on, 249–50
Love, new interpretation of, 252–3
Luther, Martin, 39
Lutheran monasteries, 40
Lyne, Joseph Leycester ('Father Ignatius'), 52–3

MacLeod, George (Lord MacLeod), 71
Macarius the Alexandrian, 23
Mandatum (feet washing), 186
Manual labour, *see* Work
Marists, 173
Martyria, Mutter (Frl. Erika Madauss), 69–70
McCabe, Fr Herbert O P, 197
Meditation, *see* Prayer
Mendicants, origin of, 35–6
Merton, Thomas O C S O, 116, 149, 157–9, 195–6, 248–9, 262–3
Methodists, in Trappist monastery, 247
Mexico, 253–5
Mirfield, *see* Church of England Communities, Community of the Resurrection
Missale monasticum, 64

Missionary Sisters of Our Lady of Apostles, qualifications of, 177

Monasteries, general; children in, 29; coin own money, 29; controlled by popes, 29–30; decadence in, 38–9; suppression of in Britain, 40–41; Lutheran, 40

Monasteries, individual; Ampleforth, 48, 99, 100, 125, 168, 177–8, 186; Beaulieu, 32–3; Bec, 171; liturgical reforms at, 246; Belmont, 106, 168; Beuron, 54, 99, 152; Bobbio, 28, 29; Boquen, 247; Buckfast Abbey, 106, 169, 259; attitudes to prayer at, 132–3; novitiate and profession at, 178–9; Bury St Edmunds, 29; Cîteaux, 5–6, 17, 31, 32; Clairvaux, 31, 32; Compostela, 47; Daventry, 39; Dorchester, 39; Douai, 100, 168; Downside, 48, 99, 100, 105, 134, 168, 171, 176; closes novitiate, 85; Ehrlach, 247; Gethsemani, 97; Kremsmünster, 97–8; La Pierre Qui Vire, 152; Maredsous, 245; Maria Laach, 99; Melk, 85, 97, 243; Montecassino, 26, 30, 47, 85, 97, 99; Montserrat, 47, 55, 261, as centre of Catalan patriotism, 99; Mount Melleray, 101; Mount St Bernard, 117–18; Mount Saviour (NY), liturgical reforms, 245–6, Nashdom, 64, 106; New Melleray, 117; Nunraw, 98, 117, 259; Ogden, 98; Padua, 47; Prinknash, 63, position of lay brothers at, 173–4; Quarr, 10w, 72; Rievaulx, 32; St Albans, 29; 38; St Benedict (Minnesota), 99; St Benoît sur Loire, 97; St Denis, 29; St Leo, 99; St Martin of Tours, 29; St Philibert of Jumièges, 29; St Rupert, 119; St Scholastica, 99; Santa Maria de la Resurreccion, 253–5; Solesmes, 54, 72; Subiaco, 99; Valladolid, 47; Weingarten, 99; Westminster, 42; Worth, 98, 100

Money, communal; use of at Taizé, 11–12; monks coin own, 29; acquisition of, 112–13; from the Stock Market, 120–22

Money, individual, 59, 66, 111, 115; weekly allowances, 120

Monks, origins of, 23 et seq.; division of day under Benedict, 27; become priests, 28; early sleeping arrangements of, 33; conscripted in Second World War, 72–3, 76; life in Community of the Resurrection, 106–8; cells of, 122–3; 10th-century timetable of, 155–6; numbers in Benedictine congregations, 168; precedence of, 172; on their vocation, 204, 208–10

Moravian Church, 67

Mortification (see also Fasting), 21, 23, 51, 52–3; hairshirts, 33; flogging, 38; Anglican, 51, 52–3; when singing offices, 64; reduced diet as, 112; when late for office, 130; among Cistercian nuns, 153; Carmelite practices of, 180–85; use of discipline, 182–3; relaxation of, 245

Murphy, Francis Xavier, 197

Napoleon I, 47, 55

Newman, Cardinal John Henry, 25, 50, 134

Nitria, 22–3

Novice Masters and Mistresses, canon law on, 164; influential position of novice mistresses, 192

Novices, disposal of their money, 115; Cistercian instruction of, 154; separate quarters for, 172; vulnerability of, 192

Novitiates, at Taizé, 8–9; effects of federation on, 89; reaction against, 159; age of entry into, 176; of Franciscan nuns, 177; of Jesuits, 178; of Benedictines, 178–9

Nugee, George, 60

Nuns, at Whitby, 34; pensions for after the dissolution of the monasteries, 41; guillotined in the French Revolution, 47; 2,000 Americans abandon vows, 91; impressions of God among, 144–5; recreation for, 150; work of, 150; timetable of, 152–5; dormitories for, 154; burial of Cistercians, 155; canon law on, 165; infantilism among, 191–5; on their vocation, 204, 205, 206–8, 210 et seq.; contemplative's account of vocation, 231–5

Obedience, 59, 198; Jewish sects and, 21; basis of, 22; in canon law, 163; Thomist doctrine of, 174–5; limits to, 175; tests of, 183–4; rebellion against, 197–8, 252; difficulties of, 223–4; re-examination of, 244–5

Oblates, women singing with monks, 246

Oblation, child, 29

O'Donnell, Br Gregory, 199–201

Offices (see also Liturgy), at Taizé, 13–14; in first Anglican community, 51; early Carthusian, 33; in Community of the Resurrection, 59; of Camaldolese hermit monks, 96; 7 times a day, 130; for contemplative nuns, 150, 152–4; lay brothers excused, 173

Oratorians, 43, 46, 170–71, 172, 204–5

Order of Fontevrault, 34, 268

Order of Preachers, see Dominicans

Order of Premonstratensians, 34, 172

Orders, Military, 35

Orders, missionary (see also Franciscans, Dominicans, Jesuits, Benedictines), 19th-century growth of, 55

Orders, nursing, 43

Orders, teaching, 43, 46–7, 55, 57; Benedictines as teachers, 99–100, 168; Trappists as teachers, 101; overwork in, 190

Orthodoxy, 203; and Taizé, 16; and prayer, 135–6

Ottaviani, Cardinal Alfredo, 255

Oxford Movement, 49–50

Palestine, early religious sects in, 21 et seq.

Pankhurst, Mrs Emily, 59

Paris, Matthew, 29

Park Village Sisterhood, 50 et seq.

Particular friendship, 188–9, 252–3

Passionists, 47, 172

Penal Laws, relaxation of, 48

Penances, see Mortification

Perfection, evangelical counsels

of, 22, 163; Luther's attitude to, 39–40; St Augustine's doctrine of, 258–9; General Congress on the States of, 259

Perrin, Henri, SJ, 109–10

Petits Frères and Petites Sœurs, *see* Little Brothers and Sisters of Jesus

Petronilla of Chemaille, 34

Philosophers, influence of modern, 247–8

Pispir, 22

Poor Clares, 48, 111, 161–2, 245

Popes, Alexander III, 34; Benedict XIII, 200; Clement XIV, 45; Gregory VII, 5; John XXIII, 6, 157, 197; Leo X, 42; Leo XIII, 54, 167; Martin IV, 37; Paul III, 44; Paul IV, 42; Pius V, 42; Pius XI, 157; Pius XII, 80, 192–3, tells nuns modifications needed, 86; popes control monasteries personally, 29–30

Portugal, persecution of orders in, 47; orders expelled, 73

Postulants, at Taizé, 8–9; bringing dowry, 164; guidance of, 177

Poverty, Jewish sects and, 21; basis of, 22; among Petits Frères, 78–9, 110, 111; in canon law, 163; religious and secular contrasted, 242–3; rethinking, 244

Prague, Benedictines in, 54

Prayer, at Taizé, 14–15; of early contemplatives, 21, 33; eclecticism of Pomeyrol, 68; of Darmstadt Sisters, 69–70; of Little Brothers and Sisters, 131–2; of Benedictines, 131; as purification, 132; as social service, 132–3; of intercession, 133–4; as act of reparation, 134; and powers of darkness, 134; as conversation, 135; Jesus prayer, 135; use of rosary in, 136; meditative prayer, 136, 137–8; definition of, 139; despair in, 141, 142; deterioration of, 160; the dance and, 161

Premontre, *see* Order of Premonstratensians

Priests, parish; compared with early monks, 33–4; hostility to friars, 37–8; 17th-century orders for training of, 46; visiting enclosure, 165; vows and promises of, 170

Profession, at Taizé, 9–10; uncertainties after, 209

Promises (*see also* Vows), in Community of the Resurrection, 59; in 17th-century societies, 170–71

Property, common, canon law on, 164

Property, private, 110–11

Protestant Communities, *see* Communities

Provida mater ecclesia, 80–81

Pusey, Edward Bouverie, 50

Raynes, Fr Raymond CR, 195

Recreation, in religious life, 127; of contemplative nuns, 150

Redemptorists, 47, 105, 172, 197

Reformation, and religious life, 39; tolerates monasticism, 40; in Britain, 40–41

Regularis concordia anglicae, 155

Religious, as theologians, 104; holidays for, 150; funerals of, 155; in Curia, 169; precedence among, 171–2; men and women working together, 246

Religious Journals: *American Benedictine Review*, 125; *Ampleforth Journal*, 125; *Gridiron*, 124; *Maintenant*, 125; *New Blackfriars*, 125, 197, 263

Religious Life, effects of crusades on, 34; isolationism in, 126; recreation in, 127; qualifications required, 176–7; secrecy about, 189–90; purpose of, 225–6; reappraisal of, 257 *et seq.*; effect of modern philosophy on, 247–8

Retreat of Pomeyrol, 68

Reuilly, 68

Richelieu, Cardinal, 46

Robert of Arbrissel, 34, 268

Robertson, Algy, s s f, 65

Roncalli, Mgr, *see* Pope John XXIII

Rosary devotions, 136

Rule, the, of St Augustine, 51, 164; of St Basil, 24–5, 164; of St Benedict, 25, 27–8, 98–9, 100, 153, 164, on poverty, 110–11, on prayer, 130, on humility, 174, on profession, 179, at Kurisumala, 249; of St Francis, 164; of St Pachomius, 23; of Taizé, 9, 11, 18, 68

Rules, canonical definition of, 164

Russia, early Dominicans in, 37

Rynne, Xavier, *see* Murphy, Francis Xavier

Sacred Congregation for Religious and Secular Institutes, studies reform projects, 86; composition of, 166; and Cuernavaca experiment, 255

Sacred Congregation of Rites, 64

St John of Jerusalem, Order of (Knights Hospitaller), 35

Saint-Sulpice, 46, 75

Saints: Antony the Hermit, 21–2, 183; Augustine of Canterbury, 28; Augustine of Hippo, 142, influence of, 257–9; Basil, 24–5; Benedict (*see also* Rule of St Benedict), 163, 241, life of, 25–6, relics of, 97; Bernard, 31–2, 142; Bruno, 33; Catherine of Siena, 51; Clement of Alexandria, 141–2; Columba, 28; Dominic, 36, 241, introduces grille, 147; Francis, 35–6, 241; Gregory the Great, 25–6; Hilda, 34; Ignatius Loyola, 44, 241, *Spiritual Exercises* of, 44, 136–9, 178; Jerome, 21; John of the Cross, 43, contemplative manuals of, 139–41; Pachomius, 23–4; Patrick, 28; Paul, attitudes to women, 191; Paul of Thebes, 21; Philip Neri, 43; Romuald, 95; Simeon Stylites, 24; Teresa of Avila, 43, 142, 184; Thomas Aquinas, 37, on obedience, 174–5, on perfection, 259; Vincent de Paul, 46, 196–7

Salesians, 57

Salvation Army, 265

Sanctification, early Cistercian, 32; J. H. Newman on, 134

Sarabaites, 27

Scalabrini Fathers, 176

Scandinavia, effects of Reform in, 40

Scholarship, medieval, 29; among religious today, 104–5

Schutz, Roger, prior of Taizé, *see also* Taizé; 69, 195, 265; early years, 4–6, comparison with René Voillaume, 259

Secular Institutes, 80–81, 264–5

Sellon, Mother Lydia, 52

Sexuality, and rebellion against authority, 197–8; recognition of, 254; repression of, 256

Sign language, 118, 149

Silence, among early Cistercians, 32; among Camaldolese hermit monks, 96; in contemplative communities, 148–9; reaction against, 159

Sisters of Charity of St Vincent de Paul, 170–71, 196–7

Sisters of the Immaculate Heart of Mary, 105

Sisters of Notre Dame de Bon Secours de Troyes, qualifications of, 177

Smythe, Sir Edward, 48

Society of Jesus, *see* Jesuits

South America, Jesuit influence in, 45; 20th-century growth in Columbia, 82

Southey, Robert, 49

Spain, Carmelite reforms in, 43; Dominican influence throughout Empire, 44; persecution of orders in, 47; mortifications today, 183; deposition of abbot in, 261

Spiritual Exercises, 44, 136–9, 178

Spiritual reading for Cistercian nuns, 153

Subiaco, 26

Succession, Oath of (1534), 41

Suenens, Cardinal Leon-Jozef, 82, 193, 244, 266

Suhard, Cardinal of Paris, 109

Suicide, 201

Sulpicians, 46, 170

Superiors, canonical ruling on, 164; power of, 169; limits to authority of, 175; modified deferences to, 244–5

Suppression, Act of (1536), 41

Switzerland, Jesuits expelled from, 54; Protestant communities in, 67–9

Tabennisi, 23

Taizé, *see also* Schutz; 3–20, 69, 246, 247, 264; influence on Vatican Council, 4; existential sign of, 5; beginning of, 6; nationalities and denominations at, 8; entry to community, 8; Rule of, 9, 11, 18; novitiate at, 9; profession at, 9; vows at, 10; 'foyers', 11; work at, 11–12, 19; art of, 13–14; use of money, 11; economy of, 11–12; worship and liturgy at, 13–15; buildings at, 7, 13; and orthodoxy, 16, 247; Franciscan friars at, 16; ecumenism at, 16; philosophy of, 4, 15–19; authoritarianism at, 194–5; Franciscan view of, 247

Teaching, *see* Orders, teaching

Teilhard de Chardin, 105, 187

Temple, Archbishop William, 61

Temple, Order of (Knights Templars), 34

Tertiaries, 79

Tertullian, 191

Teutonic Knights, 35

Theatines, 43

Theology, on obedience, 174–5; for Jesuits, 178; of perfection, 258–9

Therapeutae, 21

Third Orders, 79

Thirty Years War, 40, 45

Thurian, Max, 6

Tonsure, 62, 128

Trappists (Cistercians of the Strict Observance), 79, 104, 112, 122, 123, 126, 128, 151, 183, 259, 262–3; Roger Schutz and, 5; founding of, 46;

Trappists—*contd*
French, in England, 48;
ordered to confederate, 54–5;
numbers today, 57; migrate to
Caldey Island, 63; recent
American decline of, 91; in
Kentucky and Utah, 98; as
teachers, 101; as farmers,
117–18; as scent producers,
118; sign language of, 149;
chapter meetings of, 169;
hosts to Methodists, 247
Trinitarians, 35

Upanishads, 250
Usages, see Customary

Vatican Council, 197; Taizé
influence on, 3–4; religious
superiors at, 169
Vincentians, 46
Vocation, present shortage of,
83; of 199 British
communities, 101–3; mystical
promptings to, 207; unhappy
homes in development of,
210–13; urge to give up, 214;
homosexuality in, 220–21;
wavering in, 224; Jesuit's
account of, 227–31;
contemplative nun's account
of, 231–5; Benedictine's
account of, 235–40
Voillaume, René, prior of Petits
Frères, 75, 78, 131, 244, 265;
comparison with Roger Schutz,
247; on love and friendship, 252
Vows (*see also* Promises), at
Taizé, 10; fourth vow of
Jesuits, 44; 171; breaking of,
90–91, 248, 251; canonical
definitions of, 164;

distinctions between, 170–71;
entire community renounces,
255
Weakland, Dom Rembert O S B,
Abbot Primate of the
Benedictines, 167
Wearmouth, 28
Weil, Simone, 135
Weld, Thomas, 48
Whitby, mixed abbey of, 34, 246
Widows, 176
William the Pious, Duke of
Aquitaine, 5
Wimmer, Dom Boniface O S B, 55
Wittenberg, Articles (1536), 40
Wolsey, Cardinal, 40–41
Work, general, at Taizé, 11–12,
19; of Little Brothers and
Sisters, 77; different forms of,
101–3; worker-priest
movement, 108–10; of
Anglican sisters, 110; farming,
116–18; scent, wine and
incense making, 118–19;
among contemplative nuns,
150; reorganization of, 246
Work, manual labour, 21, 30;
abandoned by Dominicans, 36;
among Camaldolese
hermit monks, 96; for
Cistercian nuns, 153
Worker priests, 108–10; point to
future, 264–5, 269
Worship, see Prayer, Liturgy *and*
Offices
Wycliff, John, 38

Yoga, 250

Zinzendorf, Count Nikolaus von,
67
Zmud, Dr Frida, 254